Planning the Health Sector

The Tanzanian Experience

OSCAR GISH

CROOM HELM LONDON

First published 1975
Copyright © 1975 by Oscar Gish

Croom Helm Ltd, 2-10 St. Johns Road, London SW11.

ISBN 0-85664-207-X

Printed in Great Britain by Biddles of Guildford

CONTENTS

To the people of Tanzania,
their party TANU,
and their President Julius K. Nyerere

INTRODUCTION

In his speech to the Biennial Conference of TANU (Tanganyika African National Union), the national political party, in September 1973, President Nyerere of Tanzania said: ['We must determine to maintain this national policy and not again be tempted by offers of a big new hospital, with all the high running costs involved — at least until every one of our citizens has basic medical services readily available to him.]' Anyone familiar with the (health) development policies of African and other Third World countries will know just how remarkable is such a statement. This book will attempt to summarise the developments leading up to the evolution of this policy, particularly during the period between the previous TANU Biennial Conference in September 1971 and that of September 1973. It was during this precise period that I acted as de facto head of the planning and analysis unit of the Ministry of Health in Dar es Salaam, and in that capacity was able to take part in many of those developments.

Before proceeding further it might be appropriate to mention a few things about myself that are likely to have a bearing upon the presentation of the material. Probably of greatest importance is the fact that for almost the whole of my life I have consciously identified with the idea of socialism as one capable of leading to the potential development of more rational and just societies. Almost as important is the fact that I came to the university relatively late in life, and then had a mixed education, so that although I am nominally an economist, in many respects I would not properly qualify for the title. Before going to Tanzania I had been involved in health service research for approximately four years, my work being primarily concerned with questions of health manpower, and more particularly with the international movements of medical doctors and other health workers. I had come to this subject from an earlier interest in manpower and educational planning. In the course of my work I had travelled extensively in many Third World countries, but never spent an extended period of time in any of them. My recruitment to work in Tanzania was accomplished partly outside normal channels, in that it was encouraged by the Office of the President.

Much has been written about the development of socialist thinking and practice in Tanzania*, and it is not the intention to discuss these matters explicitly. What will be done instead is to illustrate the development of socialist thinking and doctrine in Tanzania in the

1

context of the country's changing pattern of health service development. However, in doing so, an attempt will also be made to broaden the issues so as to fit them into a somewhat larger context.

It is widely known that Tanzania has departed on a significantly different road to development than most other African countries. President Nyerere has clearly articulated the pattern of socialist development he sees as being appropriate for Tanzania.** The assumptions on which Tanzanian development rest were spelled out by the President in an address entitled "Socialism: The Rational Choice" that was delivered for him in January 1973, in Khartoum, Sudan. The speech was intended to show why "our present poverty and national weakness make socialism the only rational choice for us".

"Mr. President; Mr. Chairman; Ladies and Gentlemen.

My job today is to give a starting point for discussion and thought. And my subject is an examination of the alternative economic and social systems which are open to Third World countries.

In order to keep this discussion within reasonable bounds I must make certain assumptions. It is important that these should be clear before I begin: for if the assumptions are not shared, then much of what I say will be irrelevant.

Fortunately, my assumptions are not very controversial-at least within Africa.

The Assumptions:

My first assumption is that any discussion about the appropriate economic and social organization must, for the time being at least, be conducted within each nation state, and the decision must be made exclusively by the people of that nation. Thus, it is the people of Tanzania as a whole, or the Sudan as a whole, who will decide the path for their country. Tanzania cannot decide for the Sudan, nor vice versa — and I hope that nothing I say today will be understood to imply otherwise! The fact that, for example, Zanzibar within the United Republic of Tanzania, and the Southern Provinces within Sudan, have autonomy in certain matters means that in these respects the smaller units will be the unit of choice rather than the nation as a whole.

Secondly, I take it to be axiomatic that all the peoples of the Third World desire to govern themselves, and want their country to be completely independent from external control. This does not rule out the possibility of political or economic links between two or more countries; nor does it exclude a possible voluntary merger of sovereignties, provided that these things are agreed upon after

2

discussions based on the equality of all participants.

Thirdly, I shall assume that, to everyone in the Third World the present degree of poverty, and the general lack of economic development, is completely unacceptable. We have to increase our production of wealth so that we may increase the level of our collective and individual consumption.

My fourth and final assumption is that our struggles for independence were national struggles, involving the rights of all the inhabitants. We were not aiming to replace our alien rulers by local privileged elites, but to create societies which ensure human dignity and self-respect for all. The concomitant of that is that every individual has the right to the maximum economic and political freedom which is compatible with equal freedom for all others; and that neither well-fed slavery nor the necessity to beg for subsistence are acceptable human conditions.

I have said that these assumptions are not very controversial within Africa. It is equally true that they do not represent the present situation. They represent aspirations rather than facts. That is obvious from an examination of world affairs, or from the briefest visit to any of [the places where] our unskilled labourers live.

Yet because these stated assumptions are also a list of our fundamental aspirations, they must be the basis for our choice of policies. If a policy militates against the achievement of these conditions, then its acceptability must be questioned. Even more, if a social and economic system is incompatible with these goals, then it must be rejected."†

Although the development of socialist perspectives in Tanzania had been given a substantial send-off in 1967 by the Arusha Declaration (to be discussed in greater detail later) they were being very unevenly developed and applied. Although some important progress had been made in the area of health development between 1967 (the Arusha Declaration) and 1971, it was still not possible to speak of a health sector that was truly representative of the aspirations of the country as expressed in the Declaration. Accordingly, at the biennial conference of TANU in September 1971 the resolutions taken concerning the economy were intended significantly to change the pattern of development in the sectors of water supply, education and health. It was decided that "from now on the vital needs for water, schools and health shall be given priority in our expenditures except for security and defence. And to implement this, the Second Five-Year Development Plan should be adjusted accordingly."†† The ministries responsible for these services were instructed to move quickly in implementing the resolution.

My own arrival in Tanzania coincided with these directives of the Party, and also made it possible to create the planning unit which the Ministry of Health had been under pressure to develop for some years. Although major central planning responsibilities in Tanzania are held by the Ministries of Finance and Economic Affairs and Development Planning it had become apparent that unless each ministry had its own planning capacity it was unlikely that the central planning bodies could of themselves successfully ensure that each ministry developed a viable plan. Although the central planning bodies were capable of blocking resources intended for inappropriate types of development they could not guarantee that ministries put forward plans that were in keeping with overall national objectives, nor could they themselves write appropriate sectoral plans, both for technical reasons and because ministries would not feel committed to them.

By 1971 planning units had been established in all the ministries (where they enjoyed varying degrees of success) except for health. The major obstacle to founding a planning unit in health was said to be the difficulty of recruiting the necessary (expatriate) personnel; that is, a health planner defined as a medically qualified planner, and a health economist.[x] However, it was fairly apparent that the health ministry was dragging its feet on the question of the recruitment of a health economist, (if not a health planner as well). The reasons for this included not only the suspicions of traditional administrators about the role of the planner (the "treasury's man") but also the doubts of doctors about non-medical people coming into a health ministry for the express purpose of planning. Coupled with this sort of suspicion there are the very healthy doubts held by most Tanzanians about the potential value of expatriates functioning in almost any capacity. Experience has shown that relatively few expatriates, perhaps particularly those working in planning capacities, had the ability to develop policies that would be of assistance to the country. While the work of an expatriate doctor in caring for patients appears a relatively straight-forward matter the potential of an expatriate health economist is not nearly so obvious.[xx] Not only were both medical and non-medical civil servants rather reluctant to see a planning unit within the ministry but the political leadership of the ministry did not seem overly anxious either. Both the Minister and the Junior Minister were extremely active people with clear views about an appropriate pattern of health development for the country. The Minister often worked very closely with his civil servants in reaching key decisions and, not surprisingly, they felt they knew at least as well as any expatriate planner how best to plan for the health care requirements of the nation.

The period from September 1971 to February 1972 was one of progress in defining some of the problems involved and developing the sort of data needed to help clarify the situation further. It was also a period of some dispute within the ministry. In February 1972 the country experienced the most important shake-up of the President's cabinet since independence. These major changes took place as part of the preparation for the decentralisation of government which was scheduled to coincide with the next financial year, starting in July 1972. It appears that the President took the opportunity of this impending change to let eight ministers out of his cabinet, including the Minister of Health. In addition the Junior Minister and Principal Secretary (Permanent Secretary, elsewhere) were also replaced. The new incoming ministerial leadership was anxious to follow the new party directives on health and the way was now open for important changes to be brought into the health care system, especially before the next Party conference in September 1973. Because I was in a position to offer some of the technical expertise required by the new leadership in their attempt to meet the advancing political situation I found myself able to be more active than was usual for most expatriate planners.

This book will describe the results of the succeeding period, during which a new health plan frame to the year 1980 was developed by the Tanzanian Ministry of Health. Attention will be focused mainly upon the technical problems involved, although technical progress and accomplishments were possible only because of the 'rational' political environment in which they were set. It should not be necessary to add (as a safeguard against the future?) that plans have a way of changing, even in a 'rational' political environment.

---

*For example, Lionel Cliffe and John S. Saul, *Socialism in Tanzania*, East African Publishing House, 1972 (Vol.1) and 1973 (Vol.2).
**J. K. Nyerere, *Ujamaa: Essays on Socialism*, Oxford University Press, 1968.
†Reported in *The Daily News*, Dar es Salaam, 6 January 1973.
††Reported in *The Daily News*, Dar es Salaam.
xIt may be of some interest to note that a 'health planner' is defined by WHO as one with a medical qualification, and an economist may only be designated a 'health economist'. These definitions are generally adhered to by UN agencies and health ministries.
xxThe fact that I was the only expatriate (and the only economist/planner) in the ministry created some special problems, but also many opportunities. Unlike expatriates working in ministries where they were numerous it was not possible to become part of a small isolated group, one *had* to communicate with Tanzanian colleagues.

1 BACKGROUND TO HEALTH PLANNING IN TANZANIA

Part I The Country

A. Geography and Population

Tanzania is an East African country bordering the Indian Ocean and stretching inland to Lake Victoria. Its mainland portion comprises the former Tanganyika, which with the islands of Zanzibar and Pemba constitutes modern Tanzania. The bulk of the country is made up of a vast plateau with an altitude of approximately 2,000 to 3,500 feet. On the coast there is a 10 to 50 mile wide belt at sea level. There are mountains in the deep south, the far west and in the furthest north. The highest point in Africa, Mount Kilimanjaro, with an altitude of 19,000 feet is at the Tanzanian frontier with Kenya. The climate is basically dry and warm and there are distinct wet and dry seasons.

With its 360,000 sq.miles Tanzania is comparable in size to the American state of Texas. The 13.5 million residents of the country are relatively thinly spread at approximately 35 persons to the square mile; however, population is growing at a rate of 2½% to 3% per year and so parts of the country are already experiencing land pressures. The population tends to be concentrated around the borders of the country, with the centre being more thinly populated. Large stretches of the country contain arable land, although much of it lies in areas of only marginal rainfall.

Almost 95% of the population is rural. The urban population (defined as those living in towns with urban councils) numbers in all about three-quarters of a million people. Of that total about 350,000 live in Dar es Salaam, the capital city, while the other 400,000 live in 13 other urban centres ranging in size from around 10,000 to 75,000. There are said to be 120 tribes in Tanzania, depending upon definitions: the largest single group, the Sukuma, has over a million members. It takes over a dozen of the largest tribal groupings together to constitute half the Tanzanian population. Less than 1% of the country's residents are non-African. Approximately half the population is under the age of 15. It is thought that around one-quarter of the population are Moslem and another quarter Christian, while the balance retain more traditional African beliefs.

6

B. History

Tanzania emerged into European history with the coming of the Arabs to the coastal areas bordering on the Indian Ocean. By the sixteenth century the Portuguese had come to the same coast and were in conflict with the Arabs who had established themselves there, particularly on the islands of Zanzibar, Pemba, Kilwa and Lamu. These mixed coastal conditions helped to create the so-called Swahili people. The name is taken from a language developed initially by the coastal people which, although basically Bantu in structure, has been enriched by the addition of many Arabic and other imported words.

The Germans made their appearance in East Africa in the area now known as Tanzania during the second half of the nineteenth century. By the time of the First World War they were well established and had begun a settlement process, particularly in the area just south of the present Kenya frontier. The process of railroad building was well begun and various estate crops, particularly sisal, were developed. The African population of the area did not accept colonisation without resistance and there were major wars fought from the 1880s until after the turn of the twentieth century. In the interim the British had established themselves on the islands of Zanzibar and Pemba and on the mainland in Kenya. During the First World War there was significant fighting in Tanzania between German and British forces, which resulted in many thousands of Africans losing their lives. At the end of the war the major part of the area that is now Tanzania was turned into a British League of Nations mandate.

As a mandated territory there was little further settlement and relatively little investment, and Kenya came to be the centre of East African investment and development. African nationalist organisations had of course always existed, and by the early 1950s they began to take shape in the form of the Tanganyika African National Union (TANU); Julius K. Nyerere became the leader of the party and the nationalist movement, and independence was achieved by 1961.

Tanzania came to independence as one of the most undeveloped countries in the world; although in point of fact it was Tanganyika that became independent in 1961 and not Tanzania. The nation of Tanzania came into being in early 1964 as a result of the merger between Tanganyika and the islands of Zanzibar and Pemba, which had become independent in December 1963. Independence came to Zanzibar under a government headed by the Sultan, but a revolution overthrew him barely a month later and paved the way for the merger with Tanganyika, thereby creating the United Republic of Tanzania.

Even some dozen years after independence Tanzania remained one

7

of the least developed countries in the world, and was in fact designated by the United Nations as one of the world's 25 poorest. The per capita income was still below 100 US dollars* in 1971/72. Most of the population is employed in the production of such subsistence crops as maize, sorgum, cassava, bananas, rice, beans, groundnuts and fruit. For exports the country is still heavily dependent upon a few agricultural products, particularly sisal, cotton, coffee and tea. The industrial base is very slim and comprises primarily a handful of consumer products such as beer, tobacco and textiles. There are an estimated 5½ million employed persons in the country; all but three-quarters of a million of that number are self-employed in agriculture (of which 90% is at subsistence level). Of those not occupied in agriculture there are about 400,000 in urban wage employment, 150,000 in agricultural employment primarily on estates, and another 200,000 in self-employment mainly as small traders and craftsmen. Primary education extends to about half the children of the relevant age group. In 1970 there were about 65,000 students who completed their primary schooling. In 1964 the comparable figure was less than 10,000. The number of students entering secondary schools and university is strictly controlled against planned manpower requirements. Thus in 1970 nearly 7,500 students entered secondary schooling and just over 1,500 entered form 5. These totals represent around double the numbers that entered such schooling levels in 1964. The country has made substantial progress in terms of high-level manpower; in 1971, of 10,000 such personnel in the economy half were Tanzanian; this compares with the 1961 figures of 500 Tanzanians out of a total of 5,000 high-level personnel. It is expected that by 1981, of 20,000 high-level employees 18,000 will be Tanzanian.

C. Political Structure

All discussion of Tanzanian policy must make reference to the Arusha Declaration of February 1967. This document remains the most significant single statement in respect of the development of socialism in Tanzania. In it, President Nyerere said that in the past 'we [Tanzanians] have been oppressed a great deal, we have been exploited a great deal and we have been disregarded a great deal', and that the time for significant change had arrived. The Arusha Declaration put Tanzania firmly on the path of socialist development, defined as follows: the absence of exploitation; the major means of production and exchange to be under the control

---

*Approximately seven Tanzanian shillings to one US dollar, and 18 to one pound sterling. All money figures will be in sterling unless otherwise stated. For convenience, because the exchange value against sterling has changed over the years, an exchange rate of 20 shillings to the pound will be used throughout.

of the peasants and workers; the existence of democracy; and the belief in socialism as a way of life, especially by the leadership of the nation's organisations. Self-reliance was proclaimed essential to this particular socialist path of development, meaning that money, especially aid from other countries, was not to be the major instrument of development, and that industrialisation was not to be the first and immediate priority. The proper bases for development are rather agriculture, the needs of the peasant, and plain hard work. The policy of self-reliance also meant an end to privilege. Leaders are now prohibited from holding shares in any company, being a director in any privately owned enterprises, receiving two or more salaries, owning a house which is rented to others, or being associated in any way with the practices of feudalism or capitalism. The Arusha Declaration very clearly points out that a state is not socialist simply because all the means of production are controlled and owned by the government. Everything depends on how, and for whose benefit, that control is exercised.

The level of political organisation in the country is extensive and, in principle at least, every citizen is a member of a 'ten-house cell'. Every group of ten houses has its chairman, and these chairmen in turn are organised into higher bodies that lead up to the National Executive Committee of the party (TANU).* The concept of ujamaa is also critical to Tanzanian development policy. The Swahili word ujamaa is usually loosely translated into English as socialism, but comes closer in its literal sense to something like 'familyhood', or, in practice, the process of working and living together; ujamaa attempts to do just that, in both a geographic and social sense. Because such a large part of the population of Tanzania has lived in a very scattered fashion there were earlier 'villageisation' schemes intended to bring the population together. These earlier schemes tended to be built around the production of one or another cash crop and people were brought together specifically for the purpose of producing this cash crop, which became in effect the cement that held them together. By contrast ujamaa, as a villageisation concept, in the post-Arusha period and particularly since 1970, has brought a different approach to the problem: one that does not particularly concentrate upon cash cropping as such — although such production is certainly not eschewed. Because the nation's population cannot organise their lives reasonably unless they are living and producing together, ujamaa has come to mean both the gathering together of scattered populations and a 'social' method of work-in the village as well as at national level.

---

*This description, as virtually all other discussion herein, refers only to mainland Tanzania (old Tanganyika). The relationship between the two basic parts of Tanzania — i.e. Tanganyika and Zanzibar — is extremely complex and in many if not most respects they remain separate countries.

The growth of the ujamaa movement during recent years has been most impressive. From a half million ujamaa villagers at the start of 1971 it was estimated that over two million people, representing around a sixth of the country's rural population, were living in one of 5,600 villages labelled 'ujamaa' by March 1973. In practise such a label can mean a great variety of things, ranging from villages that are in all ways as they had been before except for their new label and perhaps a piece of communal land, to those where people are working and producing together, marketing together, sharing profits together and generally doing all things in a Tanzanian socialist fashion.

D. Government Structure

Of course, in addition to the political structure described above Tanzania has its formal government apparatus comprising its parliamentary and civil service wings. The country is divided into 18 regions and 63 districts*. Each district consists of four or five divisions that are further sub-divided into wards. The regional and district levels are the significant ones for planning purposes. Before their dissolution in July 1972, with the reorganisation of government, there had been local authorities known as District Councils in each of the districts. The 14 urban areas previously having Urban Councils were dissolved at the end of 1973, with most becoming districts or sub-districts and Dar es Salaam a three-district region.

The parliament has basically an elected membership. Elections are competitive and it is not unusual for sitting members to be defeated. The president's office is located in the State House (and is referred to as 'the state house'). It comprises a number of important divisions, including Central Establishments. The ministerial set-up is not unusual, although at less than 20 there are fewer ministers than in many countries. One somewhat unusual structure is the Prime Minister's Office, which since the July 1973 reorganisation and decentralisation of government, has become in effect the 'mother ministry' of the regions and districts. Two ministries with special planning responsibilities are the Ministry of Finance (Treasury) and the Ministry of Economic Affairs and Development Planning (Devplan). The decentralisation of government substantially increased the powers and responsibilities of the regions and districts, as will become clearer in the course of the section on the planning and administration of the health services.

E. Health Situation

The health and disease situation of Tanzania is similar to the rest of Black Africa. It is marked by a generally low nutritional standard and

---

*Another two regions and a number of new districts have recently been created.

10

the fact that less than 10% of the population have adequate access to clean water. The principal health problems caused by the inadequate water supply and poor sanitation are bacterial pollution and proliferation of the bilharzia vectors which are found in almost all shallow wells and local streams. In the urban areas approximately 70% of the households have access to piped water. However, less than one-third of the urban population are served with piped water inside their own houses. Only four towns have a partial sewerage system and waste water treatment is available only in part of Dar es Salaam. Rural sanitation is of a low standard, as might be expected.

The relatively limited preventive health care measures that have so far been undertaken have had only a limited effect in preventing such diseases as malaria, gastroenteritis, worm infestation, bilharzia, tuberculosis, leprosy and venereal diseases. In fact available statistics show that most morbidity and mortality in Tanzania result from diseases that are relatively simple to treat and prevent. The common, mostly preventable childhood diseases result in an infant mortality rate estimated at 160 per 1,000 live births for ages 0-1, and a child mortality rate of about 120 per 1,000 live births for ages 1-5. In addition, it has been estimated that 120 of every 1,000 conceptions fail to result in a live birth.

In addition to the many health problems of childhood, there is a wide prevalence of such diseases as leprosy and tuberculosis (an estimated total of about 150,000 cases of each disease). Each year there are as many as 30,000 new tuberculosis cases, of which only about one-third are diagnosed and one-fifth adequately treated. Although only a relatively small proportion of the sick ever reach hospital, they are an important indication of the disease patterns of the country as a whole. Thus, infectious and parasitic diseases constitute roughly one-third of all hospital mortality as well as morbidity. Diseases of the respiratory system account for one-fifth of all mortality and one-tenth of the morbidity, while nutritionally related diseases such as malnutrition and anaemia account for approximately one-tenth of all deaths and almost as high a percentage of hospital admissions. Finally, the fourth highest cause of deaths in hospital relates to diseases of the digestive system, accounting for just under one-tenth of all mortality and morbidity. In all, these four poverty-linked disease groups account for three quarters of all hospital deaths. By contrast, the diseases most common in the affluent countries play a relatively negligible role in hospital deaths, e.g. disease of the heart constitutes less than 4 per cent, and neoplasms 5 per cent.

F. Health Services

There have been five different providers of health services in Tanzania:

first the central government through the Ministry of Health; secondly the local authorities, which include the district and urban councils; thirdly the voluntary agencies, which are primarily Christian church organisations; fourthly the occupational health services; and lastly the private sector, including both the private practitioner providing modern medical care and the traditional medical practitioners.

Government services are organised in a hierarchical structure. They begin at the lowest level with the dispensary, which is at present basically a centre for curative work — essentially the dispensing of drugs. There are now 1,200 such government-run facilities and around 300 others belonging to the voluntary agencies. The average government dispensary will serve a total of over 20,000 out-patient visits per annum, as well as a number of in-patients in its two or three beds. The rural health centre is a larger institution capable of offering a higher level of curative activity as well as other health care services. There are now over 100 such centres in Tanzania, each containing an average of 30 beds and dealing with close to 70,000 out-patient visits a year. Above the dispensaries and health centres are the district, regional and supra-regional or national 'consultant' hospitals. In Tanzania there are about 65 government hospitals, of which three offer specialist consultant services. The work of these various facilities will be discussed later in some detail.

In the past, local authorities were responsible for an important part of the available health services. The District Councils had responsibility for the rural dispensaries until 1972 and for the rural health centres until 1969, when the latter came under the central government. In 1972 these councils were reorganised and these functions were taken from them. The rural dispensaries are now the responsibility of the new regional and district Development Councils, along with virtually all the other health facilities at regional and district level that had previously been managed from Dar es Salaam by the Ministry of Health. The urban councils have been reorganised so that there is a uniform structure throughout the country. The major health responsibilities of the urban councils have been such public health activities as spraying against malaria and the running of some urban clinics.

The voluntary agencies offer services primarily through their 60 or so hospitals and 300 dispensaries. The occupational health sector is made up of urban and rural components. The urban side exists primarily in the form of the Group Occupational Health Service, which offers its services on the basis of insurance schemes mainly to the industrial sector within Dar es Salaam. In addition to these urban services there are a number of estate hospitals and other health facilities, typically at sugar or tea plantations. The volume of such services in absolute terms is not large, but does claim a disproportionate

12

share of all health services in terms of the size of the population being served. The last area of the health services is the private sector (although the voluntary agency and occupational health sectors are also, strictly speaking, private). There are about 50 private practitioners left in Tanzania, mostly non-Tanzanian citizens of Asian extraction. The number of private practitioners has been declining rapidly, from 150 in 1970 to around a third of that number in 1973. In addition to the modern private practitioner there is a large traditional health care sector.

The health sector is one of the largest sources of wage employment in Tanzania. Total health employment is estimated at around 20,000, which represents about 5% of total non-agricultural wage employment. Total expenditure on modern health services in 1973 was of the order of £15 million, or over 3% of gross national product.

The Ministry of Health is headed by a minister, assisted by a junior minister. For many years the day-to-day running of the ministry was divided between a Principal Secretary (previously Permanent Secretary) and a Chief Medical Officer. The post of Chief Medical Officer has recently been done away with in a general reorganisation of the ministry, which is now organised into three divisions, all of them responsible to the Principal Secretary. The three divisions are manpower development; hospital services; and preventive services; each division is headed by a director. In addition to these divisions there is a planning and analysis section within the ministry which is directly responsible to the Principal Secretary.

The health work of each region and district of the country is headed by a Regional or District Medical Officer. Every region and district has its political leader, either the Regional Commissioner or Area (District) Commissioner. Alongside these political figures there is the Regional or District Development Director. Under the development directors, as part of their staff, are the usual regional or district officers such as the Regional Medical Officer, the Regional Engineer, the District Education Officer, etc. Since the decentralisation of government regional and district officers are not directly responsible to their mother ministries in Dar es Salaam, but to regional and district leaderships. Although there is liaison with the operational ministries with regard to the planning and development of services, the direct line of command is within the districts and regions and then to the Prime Minister's Office in Dar es Salaam.

Since the decentralisation of government the Ministry of Health in Dar es Salaam has continued to be responsible for the running of three large consultant hospitals plus one national psychiatric and one T.B. hospital, as well as certain national preventive services and units, e.g. a health education unit, a central nutrition unit, a malaria control service,

13

etc. The ministry also continues to be responsible for the central pathology and chemical laboratories, a central dental unit, and a number of institutions concerned with medical production and supplies, i.e. a vaccine plant, a pharmaceutical plant, and central and zonal medical stores. The central ministry is also responsible for about three dozen training schools and programmes for paramedical and auxiliary health workers, and handles the allocation of grants to voluntary agency hospitals and training schools, and certain external grants such as that for the World Health Organisation and a flying doctor service based in Nairobi. The regions have taken responsibility for the running of all the government hospitals in the country, except for the five mentioned above, as well as over 100 rural health centres and 1,200 dispensaries plus some other relatively minor services.

Part II Development of Health Services
A. Early Colonial Years*

As everywhere in Africa, there existed in Tanzania an extensive system of traditional medical care at the time of the coming of the first Europeans. Although there is relatively little documentation about this system of care it has probably not changed very much from that in operation today. More or less 'modern' medicine was introduced to East Africa by the first missionaries. David Livingstone, the explorer missionary, was the first doctor to enter what is now Tanzania (in the early 1850s). During the 1870s and 1880s the scattered missionary doctors who came to the country erected hospitals in connection with their missionary work, and particularly with the slave trade then continuing in this part of Africa.

The appearance of the German government in Tanzania in the late 1880s brought the establishment of the first governmental medical institutions. The first hospitals to be introduced had as their basic purpose the treatment of colonial officers and their families, who were based largely in the few existing towns. These hospitals did generally offer some sort of service to the non-European population, although only, of course, of a very fragmentary nature. In all, the German colonial government was responsible for the building of 12 general hospitals during their 26 years of rule in German East Africa. The first-ever German government-financed hospital, built in Dar es Salaam in 1897, still functions as a maternity hospital for the city.

The end of the First World War brought a change of hands in Tanzania as Britain became the new colonial ruler. The British somewhat broadened the system of medical services, particularly by

*For a detailed description of the pre-independence period see Clyde,D.F., *History of the Medical Services of Tanganyika*, Government Printer, Dar es Salaam, 1962.

extending them into the countryside with the creation of rural 'dispensaries'. These dispensaries were staffed primarily by what were called tribal dressers and were under the management of the so-called native authorities. The dispensaries tended to function primarily as poor copies of the hospitals, in that they were mainly centres for curative medicine in spite of the stated intention of making them centres of preventive health care. Although the general framework of the health services as they now exist in Tanzania was created by the British in the 1920s, their development was extremely limited. Thus the number of dispensaries grew from 35 in 1926, when they were first established, to 285 in 1931, but from that year until 1936 the number remained more or less static (see Table 1). In fact the total number of dispensaries had increased to only 334 by the end of the Second World War*. Under the pressures of depression and war Britain was unwilling to support any substantial investment in the social infrastructure of her colonies.

B. The Post-War Period

The post-war period saw some important expansion and development in the health and medical services; for example, the number of dispensaries grew from over 300 in 1946 to almost 1,000 in 1960. Many of these structures were built locally by the people, and the resulting buildings left much to be desired. However, the major problem was not building standards but the fact that government had neither the manpower nor the finance to staff most of these dispensaries. At least as important as their number was the type of work these facilities, particularly the dispensaries, were capable of performing. For many years the overall strategy of the medical department of the Tanganyikan colonial government had been to expand and improve the hospitals. It was argued that such development was an essential precondition to the further development of the health services in the territory. It may be worth noting that this pattern was being followed in spite of much discussion of the need for more preventive health work, especially in the countryside. In any event, the volume of resources being made available to the medical department was such as to make it extremely difficult for much health work of any sort to be carried out.

Until the end of the Second World War it would have been extremely difficult to speak of any organised health planning in Tanzania. Such planning as there was seemed mostly to depend upon the yearly state of finance of the medical department and on the abilities of any particular Chief Medical Officer. However, after the end of the Second World War

---

*Figures from Van Etten, G., "Towards Research on Health Development in Tanzania", *Social Science and Medicine,* 1972, Vol.6, pp.335-357.

Table 1. Growth of Some Selected Health Service Indicators: 1890 to Independence

	1890	1910	1921	1925	1930	1936	1940/1	1945/6[1]	1950	1955	1960/1[1]
Hospitals	5	–	–	–	–	–	–	–	84	86	100
Government	2	15	13	–	22	–	58	–	61	52	54
Voluntary Agencies[2]	3	–	–	–	–	–	–	–	23	34	46
Hospital Beds	–	1,200	–	–	–	–	–	6,300	–	–	10,636
Government	–	–	–	–	–	–	–	4,300	4,535	5,206	6,310
Voluntary Agencies	–	–	–	–	–	–	–	2,000	–	–	4,326
Dispensaries	–	–	–	–	–	–	–	–	–	–	942[4]
Government (local authority)	–	–	–	–	247	297	–	334	428	515	715
Voluntary Agencies	–	–	–	353	595	–	–	–	–	–	227
Qualified Doctors	–	53	31	53	–	–	–	115	154	–	403
Government	5	43	26	–	–	47	39	59	62	70	140
Voluntary Agencies	–	4	2	–	–	–	17	18	32	43	81
Private Practitioners	–	6	3	–	–	–	–	38	60	–	182
Inpatients (000's)[6]	–	–	12	28	35	38	39	63	81	111	234
Government	–	–	–	–	–	–	–	–	–	–	149
Voluntary Agencies	–	–	–	–	–	–	–	–	–	–	85
Outpatients (000's)[7]	–	–	–	–	–	–	–	–	–	–	8,870
Government (Central)	–	708	101	244	394	598	814	971	–	1,200	1,700
Local Authorities	–	–	–	–	370[9]	530	1,113	1,400	–	–	6,500
Voluntary Agencies	–	–	–	–	–	–	–	–	–	–	670
Recurrent Government Expenditure (£000's)											
Government	–	65	79	144	275	186	193	364	854	1,600	2,700

Sources:

Annual Medical Report for 1945, Dar es Salaam, 1947; History of the Medical Services of Tanganyika, D. F. Clyde, Government Printer, Dar es Salaam, 1962, as reported in "The Integration of Church Related Medical Services", in The Policy of Tanzania, T. W. J. Schulpen, Koninklijk Instituut Voor De Tropen, Amsterdam, 1973, unpublished theses; The Health Services of Tanganyika, R. Titmuss, Pitman Medical Publishing Co. Ltd, London, 1964; and (for 1960 figures) unpublished data of the Ministry of Health, Dar es Salaam.

1. Data for the earlier year was utilised when available.
2. Christian church health services.
3. The figure is for 1926.
4. Not including 19 rural health centres.
5. The figure is for 1929.
6. Hospitals only.
7. First attendances only.
8. The figure is for 1913.
9. The figure is for 1931.

a more coordinated approach to health development began to be taken by the colonial system and its administrators. A review of medical policies for Tanzania was undertaken in 1949 by Dr. E. Pridie, Chief Medical Adviser to the Colonial Office. Dr. Pridie accepted as a first principle that the curative services needed to be further developed before more preventive work or very much of a rural infrastructure could be brought under development. In fact, Pridie is often cited as the basis (one might almost say excuse) for the concentration upon curative services which for so many years followed his report. However, when Pridie's views are read more carefully they indicate that the matter was not nearly so simple as later interpretations indicated. Pridie's views are particularly important in that the first-ever Tanzanian health 'plan' of the early 1950s, although never acted upon, bore his name. The following extracts are taken from a report written by Dr. Pridie in 1950 and entitled "Reflections on Recent African Tours"*

"It is almost impossible and perhaps dangerous to attempt to define a detailed medical policy covering all the African Colonial Territories as they vary so much one from another, but in general I consider that the first aim of a medical service in tropical Africa must be to provide a balanced and efficient curative and preventive medical organisation covering the whole country, which can then be used as a foundation for implementing the various more ambitious schemes which are required to improve public health and to prevent disease. The medical services must be responsible for the public health of all communities and have a special responsibility to provide facilities for medical care and treatment of all Government officials and for all, or the majority of, the population. Although preventive and social medicine have more lasting beneficial effects it is essential to have a well-balanced medical service, giving due importance to curative medicine, as curative medicine is demanded by the people and its popularity makes preventive medicine acceptable to them. There is, however, a tendency to spend too large a proportion of funds on hospital services in some territories and not enough comparatively on preventive medicine as a whole and on curative and preventive medicine in rural areas in particular."

This quotation does imply the need for greater inputs for the curative services and yet Pridie clearly points out the tendency to allocate too large a proportion of funds to hospital services, in some territories at least. Later in his report Pridie notes that the average expenditure for medical services of the total colonial budget was about 7% and thought

---

*Pridie, E.D., 'Reflections on Recent African Tours', 1950, mimeo.

that something like 10% might be more appropriate. (The actual figure in Tanzania at that time was about 9%.) Dr. Pridie also had some interesting comments to make about hospital building, as in the following extract.

"There is a tendency, however, in some instances in Colonial Territories, to spend too much money on hospital construction owing to the very high standard aimed at. It is true that there is much to be said for the highest possible standard if it can be afforded, but in tropical countries the end result is apt to be a few magnificent hospitals and a number of filthy, squalid hospitals which there is no money to replace. It is worth considering what is the cheapest type of construction which will provide adequate accommodation to enable the doctors and nurses to carry out their work under suitable conditions and to have standard set plans for hospital wards, etcetera, for each type of hospital in each area, as a rough guide, subject to alteration with building costs, etc. I have recommended that a central hospital in the capital of the country should not cost more than £1,000 a bed, excluding quarters for staff and training schools; a Provincial Headquarters Hospital £500 a bed, and District Hospitals £250 a bed. Some hospitals under construction in Colonial Territories are likely to cost between two and three thousand pounds a bed. Another point to be settled is the number of hospital beds per thousand of the population. This varies considerably at present from one to 4,000 in Nigeria to one to 800 in British Somaliland and possibly averages about one to 1,500. I suggest that one bed per thousand of the population is about the minimum with which to provide adequate hospital facilities and about the maximum a tropical African country can afford without starving other medical and health services, and I have always worked with this proportion. It is, of course, impossible to give more than a rough guide, and it is useful to have a "yard-stick". One difficulty about hospital accommodation in Africa is that the wards tend to become crowded with cases who are really out-patients who have travelled a long distance and have nowhere else to live while under treatment. Hostels or resthouses should be provided by the appropriate local authority to accommodate these patients and save beds. This is already being done in some countries. Annexes to accommodate chronic and convalescent cases also help."

It is from the above that the target of one bed per thousand of population was to become accepted in Tanzania as an appropriate goal for hospital development; in practice this target still exists. However, what is most important about the above is that although Dr. Pridie was

18

wise enough to set targets for beds against the specific cost of those beds, what has happened in Tanzania, as in many other countries, is that the target for bed numbers has become established independently of costs which have long since exceeded those figures set by Pridie. Pridie also discusses at some length the problems connected with the organisation of rural dispensaries and health centres.

"In some territories elaborate rural health centres have been formed with a large staff of doctors, nursing sisters, sanitary inspectors, health visitors, etc., some of whom are strangers to the area, or the territory they are working in. The disadvantages of these large, elaborate rural health centres, although very useful for training staff, are that they are so expensive that it is impossible to provide a sufficient number to cover more than a fraction of the territory, and wherever you have doctors and sisters stationed, the rural health centre tends to become a hospital and the preventive and social side, which is the main objective, is forgotten. I saw one rural health centre under construction, with an operating theatre. There is another point: in my experience it is far easier for an African from the tribe a rural health centre is working among to persuade the people to change their ways of living in the interests of their health than for an African from another part of the country or an expatriate officer. For all these reasons, I personally consider that a rural health centre should be of the simplest possible type and staffed by sub-ordinate medical and health staff, who should be local Africans where possible. These rural health centres, provided they can be properly supervised, should be as numerous as can be afforded to provide some medical facilities for the bulk of the population which hospitals can never reach in addition to their more important work in preventive and social medicine, but they should not have beds — except a few for detention cases."

The basic problem discussed by Dr. Pridie, of the size of the rural health centre and therefore its running cost and the relationship of these costs to total national coverage, remains unresolved in virtually all parts of Africa. The health centres continue to be built at a level which is much too large and costly to make it possible for the country to reach the whole of its population with these centres. Dr. Pridie recommended on average one rural health centre to each 25,000 of population. More recent work would confirm this to be a realistic target. Enough has been drawn from Dr. Pridie to indicate the sound basis of much of his reasoning. Unfortunately, however, that part of the colonial heritage which gave support to the further expansion of the hospitals and the curative services in Tanzania and other parts of Africa has been singled out for repetition in various guises throughout the intervening years. Nonetheless, the coming of independence in 1961 created very different possibilities for the further development of health services in Tanzania.

C. Independence

At independence Tanzania found itself with one hundred hospitals containing 11,000 beds, of which over 40% were in voluntary agency institutions. In addition there were almost 1,000 dispensaries. Central government was employing 6,000 medical staff. There were 400 registered medical doctors in the country although only 12 of them were Tanzanians. In addition there were about 1,400 nurses. Government recurrent expenditure for the health services came to about £2.5 million per annum, which worked out at less than £0.25 per head of population. There was some additional spending on the part of the voluntary agencies, the local authorities, the occupational health services and on private practitioners. Total per capita expenditure for health care may have come to £0.35 or £0.40. The 100 hospitals admitted in 1960 over 230,000 in-patients, saw almost 2½ million new out-patient cases and had a total of 7½ million out-patient visits. In addition there were 4½ million new out-patient cases at the 1,000 rural dispensaries as part of the total number of 15 million out-patient visits.

Some two and a half years after gaining independence Tanzania began its first five-year plan. The health component of that plan was to some degree assisted by the earlier Titmuss Report*. The proposals contained in this report covered virtually every aspect of health service development in Tanzania, and were particularly important in establishing certain base line data, particularly for the non-governmental sectors, e.g. the voluntary agencies and occupational health services. In terms of implementation, especially in more recent years, the Titmuss Report is not consciously referred to by government administrators, although in earlier years somewhat more attention may have been paid to it. When comparing current health service developments in Tanzania with the recommendations of the Titmuss Report, a certain degree of overlap can be found, although this results more from a concordance of independent judgements than any other factor.

One particular development which has deflected the accuracy of the Titmuss recommendations has been the relatively rapid increase in the resources made available to the health services in the years following the report. The first and second five-year plans also significantly underestimated this volume of finance and therefore the possibilities for health service development. It is fair to add that because health

---

*R. Titmuss et al, *The Health Services of Tanganyika,* Pitman Medical Publishing Co. Ltd., London 1964.

service development policy in Tanzania had in the earliest post-independence days been largely the responsibility of a very few people, that health development unduly reflected individual rather than overall national planning policy. To some degree this was inevitable, given the basic dependence upon graduate doctors for the making of health policy and the fact that at independence there were only 12 citizen graduate doctors in Tanzania. In any event, the Titmuss Report remains an important part of the literature on health planning and an example of a good, early study of health service development in independent Black Africa. To understand Tanzanian health service development it is more important, however, to examine directly the first five-year plan and its outcome.

D. The First Five-Year Plan

The health section of the first Tanganyika Five-Year Plan for Economic and Social Development* for the years 1964-1969 was based upon the report of the medical development committee for the first five-year plan. This committee was made up of ten members; all but two, including the chairman, were Europeans. The committee worked from April 1963 through February 1964. The group went about its business efficiently, in that it first determined the cost of additional construction and the recurrent costs that would ensue from these additional facilities. It was estimated that an additional hospital ward would cost £400 per bed and new hospitals would cost £800 per bed to construct. New rural health centres were estimated at £15,000 to £18,000 each, but when combined with the average cost of upgrading a dispensary to rural health centre level the figure of £10,000 per health centre was arrived at.

The recurrent costs of these additional facilities were also calculated. District and other medium and small hospitals were estimated to run at £220 per bed and the larger hospitals in Dar es Salaam and Tanga at £400 per bed. The cost to government of a mission hospital bed, that is one which was receiving a 'grant-in-aid', was £80 per bed. The running costs of a rural health centre were estimated at £3,750 per annum. The overall health budget was calculated to grow at 4% per annum to a total of £3 million in 1969. Population growth was estimated at 2% per annum, which turned out to be a gross underestimation, to a total of 11 million people by 1969 and 14 million by 1980. Life expectancy was estimated at 35 to 45 years, with the goal of 50 years by 1980.

The committee included the following significant statement in their report: "All previous development plans in Tanganyika emphasised the importance of development in the field of preventive health as opposed

*Tanganyika Five-Year Plan for Economic and Social Development, 1st July 1964 - 30th June 1969, Government Printer, Dar es Salaam, 1964.

21

to curative medicine. In spite of this the implementation of measures designed to expand the curative services has absorbed almost all money available for development and in the event the preventive health services have tended to diminish rather than to expand. We now consider that this must in the circumstances not be allowed to occur again and therefore recommended a strictly limited expansion of the curative services. It is hoped that this limited expansion will absorb only a limited proportion of the moneys made available to medical development."

After this hopeful statement the committee went on to its specific recommendations. They began with the proposal that consultant hospitals be developed by 1969 in Dar es Salaam, Tanga, Moshi and Mwanza and that by 1980 there be an additional consultant hospital for the southern half of the country, perhaps at Masasi. In addition to the consultant hospitals it was recommended that 300 additional dispensaries be constructed, mostly through self-help. The most important manpower proposals included an increased intake of non-graduate medical students to 25 per annum, the establishment of two A nursing schools,* a sister tutor course, psychiatric nursing, and an up-grading course for medical assistants. Also, the establishment of training schools for medical aids with an intake of 100 per annum, with that intake to be from form 4 instead of from primary school; midwifery training was to be expanded and the training of village midwives systematised. A nutrition training unit would be started, as well as programmes for laboratory technicians, health inspectors, hospital dispensers, health assistants and certain other paramedical and auxiliary groups. The committee also had some brief remarks to make on the development of preventive activities, although no specific targets were set.

The total expenditure for the capital budget was to be £5.7 million, of which central government was to cover only £1.65 million. The balance was to come from the voluntary agencies (£2.9 million) the local authorities (£1 million) and from external assistance (£0.1 million). The essential strategy of the committee's report was for the local authorities to cover the cost of the dispensary and rural health centre programmes while the mission institutions were to build the bulk of the non-consultant hospital beds: central government was to put most of its money into the development of the consultant hospitals.

Of course it was possible for the Ministry of Health to guarantee the expenditures they were proposing (once they were approved) for the construction of the consultant hospitals, although it could not assure the expenditure of the voluntary agencies and there was also no full

---

*A nurses are recruited for training after secondary school education, and B nurses after primary schooling.

assurance that the local authorities would have the sums available to them for the completion of the dispensary and rural health centre building programmes. In the event, the first five-year plan incorporated the basic strategy of the medical development committee.

In the actual plan document, for the rural health services it was proposed that the 1,039 rural dispensaries existing in 1963 be increased by 300 over the five-year period to a total of 1,339: for rural health centres the comparable increase was to be from 30 to 113, an increase of 83 over the five years. In practice only 38 of the planned 300 rural dispensaries and 20 of the planned 83 rural health centres were developed by 1969. Of the services to be developed by the government sector by both central government and the local authorities, only 13% of the planned dispensaries were completed and 24% of the rural health centres, but 80% of the hospital beds; the basic reason for the very different completion rates being the ability of central government to implement the construction of the hospital beds while the health centres and dispensaries were largely left to the impoverished local authorities.

With regard to hospital development the medical committee had recommended the construction of 3,400 new and 300 replacement beds, of which about half were to be in government hospitals and half in voluntary agency institutions. Of the 1,900 government beds almost 1,400 were to be at the new consultant hospitals. As shown in Table 2, the final five-year plan allowed for the construction of only 2,245 beds, of which 1,600 were new and 600 replacement beds. Although the plan failed to distinguish explicitly between government and voluntary agency construction, it can be assumed that the indicated bed construction was for government institutions only. In the event, by 1969 there were 16,031 beds, of which 8,294 were at government hospitals and 7,737 in voluntary agency institutions. This represents an increase of 3,761 beds in the country as a whole over the plan period. There was an increase in government beds of 1,309 as opposed to the planned increase of 1,632, as well as 2,452 voluntary agency beds (although the medical committee report had recommended an increase of only about two-thirds that number).

Table 2. Hospital Bed Expansion, First Five-Year Plan

	ACTUAL 1963	PLANNED New	Replacement	TARGET 1969
General	8,307	1,933	602	10,240
Maternity	1,348	197	11	1,545
Psychiatric	1,207	242	–	1,449
Tuberculosis	1,408	260	–	1,668
	12,270	1,632	613	14,902

Planned expenditure by the Ministry of Health was to be £1.6 million, which represented 1.6% of total central government first five-year plan funding and 2% of all ministerial spending. However, actual expenditure came to only about 1.3% of all ministerial spending. It had been estimated that the recurrent budget of the health ministry would be £3 million by 1969; the actual figure turned out to be around £4 million.

The most important conclusion that can be reached about the first five-year plan is that because the bulk of government expenditure was directed towards the hospitals rather than the countryside it tended to increase health service inequalities. One of the factors involved was that the cost of building additional hospital beds, especially at the larger institutions, had increased considerably. However, in the field of manpower development some important progress had been made, and paramedical, nursing and auxiliary training had moved ahead relatively rapidly. Medical assistant training was established at Tanga and a rural medical aid school at Kibaha, as well as schools for health auxiliaries at Ifakara and Tanga. It is also important to note that a national school for graduate doctors was established in Dar es Salaam, although it is interesting that this was not one of the targets of the first five-year plan.

E. The Second Five-Year Plan

General analysis of the first five-year plan has shown that in many important respects it increased rather than decreased inequality within Tanzanian society*. However, the Arusha Declaration of 1967 laid the foundation for a different type of planning, and the second five-year plan represented progress in the direction of a more equitable society in Tanzania. Nonetheless, the second five-year plan (like the first) remained essentially a technocratic document with a distinctly limited ability to ensure the accomplishment of the fine egalitarian aspirations set out in it. However, the second plan was in many significant ways different from the first. For one thing, the second plan was more realistic in that it did not attempt to detail the expenditure pattern for each of the five years of the plan. This was done in recognition of Tanzania's inability to control, for example, its volume of exports and the prices of those exports. This question was particularly important because of the experience during the course of the first plan of having the price of sisal, the country's leading export, fall decisively. Another related experience was the breaking-off of diplomatic relations with the United Kingdom and the Federal Republic of Germany, which meant that virtually no foreign aid was accepted from the two powers that had been the major source of external assistance to Tanzania. In

*A. Van De Laar, "Arusha: Before and After," *East Africa Journal,* November 1968.

24

general the second five-year plan was couched in much more flexible terms, with specific projects being laid out only for the first two of the five years.

In his introduction to the five-year plan, the President pointed out that "There is another factor which makes it extremely difficult to assess our achievements over the past five years by comparing what we have actually done with the figures presented in the First Plan document. In 1964 we had not worked out at all clearly the implication of our socialist beliefs. As a result, we were simply trying to attract investment of any type and the role of public enterprise appeared to be that of filling in gaps left by private investment. Indeed it is worth remembering that the National Development Corporation (NDC) was not created until 1965, and its function as a promoter of socialist large-scale production was spelt out even later." The President went on to say "All this changed in 1967 when the Arusha Declaration was adopted; the NDC was then given its very heavy new responsibilities, and other parastatal organisations were created. A similar change affected agriculture. In the First Plan we talked only in terms of increased production and our efforts were directed at encouraging greater output, even when this meant helping individual peasants to become employers of labour. The policy of Ujamaa Vijijini which was adopted by the party in October 1967 meant the beginning of a change; gradually we are moving towards a programme of integrated rural development which leads in the direction of the kind of socialist policy we are trying to create. This changed policy is fully reflected in the new plan, which has socialist rural development at its very core."

"For all these reasons the Second Plan document is very different from the First. It is much more a statement of strategy and its projections into the future are not always as precise. This does not mean that we have made no forecasts; planning is impossible without them. But the general targets and forecasts are given as a basis for a continual process of progress assessment; they will enable necessary adjustments throughout the economy to meet particular changes."*

President Nyerere concluded his speech with the following words: "Running right through our development activities must be this kind of consideration for people. No one who ignores the feelings of people can be a socialist, for socialism is about people. And it is not good enough just to think of the 'masses' and how they will benefit from a particular project in the long run. The masses are the people considered together: if you do not care about a small group of people, it is at least open to doubt whether you really care about the large group. Of course, it is true that we have to proceed with nationally needed

---

*Tanzania Second Five-Year Plan for Economic and Social Development, 1st July 1969 - 30th June 1974, Government Printer, Dar es Salaam. Vol.1, p.ix.

25

projects, even though they will cause inconvenience and difficulty for particular groups; we cannot stop building a railway because some people have their farms on the proposed route or object to the noise which the trains will make. But the question I am discussing is not whether the project goes ahead, but how this inconvenience and difficulty for a few people is handled. A socialist will care about them as well as about the railway; a socialist leader will get their understanding and support for the railway, and will help them to take the opportunity of the move to organise their new lives on a basis which allows for socialist growth.*

"Friends we have a lot to do, I hope this week every delegate will work hard to understand the problems and opportunities before our people. We rely upon you to explain this Plan, and to cooperate with all your fellow citizens for its success. The people of Tanzania have shown what they can do despite great difficulties. Now that we have prepared our organisation for further development, let us go forward to even greater efforts in the future.

"To plan is to choose. Choose to go forward"*

The second five-year plan, then, was an important step forward in helping to formulate a policy of socialist development in Tanzania. Nonetheless it had many inherent weaknesses which were perhaps inevitable given the early stage of socialist development in the country.

By 1969, when the second five-year plan was begun, there was a total of 16,000 hospital beds in the country, of which something over half were located in government institutions (see Table 4). The number of rural health centres had reached 50 and the number of rural dispensaries over 1,350. Recurrent expenditure by the Ministry of Health was almost £4 million for the year 1968-69, the last year of the first plan, which figure represented an increase of roughly 60% in central government health expenditure over the seven years since independence. Annual expenditure increases had been rather modest between independence and the year 1967-68 but 1968-69 had seen a very substantial rise. The manpower situation had shown some improvement over the years but the basic shortages remained. Progress had been made in producing more nurses, and 74 Tanzanian doctors had by then been trained (at independence there were only 12).

The health section of the second five-year plan stated "The principal objectives in medical development are to bring about a society of healthy Tanzanians, in which the individual has a reasonable prospect of survival through childhood and normal adult years, free from the

*Tanzania SFYP, Vol.1, pp.XXII-XXIII.

Table 3. Ministry of Health Second Five-Year Plan Expenditure (in £000's)

	1969-1974 Planned (%)	Approved estimates (%)	1969-1971 Actual expenditure (% of App. est.)
Hospital Services	3,020 (64)	1,010 (55)	645 (64)
Rural Health Centres	1,360 (29)	415 (22)	210 (51)
Training Programmes	120 (3)	330 (18)	330 (100)
Preventive Services	190 (4)	95 (5)	85 (89)
TOTALS	4,690 (100)	1,850 (100)	1,270 (69)

incubus of infection or preventable disorders and able to obtain medical aid when he needs it. These objectives will be pursued through a coordinated, and increasingly integrated, national health service, utilising to the full the facilities made available by the central government, and local authorities, and the voluntary and other agencies." It was claimed that "The Second Plan will increase emphasis on the development of preventive and rural health services, mainly through the agency of rural health centres. One important intention during the Second Plan, therefore, is that the central government construct and manage many new Rural Health Centres, and assume full responsibility for them and partial responsibility for District Council dispensaries."*

The total planned capital allocation over the five years of the plan for the health sector came to £4.7 million; of that, some £2.8 million was earmarked for hospital services and another £200,00 was to go to hospital-related ancillary services; £1.36 million was for the construction of the new rural health centres, only £120,000 was allocated to manpower training development and £190,000 to public health/preventive health care programmes. The planned public health programmes were related to the further development of national health education and nutrition services, and the establishment of an environmental sanitation unit and a communicable disease control unit. A small sum was also allocated to the occupational health services. Manpower training expenditures were set aside, particularly for the construction of student hostels at Muhimbili Hospital, the large national institution in Dar es Salaam. A new nursing school was to be established at Tanga, a psychiatric nursing course was to be set up, and another school for medical assistants to be started. The large sum of money intended for hospital development covered a wide range of activities: in some cases the extension of existing buildings, in some the addition of new wards, and in others the construction of large new hospitals. An obstetric block in Dar es Salaam was to be built at an estimated cost of almost £300,000, and funds were allocated to the first phase of

*Tanzania SFYP, Vol.1, p.CDXII

consultant hospitals at Mtwara and Iringa as well as a new regional hospital at Musoma. In addition a number of out-patient centres were to be developed in the larger towns, and psychiatric wards were to be constructed at six hospital centres. The £200,000 allocated for ancillary services was to be used primarily for the expansion of the central medical stores and the improvement of various pathology labs and dental units around the country.

The major departure of the second five-year plan was the planned construction of 80 rural health centres, which represented the most significant development so far as the rural health sector was concerned. It had long been a matter of policy that at least one rural health centre was needed for each 50,000 of the rural population. It was accepted that this target could not be reached during the second plan period and the goal for the plan was set at 80 new rural health centres, which would have made for a national total,at the end,of 149, or one for roughly 85,000 of the rural population. The cost of constructing each health centre, including staff housing and a vehicle, was set at £17,000 and the recurrent costs, which were then running at about £4,000 per year, were expected to rise to £6,000 p.a. with the future proper staffing of the centres.

The manpower development plans included an expansion of medical school output, the establishment of two new medical assistant and four rural medical aid schools, and the beginning of a new cadre of village medical helpers that would be utilised on a non-salaried basis, especially in ujamaa villages. Nursing expansion was to be continued with the establishment of the second and third schools for A nurses, and four or five more B-level schools, including one for psychiatric nursing. It was also intended to establish courses for nurse tutors and public health nursing. Some relatively minor proposals were also made with regard to other categories of paramedical staff. The most significant positive aspect of the manpower proposals was the important expansion of medical assistant and rural medical aid training. Most of the new schools were to be constructed (and later run) by the voluntary agencies, thereby relieving the ministry of the need to include those costs in the plan estimates.

It can be seen that the largest area of health service development during the second five-year plan was to be in the hospital sector, although a substantial effort for expansion in the number of health centres was also to be made. Almost two-thirds of total expenditure was set aside for hospital and related development, not quite 30% for the rural health centres, and only 7% for manpower training schemes and preventive health programmes. In practice the expenditure pattern for the early years of the second five-year plan turned out to be even more hospital- and urban-biased than were the plan estimates.

During the first two years of the second five-year plan (1969-71) there were approved estimates for the health ministry of £1.85 million for development expenditure (see Table 3). This was almost £500,000 greater than had been originally estimated in the five-year plan document. However, during the third year of the plan the approved estimate fell to only £220,000, as opposed to the almost £1.3 million that had been called for in the plan. This fall was at least partly related to the fact that the Ministry of Health succeeded in spending only 70% of the total of the first two years' allocation, and that the actual costs of specific projects were turning out to be very different from the originally projected figures. It was also becoming increasingly clear that the health section, like other parts of the second five-year plan, were failing to live up to 'Arusha type' aspirations.

Of the £1.85 million approved for expenditure over the first two years of the plan just half was for projects to be carried out in Dar es Salaam, in addition to which other generalised national allocations included expenditures intended for the city. An important part of the Dar es Salaam projects was intended eventually to serve national purposes, e.g. teaching facilities at Muhimbili hospital, but more than half the total of expenditure approved for Dar es Salaam projects had no specific bearing upon health service development outside the city. In addition, a significant part of the balance would also be available primarily, at least in the first instance to those resident within the city. Over the two years under discussion the actual expenditure on Dar es Salaam projects came to 84% of approved expenditures, but for projects outside the city actual expenditure came to less than 60% of the approved estimates. It was of course much easier to organise and spend money on projects within the city than outside it: this was not only because of the greater number of contractors and suppliers available in Dar es Salaam but because of the more immediate interest of those in Dar es Salaam in city-based projects, and the ability of those having such interests to influence affairs in the ministries.

Of the total of approved estimates for the first two years of the plan only 5% was intended for preventive health care projects; actual expenditures were marginally lower. Of the 22% of total approved estimates intended for rural health centres over the two-year period only just over half was actually spent (although in the latter year of the two years under discussion expenditure came to 72% of estimates, compared with only 20% in the first year). Both approved estimates and actual expenditures for the extension of training institutions came to considerably more than had originally been anticipated in the plan, and the full 18% of the finally approved estimates was spent during the two years. For hospital and related services it proved possible to spend only 64% of approved expenditures. The development budget for the third year of the plan, 1971-72, was cut very sharply and only £220,000 of capital development was approved for expenditure by the health ministry. This cut-back was a reflection of the inability of the ministry to spend the sums allocated to it as well as the particular ways in which the ministry was spending; that is, the very high expenditures allocated to hospital development, and particularly Dar es Salaam development.

In summary it can be said of the first two years of the plan that development expenditure was certainly heavily biased in favour of Dar es Salaam. Of an actual expenditure of almost £1.3 million at least 60% was spent on Dar es Salaam projects. Expenditure was not only heavily biased towards the country's largest city but, in keeping with the usual nature of such expenditure, also toward the hospital services which took over half of all development spending during the first two years of the plan. By contrast, preventive health care activity received only 7% of the allocation. The most positive aspect of these two plan years was that expenditure on training programmes and rural health centre construction had taken a substantially-greater part of the development budget than in previous years and, had in fact rapidly increased their share of development expenditures even during the actual plan years. In the fiscal year 1969-70 training and rural health centre development expenditure came to only 23% of total actual expenditure, but by the fiscal year 1971-72 the estimated figure was only a little less than 50% — although of a very much smaller budget. However, virtually all of the government training expenditure continued to be concentrated at Muhimbili hospital in Dar es Salaam: of the combined total of £360,000 of such expenditure in the fiscal years 1969-72 almost 90% was spent in Dar es Salaam.

It is fair to conclude that the first years of the second five-year plan had no positive effect upon the existing imbalance between urban and rural health services: if anything they tended to increase the existing inequalities. In fact most of the hospital projects originally intended for the smaller urban centres seemed unlikely to be carried out during the balance of the plan. There had also proved to be an almost total lack of cost control over construction, particularly for the Dar es Salaam projects. During the implementation of the plan the following had become clear:

1) the original targets were often inappropriate;
2) the methodology for setting out specific programmes and projects was inadequate; most particularly cost estimates had little basis in fact; and
3) implementation had been weak, in fact the plan had not infrequently been bypassed when specific projects were being developed.

It is also of importance that a number of projects were begun in these early years of the plan that had not specifically appeared in the second five-year plan document. The most significant such example was the completion of two very large consultant hospitals in the northern part of the country. These two hospitals, which had been begun during the first plan, were built through the voluntary agencies. One of the hospitals was Protestant and the other Catholic, with the money coming primarily from the West German and Dutch governments which channel their 'humanitarian aid' funds through religious agencies. (It has been suggested that these two hospitals were supported by the West German government as a result of the earlier break with Tanzania which had resulted in the end of official West German aid. This break took place at the time of the merger between Tanganyika and Zanzibar, when President Nyerere refused to oust the East German Consulate in Zanzibar and West Germany put into practice the Hallstein Doctrine which denied the recognition of the Federal Republic to any state which recognised East Germany.) These two hospitals were built at an estimated cost of about £2.3 million each. Some of the expenditure took place during the later years of the first five-year plan, but the most significant part was in the early years of the second plan. If these expenditures were to be added to the figures cited above (Table 3) for the second five-year plan it would show the bias towards large hospital development to have been even more significant than already indicated.

The most positive achievement of the years 1969-71 was the expansion of auxiliary training that was more rapid than originally planned. By 1971 there were in existence four schools for medical assistants and five schools for rural medical aids. Nursing training continued to expand during these years and most other paramedical training was also progressing. In 1971 medical school intake reached 48. By 1971 there were 17,700 hospital beds in the country, of which about 8,000 were in voluntary agency institutions (see Table 4). The number of rural health centres had risen to 90 and the number of dispensaries to over 1,450.

Table 4. Growth of Some Selected Health Service Indicators: Independence to 1971

	1961	1969	1970	1971
Hospitals	**98**	**116**	**119**	**121**
Government	52	57	60	62
Voluntary Agencies[1]	46	59	59	59
Hospital Beds[2]	**11,166**	**16,031**	**16,312**	**17,670**
Government	6,567	8,294	8,653	9,723
Voluntary Agencies	4,604	7,737	7,659	7,947
Rural Health Centres	**22**	**50**	**69**	**87**
Dispensaries	**975**	**1,362**	**1,395**	**1,436**
Government[3]	736	–	1,126	1,156
Voluntary Agencies	239	–	269	280
Qualified Doctors	**403**	**445**	**489**	**479**
Government	140	193	216	173
Voluntary Agencies	81	106	128	110
Private Practitioners	182	146	145	96
Inpatients (000's)[4]	**221**	**396**	**458**	**498**
Government	136	243	294	331
Voluntary Agencies	85	153	164	167
Outpatients (000's)[5]	**9,167**	**21,213**	**23,525**	**25,374**
Government (Central)	1,997	4,966	6,657	5,993
Local Authorities	6,500	15,129	16,782	18,221
Voluntary Agencies	670	1,118	1,086	1,160
Recurrent Expenditure (£000's)	**2,400**	**5,376**	**6,788**	**7,715**

Source: Unpublished data of the Ministry of Health, Dar es Salaam.

1. Christian church health services.
2. Excludes 320 beds in five (private) estate hospitals.
3. All but about 20 of these dispensaries were local authority institutions.
4. Hospitals only.
5. First attendances only.

2 THE HEALTH PLAN

Part I The Structure of Planning

In most countries the government's financial year is largely built around the preparation of the annual budget, which in Tanzania runs from 1st July to 30th June. An operational ministry such as a ministry of health generally finds the period from October through December to be the quietest time of the year. It is a time when many ministry officers take their annual leave and government experiences a certain lull, particularly during the Christmas period. Sometime in January the ministry begins serious preparation for the coming financial year. Many circulars have to be prepared for consultation and discussion before actual budget sessions can be held with the Ministry of Economic Affairs and Development Planning, the Treasury (Ministry of Finance) and now, after the decentralization of government,with the regions through the Prime Minister's office. All of this work culminates in the Parliamentary session towards the end of June which approves the budget appropriations.* With the end of this session of Parliament, ministries begin the process of implementing the various projects for which allocations have been approved and during the following months they will be especially pressed with such tasks. Of course ministries also have continuing routine administrative responsibilities that go on through the whole year, although with the decentralisation of government in Tanzania many such responsibilities have been passed to the regional and district levels.

The annual budget speech of the minister offers an opportunity to explain in more detail the various expenditures included in the ministerial allocation. It also offers an opportunity to discuss some policy questions and the likely future direction of activities of the ministry concerned. In Tanzania these speeches are widely reported in the press and followed with lively interest. The speech of the Minister of Health is always among the more important ones in that it covers an area of intense interest to the people of poor countries, because it is one of those areas in which it might be possible to 'get something' now. Although steel mills and the rest are certainly recognised to be important, in the short run a dispensary is something that might

---

*This busy period of the year is made still more so by the need to complete the spending of the current year's capital budget. It is worth bearing in mind that often in government, the only thing worse than spending allocated funds badly is not to spend them at all!

actually be achieved for 'our' village during 'this very year'.

A. Policy Formulation and the Central Planning Ministries

The preparation of a budget is a long and detailed process which involves at some point or other almost anyone of any consequence in a country such as Tanzania. Of course the Tanzanian way of preparing budgets is not identical to other countries but there are many elements that are similar, if not the same. It may be that what is most significantly different in Tanzania is that planners are given a greater opportunity than they are in most other countries to participate in the reality of planning and decision making. In fact the planners are asked for assistance in implementing, in the shape of appropriate plans, the larger political aspirations of the nation. Increasingly in Tanzania there are closer ties between political thinking and planning expertise that favours the more equitable distribution of resources in a way that will maximise the opportunities of the nation's people : it is in such situations that planners are expected to give political-technical support. In most other countries (in Africa at least) there is normally a different type of political set up, in which individual ministers or other 'big men' determine the basic pattern of allocation. This is not to say that such allocations never occur in Tanzania, certainly it is possible to find such examples in the earlier development of the health services of the country, but this pattern has been changing rapidly and it is now the exception for one 'big man' to be able to force through a favoured project of a prestigious and empire building type. It can be said that rational planning, in this case for health, will lead to a greater volume of health services for a greater number of people — which is an important component of socialist politics of the Tanzanian variety.

Over all guidelines for the annual (or multi-annual) plans are put forward by the party; for example, the 1971 resolution that priority for expenditure should be given to the provision of water, schools and health services in rural areas. After such a resolution the ministries involved have the responsibility of implementing the party decision, which is not to imply that the role of the party has been completed once its initial guidelines have been put forward. This role continues through the contact between State House and all senior government and other leaders, as well as at regional, district and village level where constant discussion continues both within the party organisation and the governmental structure (which includes party representation at all levels). The discussion will concentrate on the responsibilities and functions of government in developing plans in response to party decisions.

The State House plays a key role in all that happens in Tanzania and is capable of intervening at many points in the various discussions

34

leading up to the final budget. There are frequent meetings at State House to which principal secretaries and other senior government officials are called. There are also ministerial consultations with the President and his staff so that, for example, Ministry of Health staff will go as a group to the State House to discuss problems of health sector development. The State House and Cabinet are also able to intervene in development matters through the agency of the Economic Committee of Cabinet (E.C.C.). This committee deals with many matters that in other countries might not be considered sufficiently important to be carried to this very high level. Almost any significant commitment to future expenditure, capital or recurrent, will be discussed at this cabinet committee. Papers prepared for presentation to this committee by the ministries are first circulated to all other relevant ministries and departments for comment and then the final, revised paper will be brought to the ECC by the minister concerned. It is not unusual for the committee to reject papers. It might be noted that an ECC paper is an excellent instrument for committing a ministry to a longer-term plan of development. Once such a paper is approved by the ECC the relevant ministry is committed to its fulfilment and any important departure would require another presentation to the committee. Of course the system does not work perfectly; however, these procedures are becoming increasingly effective with the passage of time.

Of course, the Ministry of Finance has a very important role to play with regard to the allocation of resources. Treasury will indicate the overall volume of resources likely to be available each year for the capital and recurrent budgets, as well as the division between sectors/ministries of these budgets. Treasury has a particular concern with the recurrent expenditures arising out of capital development. Treasury is also responsible in Tanzania for negotiations about external aid, which has come to play a very important role in the capital budget of the country. Although there will be a separate discussion about external aid later, it might be useful to indicate here that in recent years this aid has risen to a volume that is around one-half the total annual development budget of the country. (This figure may be a bit deceptive in that many projects which in earlier years had been financed directly to a private or parastatal institution, and thus were not included in the aid budget of government, are now part of the aid calculation.) This new situation is particularly striking in that the first plan, which was to have been financed largely from external sources, in the event turned out to be about three-quarters financed from local resources as a result of the diplomatic break between Tanzania and both the United Kingdom and the Federal Republic of Germany. This was the result of Tanzania's principled decision not to allow its foreign policy to be interfered with by powerful industrialised countries just because they were donors to the country's development budget.

In Tanzania the Ministry of Economic Affairs and Development Planning (Devplan) is directly responsible for the capital plan/budget. It has control over that part of the development budget for which the central ministries are responsible, as opposed to that part of the budget which now goes to district and regional projects. During the budget preparation procedures the Ministry of Health must present to Devplan its request for support for specific projects and must get them approved if the projects are to be funded. Devplan has within its structure officers who are responsible for the various sectors, so that there are one or two people with a particular brief in the area of health who will have been in close consultation with the Ministry of Health's planning unit during the period of budget and project preparation. If there has been proper coordination between these two groups, the presentation of the ministerial plan at the annual budget session need not be more than a formality, provided of course, that the total request by the ministry bears a reasonably close relationship to the amount originally allocated to the ministry by Devplan.

B. Decentralised Planning

Since the decentralisation of government the Prime Minister's Office has taken a similar parallel responsibility to Devplan in relation to the development budgets of the regions. The Prime Minister's Office has within it a planning unit which has been responsible for the holding of budget sessions with each of the 18 regions (now 19, and due to become 20) in the country since 1973. Representatives of the various ministries concerned with the projects put forward by the regions, are invited to these sessions. The process is complicated by the fact that the central ministries, although concerned with the projects being carried out at regional level, have no direct administrative or legal responsibility for them and so have had only limited interest in their detailed development. In principle, the decentralisation of government, by relieving the operational ministries of a substantial part of their day to day administrative responsibilities, was intended to allow them more time for participation in the planning process – including offering planning guidelines to the regions and districts. In practice this process has yet to become a reality in the case of most ministries, although of course, it is still at a very early stage. In general it can be claimed that although there are many problems connected with the implementation of a proper decentralisation of government, the early experience in Tanzania has certainly been encouraging.

The regions have two overall responsibilities for planning; the first is participation in the planning of new projects; the second is in the

36

implementation of the projects. In addition there is, of course, the continuing responsibility of operating regional and district institutions which are financed from the recurrent budget. The actual planning of new projects remains weak, particularly in its technical aspects. Practical steps have been taken by government to strengthen this area, by setting up substantial training programmes for regional and district officers. The general feeling is that training is most useful when carried out inside the country and the new Institute of Finance Management is taking a significant responsibility in this area. The regions have already shown marked success in implementing the local development projects, which represents a significant departure from the past when it was usual for ministries to implement their larger projects usually within the bigger urban centres reasonably well but to do far less well with smaller district projects.

One of the major problems of the proper utilisation of the development budget at regional and district levels will be the need to balance the short run interests of people in, so to speak, 'getting something for nothing' and the need to put more into immediately productive investments. In 1973-74 around 40% of the entire development budget went into regional projects; however, of that only about one-third was for directly productive investment, with another 15% or so going into cooperative and ujamaa village development and related land schemes. However, some 40-50% of the total regional investment was to go into projects for the supply of water, education and health. Of course such investment is worthwhile and it is quite natural for an immediate demand for such projects to exist at local level, especially as such demand is in keeping with national priorities. Nonetheless, there is some indication that government was becoming concerned at the situation and that the Prime Minister's office, during the budgeting procedure with the regions, was more willing to approve projects for directly productive activity more quickly than for the development of the social intrastructure. As a matter of fact, almost all requests for financing of more immediately productive projects were approved while requests for social intrastructure projects had to be controlled quite sharply. Part of the reason for this control is that such areas as education and health are heavily dependent upon the production of manpower to staff new facilities and it is the relevant ministries rather than the regions that continue to carry the responsibility for the training of teachers and health workers. It is probably the case that if the regions had their way completely in this matter it could easily result in many empty classrooms and dispensaries scattered around the country.

The most important question in decentralised planning is the need to guarantee equitable allocation between the relevant regions and districts. One of the immediate accomplishments of the regionalisation in Tanzania has been the production of data which showed clearly just how expenditures differed between the regions. An explicit goal of the decentralisation was to decrease existing inequalities between the regions, although it was also said that it was necessary to allow regions to move ahead at a pace which they themselves found comfortable. In practice this has meant that regions can move ahead by using local incentives and investments while government investment is being made more equitable between the regions. In the area of health it was found that the best way to bring about this greater equality was by calculating the distribution of new facilities against existing inequalities and allocating accordingly. And, in time, as the number of facilities became more equal in relation to population, the recurrent budget would also become more equitable. Because the Ministry of Health had worked out very clear guide lines for the equitable allocation of resources between the regions and districts it was possible for the Prime Minister's Office to press hard for the regions to accept the recommendations being made, even if it meant significantly less for the most advanced areas. This procedure presented problems, in that it took away from the regions the initiative for their own planning and there is little doubt that it will have to be substantially altered in the future. What is required, is for the regions themselves to be in a position to muster sufficient technical expertise so as to be able to come to correct conclusions about the most equitable allocation of resources. The Health Ministry will need to offer guidelines about ratios of manpower and facilities to population between regions, as well as within the regions, so that the process of more equitable distribution can be followed through the whole of the country, although continuing tension between the centre and the regions may very well continue for a time, at least as each region inevitably presses for a bit more for itself. However, this need not be a very serious problem, in that the political situation in the country is such that people generally accept the concept of equality and if data are offered to show that particular policies are likely to increase equality, then it becomes extremely difficult to oppose such policies openly. As a matter of fact it is quite clear that although many of the projects offered at the regional budgeting sessions were technically far from perfect, and may not therefore have deserved support on purely technical grounds, that because the overall concept of greater equality (which had to be seen to result from any particular pattern of allocation) was very widely accepted, the net pattern of resource allocation turned out to be quite good indeed.

The technical capacity for planning at regional level will become stronger with further training programmes and, perhaps even more importantly, with a greater stabilisation of regional manpower personnel, which can result only from increasing numbers of trained people so that emergency shifting of personnel becomes less common. The basic procedures for keeping people within specific regions already exist, in that the regional technical officers e.g. regional medical officers, do not work for any particular ministry and therefore cannot be moved at the discretion of that ministry. Instead, these officers are employed by the particular regions in which they work and it is only the Prime Minister's Office which can remove them from a region. However, the Prime Minister's Office is the mother ministry of the regions and therefore committed to them, and not to any narrow and particular needs of the ministries at the centre.

C. Ministerial and Project Planning

In the preparation of the development budget the Treasury retains overall responsibility for setting general spending ceilings. Also, the external aid division of Treasury, in discussion with those donor countries that offer assistance on a sectoral basis, will determine the volume of support to go to each sector, although each project must still be individually developed and justified — as is the case with donors that offer support only on a project to project basis. The Ministry of Development Planning will set individual ministerial spending ceilings and will also indicate the overall ceiling for spending by the regions. In addition, Devplan must also give approval to all specific projects, including those that are externally funded. The Prime Minister's Office controls individual regional ceilings and must also give approval to individual regional projects. At the ministerial level each must prepare its own development budget, as well as offering guidelines to the regions in the preparation of the various sectors making up the regional development plan.

It should be noted that if there is disagreement between the planning guidelines offered by the ministries and the intentions of the regions it is the Prime Minister's Office that must decide the matter although generally it is possible for, say the Ministry of Health to 'negotiate' the question with the regional authorities through the regional medical officer. Generally speaking disagreement between the regions and the ministries can be sorted out amicably before the Prime Minister's Office is forced to decide the issue.

At the level of the ministry it is the ministerial planning unit that has particular responsibility for planning. To a significant degree these units have been staffed by expatriates, which has led to a number of difficulties; firstly, the very nature of the 'expatriate contradiction' within the self reliant Tanzanian political environment and, secondly, the fact that expatriate contracts generally run for only two years has meant that at the time when the expatriate had settled into the job and was becoming able to make a real contribution the contract expired. In any event, these planning units generally take particular responsibility for their ministry development plans. Unfortunately too many of the units saw themselves as being responsible only for the development plan and therefore often took little interest in the administrative procedures concerned with the development and implementation of the entire budget. Nonetheless, many of the planning units were successful in their work and they continue to make an important contribution to the planning process within the ministries.

One of the more important aspects of the planning process which falls somewhat outside the structure discussed above, is the relationship of a ministry such as Health with the Ministry of Works, which in Tanzania is the Ministry of Communication and Works (Comworks). It is important to note that construction is often a very disorganised sector in Third World countries for which the reasons are numerous and discussion of them would take us too far afield, except to observe that one of the major reasons in African countries at least is the heavy dependence of the relevant ministries upon expatriates on relatively short term contracts. This is particularly important to ministries such as health which are responsible for a very substantial part of all public sector construction in many African and Asian countries.

A system has been evolved in Tanzania whereby within the buildings division of Comworks the chief architect assigns specific architects to work with different ministries, so that one architect works entirely with the Ministry of Health. This work comprises not only the design of buildings but the coordination and organisation of all that is connected with initiating a building programme, e.g. responsibility for design, bills of quantity, tendering procedures etc. The architect concerned thus becomes particularly knowledgeable about all the problems involved in health sector construction. The arrangement is particularly helpful with regard to external donors, all of whom have different building and engineering requirements to be fulfilled before funding a project. Comworks also takes responsibility for the preparation of guidelines to be sent to the regional engineers in connection with the preparation and development of standard health centres, dispensaries and other health sector buildings.

Before the creation of a planning unit in the Ministry of Health, relationships between the ministry and Comworks tended to be conducted in a very formal way; that is, through administrators with a great range of responsibilities among which the specific construction problems and relationship, or lack of relationship between Comworks and the Ministry of Health was only one. Establishment of a planning unit meant the creation of a focal point for contact with Comworks.

As a matter of fact the creation of a planning unit created a focal point for improved contact with all the other ministries responsible for, in particular, the capital budget,e.g. Treasury and Devplan.

It cannot be emphasized enough that planning must be done by planners, and no less so for health than for other areas. It is not acceptable to leave the planning to an administrator or, as is more often the case, to the medical doctor acting in an administrative capacity within a ministry of health. In practice it is often the chief medical officer or director of medical services who is the critical person in determining priorities for resource allocation. The chief medical officer is an extremely potent figure within the health system of a small country, even though the health ministry is nominally under a permanent secretary, because he is often a figure of relatively longer continuity as compared to the permanent secretary or, maybe even more so, the minister of health.

Because the chief medical officer is seen as a technical man and health decisions are supposedly of a technical nature dependent upon knowledge of things learned at medical school, the 'chief' is more often than not left with the power to determine key health development priorities. Another factor in this is that the chief medical officer is usually responsible for the posting and promotion of all government medical doctors, including the key area of secondment to post-graduate specialist training. This type of control also helps to make the chief medical officer extremely powerful in his personal capacity.

At the time of the preparation of the second five year plan the Tanzanian situation was such as to make it possible to write a health plan that apparently was consistent with overall national policy but which, when examined in detail, revealed a sharp dichotomy between its expressed purposes and the actual pattern of allocation. Although it had been possible for Devplan and Treasury to force certain overall postures into the plan this had only resulted in contradictions being written into the detail of the health (and other) sections of the plan that were dependent for implementation upon relatively narrow areas of expertise of a professional nature e.g. engineers, architects or doctors. For example, in cases of housing or roads, in which Devplan had more expertise than in health, it was possible to impose moderating influences on the standards of the professionals in the ministry concerned. However, during the period of plan implementation the engineers and architects proceeded to bypass these more moderate standards and as a result many fewer houses and roads were able to be constructed, as the standards which were actually utilised were considerably more expensive to apply. The problem was essentially the same in the health sector, except that the planning ministries were even less able to influence events in this area.

41

D. Data and Research Requirements

It is abundantly clear that ministries of health are currently expending relatively too much of their very limited data collection capacity on the gathering of disease statistics which are of doubtful usefulness.

However, given the influence of doctors on the formulation of work in ministries of health it is not surprising that this is the case. The training of doctors is based upon the diagnosis and treatment of diseases as they appear in individual patients and the collection of data by ministries of health reflects that training. The situation is also influenced by the experience of industrialised countries in which it is possible to act on the type of statistics that are now being collected by health ministries; although it must be added that even in those countries there is probably too great a dependence upon disease statistics for purposes of planning.

Any country's health service should be developed in keeping with its disease pattern and the possibility of acting upon those diseases. The broad pattern of illness and mortality in poor countries is by now quite well known, at the very least sufficiently so as to proceed with the drawing up of more suitable health plans than are now generally to be seen. For those relatively few areas in which additional disease data are needed some fairly straightforward activity could provide that minimum which will be required. It is in specific, local geographic areas that more useful disease statistics might be developed and acted upon in the context of the ongoing work of the health services.

What is needed in the first place for improved health planning is much better data about the pattern of resource allocation and the utilisation of those resources by different sections of the population, either on a geographic basis or by sex, age, class and social status. In Tanzania it was possible to develop excellent data about the allocation and utilisation of resources on a geographic basis, although the necessary work of describing resource allocation and utilisation according to population groupings, e.g. women, children, civil servants etc. has yet to be done. A very useful study of the catchment areas of institutions was carried out and it is now possible to state with some confidence the percentage of population in each district living within specified distances of different sorts of health facilities.*

It is quite remarkable just how little is known in many ministries of health about the state of most of the nation's health care facilities, although a great deal may be known about the handful of very large hospitals in the country. The facilities about which the least of all is known are the smaller rural health centres and dispensaries. In Tanzania, with the decentralisation of government, it has become less necessary

---

*Thomas, I. D., and Mascarenhas, A. C., Health Facilities and Population in Tanzania, Bureau of Resource Assessment and Land Use Planning, University of Dar es Salaam, Research Paper No. 21.1.1973.

42

for the central ministry to know in detail what is happening at these institutions, and the problem becomes more one of regional staff knowing what is necessary in the first place to improve this type of facility. The centre can assist with this by developing guidelines concerning the needs of small institutions, e.g. water supply, electricity, equipment.

In discussing disease statistics it is necessary to distinguish between hospital disease data, which may be relatively limited, and more potentially useful epidemiological statistics. The problem is that often epidemiological data seem to be collected more for their own sake, frequently by staff of the medical faculty (often expatriates) who retire to the countryside from time to time to do a survey of the level of anaemia or malaria in one or another part of the country, than in connection with any planned health activities. These data are often collected without any real possibility of using them except for the writing of a paper or, at most, as a means of instructing medical students in data collection techniques. In practice in Tanzania it proved to be extremely difficult to link data collection with campaigns of action against specified diseases There were many suggestions for the setting up of epidemiological surveillance units, which may not be a bad thing by itself, but it proved to be virtually impossible to get help for the development of disease control programmes. It may very well be that useful disease statistics can best be developed only as part of ongoing campaigns or activities. It is true, of course, that some preliminary data are needed before embarking on specific activities but it is probably the case that there is already more than enough data in most fields to embark on many more preventive health activities than are now being undertaken. Further collection of disease data should be limited basically to those areas for which active programmes are planned. Priority areas need to be selected and assessment should then be made of the knowledge needed to carry out any particular programme. Such an approach would be eminently more satisfactory than the more usual one of looking at a body of (theoretical) knowledge to determine the next pieces of data needed for the further development of that particular body of knowledge, even in the absence of any plans to utilize the material as it is developed.

The following is a summary check list of the most important data required for the making of national health plans.

1. Economic and financial data: the total volume of expenditure by central government, local government and the private sector (including the voluntary agencies, occupational health and/or insurance schemes, and private practitioners); expenditure according to administrative function, e.g. preventive and curative

activities, manpower training, etc; the geographic distribution of expenditure by national administrative categories, especially according to urban and rural divisions; distribution according to sections of the population, e.g. civil servants, those in industrial/wage employment etc; distribution according to age and sex groupings; distribution by type of facility in which the health service is being offered, e.g. hospital, health centre, dispensary, etc. Expenditure by disease category would also be useful.

2. Facilities: such information as number of in-patient days, average length of hospital stay, number of 'under fives' visits, number of vaccinations, etc; all types of data concerning the recurrent cost of health facilities are useful, e.g. expenditure for inpatients broken down into such major cost categories as personnel, drugs and diet; also such costs as that for an inpatient day, an outpatient visit, a vaccination, etc; the capital costs of different types of facilities, and the capital costs of alternative types of hospitals and the resultant recurrent costs; also the utilisation of the services offered by different health facilities, the size of catchment areas and the disease categories for which people visit institutions.

3. Manpower: the data here fall into the two major categories of training and utilisation. On the training side there is need to know the type and number of training institutions in the country, their cost per unit of output, staffing, and wastage rates from training. On the utilisation side it is necessary to know the numbers of different sorts of manpower in employment in all public and private health facilities, their wastage rates from employment, costs of employment, possibilities for upgrading, migratory patterns — national and international — and so on.

As indicated above, gaps in disease statistics need not defer the further development of appropriate health services; in very few countries would there be so little data of this sort available as to prevent substantial progress being made with the development of reasonable health plans. It must be stressed that what should be aimed for are minimum levels of data aimed at the prerequisites necessary for the making of the health plan.

Pilot projects have become a sore point with many health care administrators. All too many such projects never seem to get beyond the stage of being just pilots, primarily because the cost of the pilot has been such that it cannot be reproduced on a national basis. Pilot projects are only justifiable if in the foreseeable future they could be expected to become the basis of much more extensive programmes.

It is the case that in Tanzania the pressure for the creation of appropriate rural services has created a recognition of the need for appropriate research in this area. Offers of international assistance for research programmes have been substantial, with many of them being sophisticated and expensive efforts requiring many high level expatriate personnel. This type of research often contrasts rather sharply with more essential but rather prosaic work carrying a higher priority in relation to the current possibilities for the development of health care services. For example, ways of improving the registration of births and deaths; or with regard to health facilities, the problem of increasing the range of hospital services — which is connected to that of an appropriate balance between the volume and size of the most basic rural facility (the sub-centre or dispensary) and the middle level facility (the rural health centre), and the relationship between these rural facilities and the hospitals. The whole question of mobile services needs proper exploration, not only in terms of the operation of the mobile teams themselves but the ways in which they can be used to strengthen the entire rural health infrastructure. Related to this is the broader problem of improving communication, particularly the ways in which radio might be used for this purpose. Another important question has to do with the improved management and utilisation of the urban hospitals in relation to the whole of the urban environment. A great many problems arise with manpower development, most particularly those relating to the more efficient production of improved auxiliaries. Many questions about resource allocation also remain, particularly the ways in which resources are being used for the control of specific diseases and alternative ways of meeting disease problems. A particularly difficult area is that of drug purchasing, distribution, prescribing and utilisation. The above is far from being a complete list — and represents only some of the most important current possibilities for useful health sector research.

Part II The Plan Frame

This section will return to the historical development of the situation in Tanzania (which had been left at the end of 1971). During the first half of 1972 the framework for a new health plan to run to the year 1980, was prepared and accepted by government. The main features of the plan will be set out, although most of the more precise material will be left for later discussion within the context of specific issues, e.g. finance, manpower, buildings etc.

A. Background

The creation of the document which has become the basis of health sector development in Tanzania to the year 1980 resulted from a number of different pressures; the most significant was undoubtedly the TANU decision to give priority to the provision of health services, education and water supply to the rural population and the consequent need for the health ministry to respond to this. A second significant influence was 'the mid-plan review' conducted in late 1971, which was charged with the responsibility of evaluating the progress of the second five year plan that had by then reached its mid-point. The review turned out to be quite critical of the plan as it was being developed by the Ministry of Health; critical not only in terms of the serious lack of implementation of the second five year plan as set out, but as to the very conception of the plan itself.

Another immediate pressure in favour of a new health plan framework had arisen with the possibility of achieving a significant volume of foreign aid for health programmes. For sometime there had been discussion going on with Sweden for support for the construction of a very significant number of rural health centres. In addition, by this time, contact had been made with a number of other (especially Nordic) countries concerning additional external support for different types of health sector activities. All of the external donors required some framework of health sector development into which they could fit their potential support. Another factor adding to the pressure to develop an overall health sector plan arose from the possibility of World Bank support for the expansion of the medical faculty. However, there existed on the Tanzanian side some considerable differences about the proper expansion of the faculty, both as to the volume as well as the form of that expansion. As the Ministry of Health was the main consumer of the product of the medical faculty it was up to the ministry to determine its likely demand for medical graduates over the rest of the decade, this demand would in turn determine the size of the expansion of the faculty. There were considerable differences over this question and they were to be resolved in the context of an Economic Committee of Cabinet (ECC) paper which was to set out the overall development of rural health services to the year 1980.

B. The Health Facility Network

All of these pressures made necessary the rather quick preparation of a document for the Economic Committee of Cabinet. Although at first it was not thought necessary to prepare one document that would be concerned with all of the various problems involved, it became obvious that this was the best way to proceed. The paper resolved itself around the question of the kind of network of basic rural health facilities that

46

would have to be developed and the best way to staff this network. The paper argued that for the vast majority of the population, contact with health services of any description would necessarily be with small basic facilities located within the rural areas. The rural health centre had been conceived as the nucleus of local coverage, where reasonably well qualified health workers using elementary facilities would support surrounding dispensaries as well as being points from which national health campaigns might be launched and sustained. In addition they would provide a link between the rural population and a limited number of superior health facilities in larger centres. It was agreed that the general goal of one rural health centre for each 50,000 of population was basically sound, although it was fairly well known that a rural health centre could not in fact, under existing circumstances, directly serve 50,000 of the population (except perhaps in conjunction with its satellite dispensaries). However, it was unrealistic at the time to put forward the goal of a greater number of health centres. It was considered an accomplishment if 25 or so new rural health centres could be constructed each year during the balance of the 1970's to a total of 300 by the year 1980, thereby assuring the goal of one centre to each 50,000 of rural population.

The target of 25 new rural health centres per year necessitated a re-examination of the cost of each centre. The cost of constructing the then current standard rural health centre design was substantially greater than the volume of resources available, if 25 per year were actually to be built. A review of the existing standard plan and consequent staffing pattern had been ongoing, and a new design was accepted that would cost perhaps half the old one to construct and would require for operation only about two-thirds of the staff. Although the new design reduced capital costs considerably it did not lower the standard of construction. The reduction in costs was obtained at the expense of space. The main areas of saving were staff houses, not so much in their number as design, in the ward accommodation which was reduced from 20 to 14 beds and in the 'hotel standard' of accommodation, thus allowing considerable savings in the service areas, e.g. laundry, kitchen etc.

The second significant type of construction in the countryside was to be the dispensaries. It was recognised that the great bulk of existing dispensaries, which had previously been operated by the local authorities, and were now being transferred to the Ministry of Health, were not well equipped, staffed or managed. The work of the dispensaries was almost entirely curative in its orientation and usually of a very low standard. For the first time a standard design for dispensary building was developed for utilisation in all parts of the country (with minor variations). This plan was based upon simplicity of construction and a standard staffing pattern that assumed at least two well trained health workers at each dispensary. It was determined that 100 dispensaries a year would be constructed to a national total of 2,300 by 1980, resulting in approximately one dispensary to around 6,500 of rural population. The ratio of dispensaries to health centres was not very scientifically fixed; in effect there were to be about 7 dispensaries to each health centre, which seemed a reasonable figure. The number of new dispensaries to be developed was also constrained by the very large number of those already in operation that required substantial improvement, particularly in their staffing. Calculations had been worked out as to the likely number of outpatient visits and other services that would result from a population of six or seven thousand per dispensary and the new design appeared to be adequate for such a population provided, of course, that the staffing at the institution was appropriate. In any event, experience had shown that demand for health services largely resulted from the supply of facilities,e.g. when people lived closer to a facility they would use it more readily, therefore the more facilities that were constructed the greater the demand for their services. As it had already been accepted that the controlling factor for the development plan was the real volume of resources available rather than some abstract concept of the 'need' for health services, the relevant factor became the number of facilities that could in practice be constructed and staffed and the appropriate balance between the different types of facilities.

Hospitals were left as 'the residual' after allowance had been made for the construction of other, smaller, mostly rural facilities. It was fairly obvious that the growth in the number of government hospital beds would have to be limited if the rest of the plan were to be fulfilled, and after some discussion it was agreed that the growth of hospital beds should be no more rapid than that of population, say 3% per annum, which meant initially about 300 additional beds per year.

The construction costs of the new facilities were known. The capital cost of a new dispensary was under £2,500, a health centre almost £25,000, a new 80 bed district hospital around £100,000 and a 26 bed hospital ward £10,000. However, the more significant constraint on the building of additional health facilities was the ensuing recurrent costs, which were primarily dependent on the staffing pattern. In practice the decisions about the number of facilities to be constructed were made more with a view to the resulting recurrent costs and, therefore, on manpower patterns than any other single factor.

C. Budgeting

In the setting out of the overall plan to the year 1980, the starting point was the size of the expected recurrent budget for that year. The size of

48

the current recurrent budget was known and assumptions were made about the rate of growth of that budget to the year 1980. The assumed figure for rate of growth was 10% per annum which, given the rate of inflation in the country, meant a real growth rate of perhaps 6% to 7% per annum, a figure that was not too much greater than the expected rate of overall economic growth of the country.

After having calculated the expected total health budget for the year 1980, which was to be about £20 million, estimates were made of the running cost of those facilities holding the highest development priorities, i.e. rural health centres and dispensaries. Staffing levels for these institutions were also calculated, based upon employment costs and the capacity of the country to produce the mix of manpower that was considered to be optimal on a national basis. It was determined that the annual running cost of each new standard rural health centre would be about £7,000. The same exercise was conducted for dispensaries and it was determined that the operating cost of the new standard dispensary would be under £1,400 per annum. The cost of running different sorts of hospital beds was known and a limited growth in these expenditures was allowed for in the case of existing institutions, in addition to making provision for an expansion of the number of hospital beds roughly equivalent to the growth of population.

In addition to the running of these various institutions, which encompassed the bulk of the expected expenditures from the recurrent budget, it was also necessary to make allowances for the running of preventive services, training institutions, laboratories and the general administration of the services. The outcome of these calculations were such as to indicate that the largest single item of expenditure, the hospital services, would decline from approximately 75% of the health budget in fiscal year 1970-71 to around 50% by 1980-81. The cost of running the dispensaries and the rural health centres would rise from about 10% of expenditure to around 25% in 1980-1. Preventive services would rise from less than 5% of recurrent expenditure to two to three times that figure by 1980 (this was the weakest of all the estimates). Training costs would rise from 2% of budget to around 7%. Laboratories and other ancillary services would continue to take around 3% of budget and administrative costs would decline slightly at about 3% of budget.

The framework of the recurrent budget until 1980 was therefore set; the most significant changes being the decline of the hospital service from roughly three quarters of total expenditure to about half, coupled with an increase from about 15% of total recurrent expenditure for small rural units and preventive activities to about 35% to 40%. The estimated figure for preventive activities, of between 10% and 15% of total budget, was extremely rough not only because separate preventive health programmes hardly existed and specific new plans were not yet ready for costing, but so much of preventive activity will continue to be incorporated into the rural health infrastructure itself and thus is unlikely to have its costs estimated on a separate basis.

A great deal of attention was also given to the question of developing an appropriate manpower mix for the expanding health network;(this question will be discussed in a separate chapter later.) It is worth pointing out that the nature of the development pattern decided upon, that is concentration upon the development of a widespread rural network of small facilities, meant that the manpower to be produced had to fit such a structure and required a massive expansion of the country's auxiliary manpower training facilities.

Given the Tanzanian environment it proved to be relatively easy to reach agreement over the need for the expansion of rural facilities and even for the production of a great many auxiliaries to staff those facilities. However it was not so easy a matter to reach agreement that, concomitant to the development of this rural intrastructure, there was the need to control the expansion of the number of hospital beds, and the doctors to staff those beds. There was a tendency on the part of some, particularly the medical doctors, to argue that this was really a problem for the Ministry of Finance i.e. that it was up to Treasury to find the necessary resources both to expand the rural facilities rapidly and continue with the rapid development of the hospitals and other specialised services. Of course, President Nyerere has emphasized many times that 'to plan was to choose', and that no solutions were to be found in simply arguing that all things were needed; what was required was a choice between competing priorities.

In point of fact it was a quite revolutionary development to reach agreement that the growth of hospital beds was actually to be limited, especially in the face of the quite recent developments of the late 1960's during which a relatively rapid expansion of hospital building had taken place. At least as important as the growth in the number of hospital beds had been the fact that the cost of running them had become much more costly. Some budget items had risen very sharply; for example, the item "Diet" had risen from a figure of £110,000 in 1961-62 to £385,000 in 1971-72, for an annual average increase of 14%. The most impressive rise in costs however had been in the budget item labelled "Hospital services and supplies" which is primarily composed of drugs. This item had risen from £450,000 in 1961-62 to an estimate of £1.7 million for 1972-73, with the actual expenditure figure likely to be considerably higher. Over a period of 11 years the average increase for this item had been 17% per annum, however, over the last four years of that period the average annual increase had come to 28% and the figure for the year 1971-72 was 43%.

The basic planning issue had become that of a tradeoff between a more rapid growth of preventive programmes, dispensaries, rural health centres and the basic staff for such facilities, on the one hand, and a less rapid growth of hospital beds and (especially more expensive) drugs, on the other. The question of drugs turned out to be extremely complex (undoubtedly one of the most intractable from the point of view of control). If countries such as Tanzania can move away from hospital beds and expensive drugs towards the preventive programme and the dispensary and rural health centre it would prove to be a major achievement in taking advantage of their one really natural advantage, a large supply of labour that is relatively inexpensive to train and employ. Whereas the comparable cost of labour in countries like Tanzania is much cheaper than in industrialised countries the price of drugs and hospital equipment is as least as high and generally considerably more so.

The plan set out above (including the manpower section to be discussed later) was sent to the Economic Committee of Cabinet and approved in July 1972. This plan marked one important juncture for the health care sector in Tanzania and offered a point of departure for the third five-year plan which will extend to the year 1980.*

---

*The formalisation and beginning of the plan has since been postponed due to the economic situation currently (1975) prevailing in Tanzania (and the world). However, judging from the June 1975 budget speech of the Minister of Health, it appears that the 1975-76 development budget of the ministry is following very closely the pattern of allocation described above.

3. FINANCING THE HEALTH SERVICES

A. The Volume and Distribution of Expenditure

Very little can be said authoritatively about how much any particular country should be spending on its health services. A report of the volume of expenditure on a country by country basis would not constitute an assessment of a correct level of expenditure. In fact it is even difficult to know the amounts actually being spent today on health care in most Third World countries. Data on the distribution or utilisation of health care resources in such countries are even more sketchy.* Expenditures for health care have been rising rapidly over the last several decades in most industrialised countries, and in many developing ones. It is now usual for an economically advanced country to devote 6 to 7 per cent of its gross national product to direct health care expenditure, not including such public health factors as provision of fresh water and improved diet. In poor countries the comparable figure is very likely to be closer to 2 or 3 per cent of GNP.

In Tanzania the volume of central government health care expenditure has risen from £2.4 million during fiscal year 1961/62 — the first after independence — to over three times that amount in FY 1971/72. These sums represented an increased share of total central government spending from 7.7 to almost 10 per cent. Virtually all the percentage increase took place over the 3 years 1968/69-1971/72, when health sector expenditure almost doubled. Over those same 10 years the volume of educational expenditure by central government rose by one-half, though the share of total budget expenditure going to education increased only marginally. Nonetheless, the share of central government spending going to education is still double that for health. Notwithstanding this rapid growth of expenditure for health care, the absolute volume of expenditure in money terms is small. Total annual government recurrent health expenditure (including that for the former local authority dispensaries) in 1972/73 amounted to approximately £.75 per head, to which must be added about £.20 for capital expenditure plus private sector spending of about another £.20, for a total of £1.15 per head. Tanzania's very low per capita income of about £35 means that around 3 per cent of GNP is being spent directly on

---

*For example see Abel-Smith, B. An International Study of Health Expenditure, WHO Public Health Paper No.31, Geneva, 1967; and Gish, O. Doctor Migration and World Health, Occasional Paper on Social Administration No.43, G. Bell and Sons, London, 1971.

modern health care, again excluding expenditure in such areas as water supply, improved nutrition, medical education at university level, social welfare related activities, medical research, and traditional health practitioners and medicines.

Tanzania's figure of 3 per cent of GNP for health care stands up well when compared with other countries at similar levels of per capita income. Moreover, the fact that a high percentage of total health care expenditure in Tanzania is to be found in the public sector, makes for effective utilisation of that expenditure in terms of equitable allocation of resources in relation to population distribution and existing disease patterns. In fact, it is axiomatic to health care planning in virtually all poor countries that the "thinner" the spread of any given volume of resources, the greater the return in terms of better health (or at least the lessening of morbidity and mortality). This follows from the relatively widespread distribution of population combined with poor transport. The simple technology required to prevent and treat the great majority of medical cases to be found in most Third World countries reduces the problem effectively to one of getting the health care to the people. Of course there is a minimum level of "thinness" below which it is not possible to go if coherence is to be retained within a given health care delivery system. The appropriate level of "thinness" to be aimed for in any specific country is a matter of experience and research. However, the question remains essentially academic for virtually all Third World countries in that, probably without exception, the present pattern of health sector expenditure is far too intensive and can with complete safety be very extensively "thinned" before problems of the other extreme are likely to occur.

The additional spending described above has been primarily directed to the growth of number of hospital beds. In 1961 there were only 6,567 government hospital beds, and during the next 6 years less than 1,000 beds were added to that total. However, the four year period 1967/71 saw an increase of over 2,200 new beds. In addition, the subsidies granted to the voluntary agency (mission operated) hospitals were increased as the number of beds in such hospitals grew in number. Half the increase in government health expenditures went into additional staff (the number of government employed nurses doubled), while 25 per cent went for drugs and the remainder to other expenditures primarily related to the growth of hospital services. At the same time, Tanzania had been developing its rural services more rapidly than was the case in most other similarly placed countries. Thus, while the total number of government beds increased by 50 per cent over the 10 years between 1961 and 1971, the number of rural health centers (RHCs) increased from 22 to 87 (300 per cent). Although the percentage growth of dispensaries in comparison to hospital beds had been less rapid over recent years, this has largely been made up by the rapidly growing number of RHCs. (Some of these comparisons are rather difficult because dispensaries only became the responsibility of the Ministry of Health in 1972/73, while RHCs were transferred from the district councils to the Ministry in 1968/69. All government hospitals, on the other hand, have always been the direct responsibility of the Ministry. Therefore, the activities of the different health facilities have been influenced by policies followed by separate agencies of government at different times.)

A critical measure of equality of access to health care is the distribution of expenditure. In FY 1970/71 the public sector spent £.60 per capita for recurrent health care expenditures. In one-fifth of Tanzania's 60 districts, containing a quarter of the total population of the country, less than £.25 per head was spent for health care. Only 15 districts, with just under a quarter of the population, were allocated more than the public sector average of £.60 per head. Those 15 districts included 10 of the 11 towns in the country with a population greater than 20,000, as well as the three districts with the least population (so that even relatively small expenditures led to high per capita levels). The districts with urban concentrations obviously did well as a result of the location of the larger hospitals within those urban centers. (It is important to note that the pattern of expenditure was so calculated as to assign spending to the district where the beneficiaries of that expenditure lived, and not to the actual place of spending. Thus, based on surveys, it was possible to estimate the percentage of those utilising the largest hospitals who were actually resident within the town in which the hospital was located and to adjust the per capita expenditure data accordingly.)

Private sector expenditure (defined as spending by non-central or local government) had the effect of moving the pattern of total expenditure for FY 1970/71 marginally towards the rural areas, mostly as a result of the voluntary agency (mission) spending which was heavily concentrated in those parts of the country. However, that expenditure was largely cancelled out in total volume by expenditure for private doctors in the towns. The occupational health services, in terms of expenditures, were about equally divided on a rural-urban basis. Because the latter types of spending were concentrated among the urban few while the mission expenditures were spread widely in the countryside, the net effect on a per capita basis of this combined non-governmental spending was to widen in absolute terms the rural-urban gap, even though the relative gap was decreased. Moreover, when expenditure on a district basis is related to the size of the urban population within the districts, there is a very high rank-order correlation. For example, the capital city (with 350,000 people) spent

54

around £4.50 per head for health care; Tanga District, containing the second city (with a population of 70,000), spent £1.75; Arusha and Mwanza Districts (with towns of just under 35,000) spend £1.30 and £1.10 per capita, respectively, and so on.

B. The Development Budget

It can be seen from the above discussion that in Tanzania the absolute volume of expenditure for health care is small and the question of its distribution is therefore particularly important, assuming of course that it is the intention to reach the whole of the population of the country with the available resources. The question of national coverage is especially important with regard to the capital budget, in that 'this year's capital budget becomes next year's recurrent budget'. The sensitivity of the recurrent budget to the capital budget in sectors such as health is often underestimated. For example, in Tanzania the ratio of the capital to the recurrent budget of the Ministry of Water and Power is roughly in the order of three to two, and for the Ministry of Communication and Works it is about one to one. However, for the Ministry of Health the ratio had been running at about one to eight. Such a ratio reflects the labour intensivity of the health sector: the fact that so much of health sector expenditure goes for wages − in Tanzania almost half. If a firm policy of equitable distribution of expenditure is to be followed it would begin with measures directed towards equalisation of the number and type of facilities in the different parts of the country, followed by a more equitable pattern of staffing between the institutions.

The following two tables show the changing pattern of the Tanzanian capital budget for health during the period of the second five year plan. It can be seen that the budget, after an initial rise, declined before showing marked increases during more recent years. This progress was largely the result of the new policies being followed by the health ministry, as reflected in the more detailed data shown in Table 5b. Whereas over half the budget had been made available for hospital services in the first three years of the plan period, and of that amount about two-thirds was spent in Dar es Salaam, in the last two years of the period the percentages of the capital budget allocated for hospital services had fallen to 27% and 15% respectively, of which less than 10% was spent in Dar es Salaam. The other significant shifts in the budget were the increased expenditures available for rural health centres and dispensaries, and the massive increase in expenditure for the construction of additional training institutions. These training institutions were intended almost entirely for the production of manpower to staff rural facilities. Given a 'reasonable' capital budget, a ministry of health could, over a relatively short period of time achieve

55

Table 5a Health Development Budget: 1969/70 – 1973/74

	(1) Approved Estimates (£000's)	(2) Actual Expenditure (£000's)	(3) (2) as % of (1)
1969/70	754	416	55
1970/71	1,102	799	73
1971/72	219	193	88
1972/73	766	n.a.	90 +(est)
1973/74	2,914	—	—

Table 5b

Health Development Budget Expenditures: 1969/70 – 1973/74
(in %'s)

	1969/70	1970/71	1971/72	1972/73	1973/74
Hospital and ancillary services	63	52^1	52^1	27^2	15^2
Rural health centres and dispensaries	7	24	33	35	33
Manpower development	16^3	22^3	13^3	18^4	48^4
Preventive services	9	1	2	10	2
Manufacturing	5^5	1^5	0	10^6	2^6

[1] Between 60% and 70% in Dar es Salaam
[2] Less than 10% in Dar es Salaam
[3] Around 85% in Dar es Salaam
[4] About 1% in Dar es Salaam
[5] Vaccine plant construction
[6] Pharmaceutical plant construction

a significant level of health service equality, provided a sharp brake were to be put upon hospital, and especially large hospital development.

It is of interest that the control of hospital development, with a view to equalising the health budget of Tanzania, has led to more districts increasing their number of hospital beds than probably would have been the case with a policy of (theoretically) unlimited expansion of bed numbers. The decision to control hospital building to the level of population growth means that, for a time, roughly 300 beds per year

56

will be added to the total of hospital beds; however, because the policy is to equalise the ratio of beds to population between the districts means that these 300 beds are mostly being allocated to those districts with the worst bed population ratios. For example, in 1973/74 of the 307 planned additional hospital beds all but 52 went into the lowest level of government hospital i.e. district hospitals. It is likely that if the previous policy of not controlling hospital bed building had been adhered to, these smaller hospitals would not have benefited to the same degree as they do now. Although, in all probability, a significant number of beds (probably greater than the 300) would have been added to the larger of the government hospitals relatively few would have been left for the smaller institutions. Although full parity of bed population ratios between all the districts will not have been achieved by 1980 a very high level of equality will have been reached in all but a very few.

The decisions about the distribution of health centres and dispensaries were also taken with some care. For the first time it was possible to project seriously the building of 25 rural health centres during any one year; for the balance of the second five year plan it was decided to carry on with completion of those centres which had originally been projected for construction during the plan period. The distribution of the roughly 150 health centres to be built over the last six years of the 1970's (essentially during the third five year plan) would be based primarily upon district populations, so as to reach the long standing goal of one centre to roughly 50,000 of rural population in every district.

The distribution of dispensaries was of particular interest to those involved with ujamaa village development. It must be appreciated that the dispensary acts as the village hospital, and that although true hospitals can be established at relatively few places, dispensaries can be sited at a relatively great number. After some discussion, a system for the distribution of dispensaries on a district basis was agreed, based upon the following three variables; (1) the existing dispensary-population ratio, (2) the accessibility of the population to existing health facilities, and, (3) the percentage of district population living in ujamaa villages. Weights were attached to each of these variables on a district basis, the three weightings were combined and the hundred dispensaries to be built in the year 1973-74 allocated accordingly. The result was that slightly over 40% of all districts were allocated at least one dispensary (only two districts received more than six).

C. The Recurrent Budget

The rapid growth of recurrent expenditures in the health sector represents a most serious problem for those concerned with the development of health services. Coupled with the problem of the absolute rate of growth is the fact that this growth most commonly occurs in the hospital sector. The very limited catchment areas of health care facilities in countries such as Tanzania means that a rapid rise in hospital expenditures will lead to greater inequality in the distribution of the recurrent budget. This happens because the number of those able to reach the hospitals is so limited that those living in the towns, where the hospitals are sited, will be in a position to absorb an ever greater share of the health budget. However, it is not only expenditure for hospitals in general that increases inequality, but the fact that it is extremely common for these increased hospital expenditures to be concentrated at the larger institutions, particularly the consultant hospitals, so that the benefits of the increased hospital expenditures are primarily restricted to those resident only in the very largest towns. In this connection it is worth noting that in the preparation of the Tanzanian first five year plan it was estimated that the recurrent cost of running a bed at a district or other small hospital was £220 per annum, while the estimate for the large hospitals in Dar es Salaam and Tanga was £400 per bed. Eight years later the average cost per district hospital bed was up by less than 20%, at £275 per year, however, the annual running cost of a bed in Dar es Salaam had become two and one-half times as costly at over £1,000 per bed.

The following table shows the costs of in-patient days at different types of institutions in Tanzania. It should be noted that on a comparative African basis these figures are extremely low.

Table 6 Cost Per In-Patient Day: 1970/71 (in £'s)

| | Cost per In-patient Day | |
	Average	Range
Dispensary	.20	n.a.
Rural Health Centre	.35	n.a.
District Hospital	.65	.35 – 1.05
Regional Hospital	1.20	.75 – 2.60
National Consultant Hospital	2.50	1.40 – 3.00

It can be seen that the average cost of an in-patient day rises from £.20 at a dispensary, to £.35 at a rural health centre, to £.65 at a district hospital, to £1.20 at a regional hospital, to £2.50 at a national consultant hospital: the average cost at these different service levels almost doubles at each step. It is also worth noting that the range of operating costs at similar types of institutions varied from about

58

one-half to double the average.

The problem of controlling the recurrent budget can be broken down into two parts. The first, at 'macro' level, involves the overall division of the budget between hospitals and smaller facilities. The second, at 'micro' level, concerns the actual running cost of individual institutions. Recommendations concerning the volume and distribution of expenditure in the health sector must, of necessity be concerned at the same time with both these aspects of expenditure so as to avoid control of health sector expenditures becoming the basis of denying to those having least access to health services an increasing share of those services.

It ought not to be necessary to point out that the health sector is amenable to rational planning and control even though it is concerned with human illness and, sometimes life itself. To accept the argument that health is above monetary considerations, and that consequently all who present themselves for treatment must have made available to them any volume of resources necessary to effect an immediate cure, is to perpetuate the sharp inequalities now existing in the health care systems of most countries. The fact is that rationing of health care does exist, everywhere. If that rationing is not accomplished through the market system it is accomplished by constraint on the supply of services, and if those services are unequally provided then rationing will be more sharply applied to those who do not have easy access to those services which are available.

It is worth noting that in those countries in which health services are nominally provided free of charge to recipients, it is often the only service which is so provided (in principle) to an unlimited extent. Although many African and other Third World countries are providing primary schooling without any charge fees are often required at secondary school level (though not in Tanzania). In any event, secondary schooling and university education are not considered to be rights that must be available to all. Rationing is explicitly accepted in these areas although the form of rationing, usually passing an examination, supposedly gives equal opportunity to all to enter into secondary and higher education. In practice, of course, the system is weighted heavily against the lower income groups and in favour of the upper social classes. However, in the case of health care it is seldom overtly stated that all do not have the complete right to go through the entire system of care including the consultant hospitals in the capital city, even to the extent of being sent abroad if the required medical attention is not available within the country. In practice this open ended commitment is available to only a few. Most urban dwellers can get themselves to a large hospital and can, if necessary, be seen by a qualified doctor, although the problems of actually getting a hospital bed and being seen in some reasonable period of time by a specialist may often be substantial. Although data are not available there can be no doubt that in the Third World a very substantial proportion of all specialist hospital services is being taken up by expatriates, civil servants and other important members of the community. For the rural population the problem of entering the upper reaches of the health care system is virtually insurmountable.

As has been discussed earlier, the very rapid increase of expenditure for health care in Tanzania between 1967 and 1971 had been substantially concentrated in the larger hospitals. The Arusha Declaration of 1967 gave a major impetus to increased spending for health care. However, although it was easy to spend more money for expanded hospital construction and services — and particularly those of the larger variety — it was not nearly so straightforward a matter to direct funds toward preventive programmes or simple rural dispensaries and health centres. The increased spending had the effect of increasing the demand for health services, as is known to accompany any increase in the supply of such services. Thus during the first six years of independence (1961-1967), while the rate of growth of health expenditure by the Ministry of Health averaged 6.5 per cent per annum, the rate of in-patient care grew at a rate of about 8.5 per cent. However, over the years 1967-1971 the rate of in-patient care rose 15 per cent per year, in response to a ministry expenditure growth-rate of around 30 per cent per annum. It is the case that health care expenditures had proceeded virtually independently of patient loads and were mostly policy determined, with patient loads responding later to the increased expenditures (which is not to say that there had not been a popular desire and probably substantial 'need' for these additional facilities). During these years of rapid increase of Ministry of Health expenditures almost half the increase had gone into additional salaries, a quarter to 'hospital services and supplies' (basically drugs) and a fairly significant sum for increased 'diet' costs.

As stated earlier, the control of health care expenditure falls into the two categories of the appropriate distribution of expenditure between different types of facilities, and the control of costs at individual institutions. In so far as the first aspect is concerned, for reasons already discussed, it is absolutely necessary for virtually all Third World countries to decrease their rate of hospital development in favour of that of the smaller health facilities. The question of control of expenditure at individual institutions falls into two distinct categories; firstly, ways of controlling the supply of resources to given institutions and, secondly, ways of controlling the demand for the services offered at these institutions. As pointed out earlier, the costs between different institutions for the operation of similar services can vary considerably.

60

These differences are largely the result of historical accident and bear little particular relationship to the health or disease situation in the different areas of Tanzania or other countries. It would therefore be appropriate for all hospitals or other institutions of a similar category to receive fixed sums for the operation of each of their services e.g. per bed, per outpatient visit etc. These sums might be adjusted for such factors as bed occupancy rates, volume of new outpatients, district population, or other special factors which might exist in the particular area. Because about half of all expenditure in the health sector goes on payment of wages and salaries it is also necessary to standardise the staffing patterns for institutions of a similar category. It should be realised however, that full equality of expenditure on a district or other similar basis cannot be achieved until the facilities themselves have been equalised in relation to population.

Some other budget items requiring control are those of 'diet' and drugs. Equalising between hospitals the diet expenditure allowed per in-patient day ought not to be a complex question, but often turns out to be so. It is certainly the case that in many countries the amount allowed per in-patient day at a district hospital is considerably less than that allowed at a large consultant hospital; this occurs for a number of reasons, mostly having to do with the same factors that allow privilege for consultant hospitals in most other respects, however, stronger administrative control certainly can be brought to bear in this area more easily than in some others. It was found in Tanzania that the average cost of feeding an in-patient at regional and district hospitals was a little less than £0.10 per day; however, at the three large consultant hospitals in the country the equivalent figure ranged from £.15 per day to £.25.

Another key area of financial control in the health sector, over volume as well as distribution, is that of drugs. This is an area that is critical not only to the health sector but the national economy as well, in that pharmaceutical import bills are generally considerable in Third World countries. This question will be discussed in some detail in a later chapter.

Another aspect of the control of expenditure is the critical need for trained health service administrators and other managerial staff within the health delivery system. In countries like Britain it has taken a considerable time for the medical men to give way at hospital level to professional managers, and the process is still far from complete. In countries like Tanzania it is still basically the doctors who manage the hospital and other health service institutions in which they work; in contrast, the hospital administrators have little training and hold only low level status.

Mention has already been made of the sharp differences in the running costs of similar institutions in Tanzania. Of the three largest hospitals, the so-called referral hospitals, one was able to run at roughly half the cost of the other two, as a result of excellent administrative practice. This hospital was able to operate in-patient days at roughly half the cost of the other two large institutions in the country. It was also able to function with a remarkably small drug bill when compared to the other institutions; this was at least partly the result of pre-packaging of the drugs dispensed to out-patients by medical assistants. These medical assistants had a list of twenty or so drugs they could prescribe to out-patients; if the medical assistant thought that something else was required, the patient was referred to a qualified doctor.

A very high priority for Third World countries is the establishment of training programmes for health service administrators: to depend longer than is absolutely necessary on overseas training in this area is a grave error. The following figures may be of some comparative interest. The whole of the Tanzanian government health service containing almost 15,000 workers, over 60 hospitals and around 1,500 smaller facilities had for administrative purposes in 1970 three hospital secretaries, 10 hospital administrative assistants, 28 higher executive officers, just over 200 clerical officers and assistants, and another 120 records assistants; in all 360 people, of whom only a handful had any substantial level of training. Various training possibilities exist. For the few people who would work at central administrative tasks and in the very largest hospitals a small volume of regional training (e.g. Commonwealth West Africa) might be justified. Local training courses should be created for the middle and lower level personnel who will run the great bulk of hospital and other health services. In addition in-service training is possible, especially at some of the hospitals which already have an acceptable level of administration. Of course having the personnel is not enough by itself; it is also necessary that they be given authority and status sufficient for them to put their good training into effective use.

D. Charges

The other aspect of expenditure control is related to the demand for health services. Where health care has been removed from the market place (in so far as the public is concerned) demand is primarily controlled by limiting the supply of services. The alternative is to limit demand through the imposition of some form of charges for the services provided. There are three basic reasons for charging for health services. The first is to raise revenue; the second is to increase the efficiency of the service by reducing over-utilisation and by increasing cost consciousness on the part of both the providers and consumers of the services; and the third would be directed towards the improved distribution of services through the use of selective charges intended to act as a counterbalance to relative over-utilisation of services by those with easiest access to health facilities.

The imposition of health service charges upon the sick at the point at which the service is provided *for the express purpose of raising revenue* (with the possible exception of certain amenity fees) is increasingly being rejected almost everywhere. However, having selective charges for the purpose of increasing the efficiency of health service institutions and for redressing present imbalances in the utilisation of facilities can be perfectly justifiable. The major argument against having any charges at all is the risk that someone needing health care might be excluded from that required care, which is indeed a possibility. However, if selective charges were to help create a more equitable distribution of health services, thereby making them available to many now left outside the system, there would be ample justification for the relatively small risk involved. It is worth noting that under the conditions of most African and Asian countries it is not feasible to utilise income criteria for the bulk of the population as the basis of charges i.e. relating fees to incomes, because incomes are mainly derived from subsistence agriculture and, in any event the administration of such systems is beyond the capacity of these countries.

What is being argued here is that selective charges need to be related to national health care requirements and that these requirements can best be met by the more equal distribution of available services so that, for example, charges might exist at the out-patient departments of urban hospitals but not at rural dispensaries. Relatively small charges imposed at hospital out-patient departments should be sufficient to discourage some percentage of those making relative over-use of these facilities thereby making it possible for government to transfer resources to the smaller rural facilities. The selected charges should not only be intended to increase equality of allocation, but must be administratively feasible as well. For example, if there were to be no charges for pregnant women, a question would be likely to arise in connection with such women attending an out-patient clinic for some condition totally unrelated to their pregnancy. However, some groups could relatively clearly be excluded from charges, for example pre-school children (although even here, under African conditions at least, there could be dispute over definitions).

As has already been stated the rationing of health services in poor countries is a reality based upon limited accessibility to health care facilities and not upon such factors as seriousness of illness or immediate ability to pay for services rendered, except that those with the least potential ability to pay (and often bearing the most substantial burden of illness) are usually most severely rationed in relation to their accessibility to health care. Conversely, those with the greatest ability to pay (and a lesser volume of illness) generally enjoy the greater level of accessibility. One way of illustrating this fact is by comparing the volume of in-patients per 1,000 of Tanzanian population according to different possibilities of access to health facilities. The range of hospitalisation per thousand of population varied from a low of seven per annum in Maswa district to a high of over 100 in Dar es Salaam, with the national average being 35. The five districts in the country with the worst bed-population ratios and the lowest rates of hospitalisation showed a perfect rank-order correlation. Out-patient visits by district showed a similar pattern. To recapitulate: to control growth of health care expenditures and to ensure its more equitable distribution there is need to introduce some deterrent to the present often indiscriminate and sometimes abusive use of health services in Third World countries. Selected small fees should be introduced for the purpose of ensuring that the best possible use is made of the scarce resources now available for health care. As stated earlier the intention ought not to be to raise revenue for the health services or to present a barrier to the sick, but to make the services more efficient and equitable by deterring those who are over-using them relatively or absolutely. In this connection it is worth bearing in mind that even such countries as China and Cuba find it advisable to levy certain charges for some health care services.

Any imposition of fees raises certain problems of an administrative nature. In the first place it is necessary that the schedule of charges be small enough so as not to discourage anyone suffering from any significant level of illness and yet large enough to have some minimum effect, as well as at least covering the costs of administration. The scheme must also be (seen to be) simple and fair in its application, although no arrangement is likely to be perfect. In general there should not be any in-patient fees as these are not "self-referred" illnesses in that people are hospitalised as a result of a medical worker's recommendation. It would be possible to establish a system of charges for all (out)patients although a simpler and better controlled method, that could accomplish the same ends, would charge a set fee for all drugs on a 'standard schedule'. It would be important that each drug be charged for separately in order to discourage the very common practice (in Africa at least) of prescribing many more different drugs than is medically required. All outpatients should pay this fee, except those attending specially organised preventive clinics e.g. ante-natal, child welfare, nutrition etc. Any drug not on the standard schedule should be charged for at its economic cost. The designated fees might be £.05 to £.10 per prescribed scheduled drug at a hospital or urban outpatient clinic in the larger towns, and perhaps half that at a rural health centre or dispensary; although the suitability of charging any fees at all at the health centre or dispensary level would vary from country to country.

The system of collection must be as simple as possible, with the drug prescription itself being the receipt of payment. Prescription books should be made up of numbered, perforated pages so that the bottom half could be given to the patient as the receipt of payment. There might be two colours utilised in printing the prescription/receipt books, one colour for drugs on the standard list and another for special items to be charged at economic rates. In larger hospital pharmacies it might be necessary to have a separate fee collector, but in most smaller institutions the pharmacy dispenser should be able to collect the fee in exchange for the drug. Because the intention in setting fee schedules is to make the health service more efficient and equitable, and not to raise revenue, it would probably be necessary from time to time to adjust schedules in keeping with greater knowledge as to the ways in which the expressed purposes for charging fees were being accomplished.

The question of insurance schemes designed to support health services *in the specific context of Third World situations* has been relatively little explored. In practice, most of the programmes in operation tend to reinforce already existing inequalities in health service resource allocations. These schemes have been set up essentially for those in wage employment — primarily industrial workers and civil servants — and sometimes their families. They follow the pattern of those in the industrialised Western countries where, historically, they had helped to bring about greater equality of access to health care for those in wage employment. In Third World countries, however, those in wage employment do not usually represent the least well off and to shift a greater volume of health resources to those in such employment is likely to increase inequality. (This question will be discussed later in greater detail.)

The question of creating health insurance schemes for rural populations has seldom been seriously considered. It may be that the situation in Tanzania allows for the development of such a scheme because once villagers are organised, as is the case with those in ujamaa villages, such programmes become a possibility. However, if such schemes were to be economically viable one critical element would be that a significant part of the services provided must be created out of village resources. This would require substantial participation on the part of villagers themselves, to carry out preventive activities as well for the support of village medical aids drawn from amongst their own number. Use would also be made of certain traditional herbs and local medicines. Actually the above seems to be the basis of much of Chinese local health services in that the commune produces and provides all basic health care requirements as well as taking the additional responsibility of paying for certain of the health care needs of its members when they make use of health facilities above the level of the commune.

4. STAFFING THE HEALTH SERVICES

There is no single question more significant than that of appropriate manpower training for the proper development of health services in both rich and poor countries. In many respects, the planning of health services is the planning of health manpower. It is also the case that there is a positive correlation between labour intensity and success in health services, although, of course, labour intensity must be measured against the particular economy under consideration (obviously the labour intensity of health care services in Tanzania must be relatively greater than in the United Kingdom). To argue this way is not to imply that it is only the number of health workers in employment that matters; clearly the training and utilisation of this greater number of health workers must also be appropriate to particular circumstances and possibilities.

A. Some Principles

Before entering into the discussion it would be useful to describe the most important types of health manpower that exist in Tanzania. Firstly, there are the usual distinctions between doctors, nurses, pharmacists etc., although within each of these (vertical) divisions there are almost always three (horizontal) levels. At the top is the internationally recognisable professional e.g. the graduate of the medical school, the A nurse (equivalent to the state registered nurse), the radiographer, and so on. There is also a second (or middle) level of health worker in most of these categories; these cadres generally have eleven years of schooling followed by three years of training. Some examples are the laboratory technician, the pharmaceutical assistant, the dental assistant and the medical assistant. (There is also an upgraded medical assistant bearing the title of assistant medical officer.) In the case of nursing the second level is that of the B nurse, with seven years of primary school plus three years of training. In addition to these two levels there is also a third, the auxiliary level, drawn from primary school leavers and having usually twelve to eighteen months of additional training: some examples are pharmaceutical, laboratory and radiographic auxiliaries. However, the third level of medical practitioner, the rural medical aid, has three years of training following primary schooling. The third level of nurse is the maternal and child health aid, a primary school leaver with eighteen months of additional training.

The discussion will turn to some general principles of health manpower planning before coming back to the development of the Tanzanian situation, and some issues arising from that development. Undoubtedly the most important overall point that can be made about health manpower planning is that it must be based upon the principle of national coverage; that is, the realistic possibility of reaching the whole of a population with the services of any particular manpower cadre. If this principle is followed it will protect against the production of relatively overtrained and therefore too expensive groups. This is a particularly important consideration in that some 40% to 60% of the total of a health ministry's budget will be needed to cover personnel costs — of which one-half to three-quarters for the employment of health workers and the balance for such personnel as cleaners, watchmen, cooks, drivers etc. Although the total volume of personnel to be employed is subject to the constraint of available finance, the specific problem is to determine the precise numbers of different types of workers to be trained given the size of the budget. Any particular category of worker must be seen in relation to all other categories of health staff, and both vertical and horizontal divisions of staff need to be considered: there must be balanced pyramids of doctors, nurses, lab workers, etc. An appropriate division of labour would mean that, say, the 'doctor' pyramid would contain relatively few of those with the highest level of training, a greater number with some middle level of training and a significantly greater number with still less training. (In discussing manpower pyramids it is convenient to distinguish between auxiliary and paramedical personnel. Paramedical personnel include such categories as nurses, laboratory technicians, radiographers, etc. Auxiliaries refer to health workers of all categories with less than professional level training.)

Of course the number of personnel in each of the various horizontal or vertical categories must bear relationship to the physical facilities comprising the national health delivery system; that is, there must be a match between the number of beds and the number of nurses doing bedside nursing, or between the number of rural medical aids and the number of dispensaries in which they will work. In practice it is more likely that the planned numbers of different types of personnel should determine the development of facilities than the other way around.

It is important that health manpower numbers be planned in relationship to facilities or specified activities rather than with regard to population ratios. It is the facilities that should be planned in relationship to population, thereby becoming the instrument for an equitable distribution of health personnel. However, there can be no specific fixed ratios of manpower to facilities or of one category of

68

manpower to another; the situation will vary depending upon economic possibilities, historical development, the political situation etc.

Nonetheless, although there cannot be fixed ratios of manpower to facilities or of one category of manpower to another, the principle of pyramidal manpower structures must be upheld, thereby following the economic concept of the division of labour as the basis of increased productivity, or the management concept of delegation of authority being the basis of increased efficiency. These principles lead to the obvious need for personnel such as medical assistants and rural medical aids, although the specific training levels for each category of such personnel will vary depending upon particular conditions in different countries.

In working out the health manpower plan there will be need for certain basic data. The following chart shows the information most needed, after the size of individual cadres have been determined (based upon the size of the recurrent budget and the share to be taken by personnel costs, and the type of health programmes and facilities to be developed). The type of data shown would provide sufficient basic information on which to base a manpower plan for most countries.

Basic Manpower Data Requirements+

A. Stock
   1. Employment distribution: geographic, by facility.
   2.* Age structure and/or years of service.
   3. Intake: newly trained, upgraded.
   4. Wastage: resignations, retirements, deaths.

B. Demand
   1. Vacant posts.
   2. Planned expansion.

C. Supply (newly trained and upgraded)
   1. Availability of candidates for training.
   2. Cost of training.
   3. Availability of places: schools, teachers, curricula.
   4. Wastage from training.

+These data are necessary for planning the output of a given cadre *after* its basic size, in relation to other cadres, has been determined (see text): although revisions as to its size may be required during the development of the type of data shown here.

*Useful for longer term projections but less significant in the short run.

Many otherwise excellent training schemes for health personnel have failed either because no proper career structure for them existed within government or insufficient control was brought to bear upon their later careers. The control factor is particularly important in a situation in which it is possible for health manpower to move from one cadre to another, as is commonly the case in Tanzania. Manpower plans are often frustrated when those trained for duties in a particular cadre/grade too quickly leave for a higher one (or perhaps resign from the service). Although there is much to commend the idea of upgrading between cadres, it is also true that more often than not such systems tend to break down because of the tremendous pressure for upgrading which will almost certainly arise. Especially in situations of health manpower shortages, such pressures are likely to become unmanageable as people leave the government service for better opportunities elsewhere; therefore, while it may be desirable, and it is almost certainly necessary, to leave open the upgrading door it is also necessary to allow only that amount of movement between cadres which is compatible with the fulfilment of overall health manpower objectives. The problem is one of designing schemes which satisfy an upward moving career structure yet do not frustrate planned manpower requirements. One possible way of achieving this objective is to elongate each grade so that there is a very substantial salary overlap with the next higher one, such a scheme could reduce the pressure for upgrading substantially. To satisfy that part of the pressure for upgrading which would still exist primarily due to professional as opposed to strictly monetary considerations it would be necessary to allow some upgrading, at a strictly controlled rate. The movement between cadres,e.g. rural medical aid to medical assistant,ought not to be a matter of right as a result of length of service, but a reward for outstanding service. It would not be impossible to set a target figure for annual upgrading as a percentage of a total cadre, say 2% to 3%. (It is always possible, however, that in keeping with planned major changes of the structure of the services there might be need for substantial upgrading schemes at particular times.)

This discussion of health manpower planning has not taken into consideration any aspects of the training and employment of village medical helpers of the Chinese 'barefoot doctor' type. It is not because such groups, based essentially upon the ability of villagers to provide their own health services and health workers, are considered to be unimportant. It is just that ministries of health as we conventionally know them are seldom concerned with such approaches. It may very well be that answers to such questions are more to be sought within discussions of the workings of national political structures than that of ministries of health as such. (see Chapter 6.)

B. The Manpower Plan: An Overview

Between 1961 and 1970 the total employment of the Ministry of Health in Tanzania had almost doubled from 6,300 to 12,400. Over that period there had been some important increases in numbers of health workers, for example the total number of nurses in employment by government and the voluntary agencies had doubled (the number of A nurses had increased from just under 400 to almost 800 and the number of B nurses from about 1,000 to almost 1,900), however, a number of other key cadres of health workers had remained virtually static. For example, the total number of registered doctors in the country had increased only marginally from 403 in 1961 to only 489 in 1970, although it is important to note that the number of citizen doctors had increased from 12 at independence to 123 in 1970.

As a result of the Arusha Declaration a move was made in the late 1960's to expand the output of a number of medical auxiliary categories. However, it was not until the frame for a new health plan was created in 1972/73 that a truly massive reorientation and expansion of health manpower was undertaken. In keeping with the adjusted priorities of the new plan the expected volume of expenditure available for employment purposes was distributed over the various categories of health workers needed to staff the existing and planned new facilities. It was determined that if the Ministry of Health was to accomplish its rural health development programmes it was essential that there be a balanced and coordinated plan for the training of all categories of health workers. The programme that was developed took into account the overall costs involved in training and employing the needed health manpower, the training periods involved and the balance between the different types and levels of personnel. The question of self-sufficiency and localisation of health staff was also incorporated into the projections. It is expected that by 1980 (and in most cases much sooner) there will be no need for expatriate health personnel in public sector employment, except for a couple of dozen specialists employed mostly at the medical faculty as teachers. It is also likely that in the private sector the voluntary agencies will continue to employ anywhere up to 100 medical doctors; in addition, a handful of expatriate private practitioners might remain in practice. The projections included the employment requirements of all public sector institutions as well as those of the voluntary agencies. It was also determined by the plan that the creation of new vacancies for staff within government services would be closely coordinated with expected outputs from training centres.

Of the 21 different categories of health manpower for which explicit targets were set, all but two in future will be trained within Tanzania, the exceptions being pharmacists and dentists. All of the needed training institutions and courses for the 19 categories of manpower were already either functioning or under construction, with the exception of a local training course for health service and hospital administrators. The regulation of numbers and types of health manpower will entail close control of intakes and outputs from the training institutions. Wastage rates from different institutions have been estimated, and it is expected that each year's intake will be marginally adjusted to allow for variations in those rates.

The largest groups of people to be trained fall into the categories of medical practitioners and nursing; thus the expected output between 1972 and 1980 of professional and auxiliary medical practitioners will amount to about 4,400, and of all nursing categories about 6,100. The expected output of public health 'inspectors' (health education officers and health auxiliaries) will be about 700, laboratory workers about 600, pharmaceutical output will amount to over 300 and dental personnel about 150. In all it is expected that there will be an output of almost 13,000 health workers between 1972 and 1980 of which only slightly over 2,000 will be of professional standing; that is, a little over 500 graduate doctors, 1,100 A level nurses, 200 lab technicians, 100 public health inspectors and several dozen each of dentists, pharmacists and radiographers.

In 1972 in Tanzania there were about 500 registered doctors, a similar number of medical assistants and assistant medical officers (upgraded medical assistants), and only slightly more rural medical aids. By 1980 it is expected that there will be around 800 registered medical doctors in the country, of whom about 700 will be Tanzanian. For each registered medical doctor there will be approximately two medical assistants and assistant medical officers (about 1,500 in all), as well as roughly four rural medical aids (a total of close to 3,000). There will be enough rural medical aids by 1980 so that one can be posted to each of 2,300 dispensaries and two to each of the 300 rural health centres expected to be functioning by that time. The medical assistants will be in charge of the rural health centres and will also be covering a significant part of the hospital outpatient work. Of the 800 medical doctors in the country it is expected that about 100 will be expatriates working for voluntary agencies. Of the roughly 700 citizen doctors all but a relative handful should be working in the public sector. (A more detailed discussion of the problems connected with the training and utilisation of medical practitioners will follow in the next section of this chapter.)

In 1972 there were over 3,200 A and B nurses (one-third of them in the A category) in Tanzania. Based upon present levels of intake it is expected that by 1980 there will be a total of about 2,000 A nurses and around 5,200 B nurses, which should cover both the needs of the public sector and the voluntary agencies reasonably well. Most of these nurses are likely to be employed in the hospital sector, although a fairly large number will be scattered through the rural health centres and be involved in public health activities. An important departure in nursing training was the development in 1972/73 of a new cadre called the maternal and child health aid.* It is expected that by the year 1980 about 2,700 such young women will have been trained and employed. Other categories of dental, pharmaceutical, laboratory and other para-medical and auxiliary personnel were also planned for in considerable detail. Some groups, such as the health auxiliary (rural sanitarians) will be significantly expanded. (More detailed discussion of these groups will follow later in the chapter.)

Although the plan for the training of manpower also takes into account the needs of non-governmental institutions, particularly the voluntary agencies, it was of prime importance that the cost to central government of the expected increase in personnel be carefully calculated. Tables were drawn up showing the stock and employment costs of the various categories of health workers in employment by central government in 1972, and the expected numbers and consequent costs of employment in 1980. The changing cost pattern for each group was then calculated; for example, medical assistants who were absorbing just over 4% of all personnel emoluments would by 1980-81 be taking over 9%; although A and B nurses would be held constant at 25% of the total ministry wage bill.

The total number of training institutions for health manpower in Tanzania is substantial. Although it might appear to be more efficient to have fewer and larger schools, in the conditions of Tanzania and similar countries there is very substantial value attached to the training of people as close to their homes as possible. By the time the building programme of new training institutions is completed there will be in Tanzania, in addition to the faculty of medicine, seven schools for medical assistants, 16 for rural medical aids, 3 for A nurses, twenty for B nurses and 19 for maternal and child health aids. There will also be a number of other training programmes (e.g. midwifery) at some of the above mentioned schools as well as at some other places. In all, training will be going on at over 60 different centres in Tanzania. In addition to making it possible to train the greatest part of all health workers within reasonable distance of their homes all of these centres

---

*Not completely new, as there had been an earlier related category called the village midwife. These 600 or so women will be retrained and become part of the new cadre of maternal and child health aids.

represent some form of growth point for the districts in which they are located. In time it will also become possible for many of the centres to become regional training institutions rather than continue to be operated by the health ministry from Dar es Salaam, which would be a logical extension of present government policy on decentralisation.

The question of replacing expatriate health workers was given high priority in the manpower plan. There were in 1972 around 700 expatriate health workers in Tanzania. More than half of this total worked in the mission institutions, made up mostly of nurses and just over 100 doctors. There were in private practice around 100 doctors, dentists and pharmacists. In the public sector there were about 200 expatriate health workers, of whom about 30 were teaching at the medical faculty while the balance worked within the Ministry of Health. Of those working for the ministry about 100 were medical doctors, another sixty or seventy were nurses and the rest paramedicals. All expatriate health workers will have been localised by 1980 except some few dozen specialists in the medical faculty and perhaps a few in the ministry, as well as those medical doctors who will continue in voluntary agency employment. A handful of expatriate private practitioners may also remain.

C. Medical Practitioners

The discussion will continue with more detailed consideration of some of the problems connected with different types of health manpower, beginning with the several types of medical practitioner.

Medical Auxiliaries*

Although much as been written about the need for medical auxiliaries, and although the need is accepted by just about everyone *academically* involved in problems falling under the headings of health planning or health manpower planning, in practice no more than a handful of countries are seriously expanding the output of medical auxiliaries. In fact, in most places where medical auxiliaries already exist their numbers are being steadily reduced. For example, in francophone Africa, where the use of medical auxiliaries was very widespread until quite recently, the "Central African Republic is today the only State planning to train medical assistants".†

During the colonial period, 'proper doctoring' in Tanzania and the rest of Africa was basically confined to Europeans (even Asian doctors recruited for work in Africa were generally of the licensed and not the

---

*Some of the first parts of this section were published by the author in *The Lancet,* Dec. 1, 1973, pp.1251-1254.

†Pene, P. *The Lancet,* 1973, i, 1047.

registered variety). Africans could become medical auxiliaries, and those who succeeded to this high status job (for Africans anyway) were often outstanding men. Despite the high status attached to the post the medical auxiliary was in a distinctly inferior position relative to the proper medical doctor. Inevitably then, especially with the growth of independence movements, the category 'medical auxiliary' came to be seen as a colonial invention intended to keep the African away from true medical practice. Subsequently, with the coming of independence, there was a move away from the training of medical auxiliaries.

Although the feelings against 'second-class doctors' had already come into existence during the colonial period independence brought new factors to the situation. The most important was the emergent class structure in most of the newly independent countries. Very quickly an indigenous elite came into being that had similar demands — medical included — to those of the replaced colonial masters. The new leadership required large hospitals staffed with 'real' doctors. And, of course, the emergent national medical leadership — as part of the new national elite — shared those feelings and, in fact, strengthened them, since the most immediate effect of such medical policies was to enhance the career prospects of the new medical professionals. The doctors, as an organised body, proceeded to lend 'scientific' substance to the shared preference for doctors rather than auxiliaries. Despite the views held by individual doctors in public health and preventive medicine and by some other outstanding and courageous individuals, the profession as an organised body and as part of the new national elites succeeded in recreating European systems of medical care in the newly independent nations of Asia and Africa that were totally inappropriate to countries with conditions vastly different from those in the industrialised world. Medical doctors are basic decision makers, within the existing socio-political framework, in the shaping and implementation of health care policy and they have argued successfully that because any individual doctor is likely to be a better clinician than any individual medical auxiliary it is therefore proper to train only medical doctors. The fact that 20 or 30, or 40 auxiliaries can be trained for the same cost and much better utilised than any one doctor is ignored.

No conspiracies were formed in order to create the inappropriate conditions that now exist. Perhaps, unfortunately, no conspiracies were necessary. The coalescence of interests was such that non-European type medical practitioners came to be regarded as not really acceptable. It is noteworthy, however, that in many countries the demand for people who could take over tasks ordinarily reserved for doctors has led to the 'subversion' of the traditional work of nurses; that is, nurses are often being used to run the smaller, mostly rural health facilities such as dispensaries and health centres. Not that it is necessarily a bad thing to turn the nurse away from the bed and more toward outpatient and community work; but she, or the male nurse who is often preferred for this type of work, is highly unlikely to prove nearly as satisfactory in this role as a *properly* trained medical auxiliary i.e., one who has been purpose-trained as a different sort of medical practitioner (but not as a second-class doctor with only an abbreviated medical faculty curriculum). However, the planners seem to find it much easier to accept new roles for nurses and new types of nursing auxiliaries than to train other levels of medical practitioners who could function either as assistants or as substitutes for the registered doctor.

Tanzania has for a long time had four distinct types of medical practitioner (apart from the medical specialist or consultant). Of these four types, only the university graduate is to be found in the Medical Register: this particular type of practitioner has had a full secondary education followed by a university medical course of five years, plus one year of preregistration medical employment. A second type of medical practitioner is the assistant medical officer (A.M.O.). The A.M.O., who bears the title doctor, is originally trained as a medical assistant (M.A.) and then has at least four years of work experience plus an additional 18 months upgrading course. The medical assistant, in turn, has eleven years of schooling plus three years of medical training. The final category of Tanzanian medical practitioner, the rural medical aide (R.M.A.), differs from the M.A. in that he has only seven years of (primary) schooling before his three years' medical training.

Through upgrading courses that follow a prescribed number of years in employment at the lower level it has been possible for the R.M.A. to become an M.A., the M.A. an A.M.O., and the A.M.O. a registered doctor. In fact it is now possible, at least in principle, for a rural medical aide to become a registered doctor. This possibility was established in 1972 when five assistant medical officers were accepted into the medical faculty for a reduced course of four years' duration leading to a medical degree. As a result of past practice it has proved possible over the years for a substantial proportion of R.M.A.s to become M.A.s and M.A.s to become A.M.O.s. In fact, a number of R.M.A.s have even managed to become A.M.O.s. As has already been pointed out, although the different categories of medical practitioner have been in existence for many years their numbers had not grown much, up until the 1970s. As in most African countries there existed in Tanzania mixed feelings about the value of extending the training of medical auxiliaries. At different times the training of assistant medical officers and medical assistants had been stopped: especially after the opening of the medical school it was believed that such auxiliaries would no longer be required.

With the Arusha Declaration of 1967 the entire basis of the country's development policies had to be re-examined, in health no less than in other areas. From the principles laid down in the declaration it followed that Tanzania would have to create a health care system that was accessible to, and that would serve, the whole population. Because there is no way in Africa (as in other low income countries) to create such a system with the registered doctor as the primary medical practitioner a major expansion in the number of medical auxiliaries was clearly required. Consequently, in contrast to the four medical auxiliary schools having an output of 74 that existed in 1961, there were ten such training centres in 1971 with an intake capacity of 260. All but three of these ten schools were established between 1969 and 1971 (see Table 7).

Table 7 shows the marked acceleration of auxiliary training that followed the 1971 TANU directive to give absolute priority to the provision of water, primary schooling and basic health services to the rural population.

In Tanzania too there had been considerable hesitation about the appropriateness of having a primary school leaver, i.e. the rural medical aid, as the basic medical practitioner in the country. In fact during the years preceeding the decision to expand the number of R.M.A.s significantly some steps had been taken that seriously prejudiced the very future of this cadre. For example, the training period of the RMA was extended from two to three years which, of course, was followed by increasing pressure for salary upgrading. An increased salary scale would, in turn, have raised the question of a higher schooling requirement before entering RMA training, in effect from secondary rather than primary school, thereby significantly diminishing the gap between RMA's and medical assistants (the difference then being that although both would be secondary school leavers only the medical assistants would have had science training). Such changes would have clearly lessened the desirability of the RMA as a cadre, as the cost of training and employing them would have risen to just about that of the medical assistant. The final result would have been the destruction of the RMA cadre, and although a somewhat greater number of medical assistants might have become available the dispensaries would have continued to be staffed primarily by untrained people; over three-quarters of the nation's dispensaries were staffed by dispensary assistants — the former tribal dressers — who generally have had little or no formal training for the posts they hold. Of course it is laudable to desire more highly trained health workers; however, desire is not enough and it is not possible to 'jump steps'. If a nation such as Tanzania wishes to get away from the untrained and unacceptable

77

Table 7. Medical Practitioners in Tanzania: Independence to 1973

	1961	1970	1971	Training intake	1972	Training intake	1973	Training intake	Training 1974-1980 Planned annual training intake
Graduate doctors	403[1]	489	479	48	494[2]	48	533	64	64[3]
Assistant medical officers	32	100	115	22	140	–	140	24	35[4]
Medical assistants	200	285	289	115	335	146	335	201	210-250[5]
Rural medical aides	380	473	544	124	578	146	621	338	560[5]

[1] Of the total: 35% in government service; 20% employed by the voluntary agencies (missions); and 45% in private practice. Of the 403 medical graduates only 12 were citizens.

[2] Of the total: 62% in government service; 23% employed by the voluntary agencies; and 15% in private practice. Of the 494 medical graduates, 195 were citizens.

[3] Does not include students going to Cuba for a 7-year course in medicine.

[4] Biennial intake

[5] Wastage from training approximately 15%.

dispensary assistant it is then necessary to move to that cadre (the RMA) which can be produced quickly and in sufficient numbers so as to cover the whole of the country.

Although choices of the kind discussed here are often presented in the light of an abstract preference for a rural medical aid or a medical assistant, the actual choice is between a rural medical aid and a dispensary assistant. The same principle applies to the question of medical doctors or auxiliaries. For almost the whole of the population the choice is not really between a medical doctor and an auxiliary but between a medical auxiliary and *no one at all* (at least in the modern health sector): this being a classic example of the rejection of planning in favour of an abstract desire for the best, in the absence of any real economic or manpower considerations, thereby making the best the enemy of the good. The net result of such an approach being the output of a few 'good' health workers of whom only a handful will be available to the bulk of the population, instead of a much greater number of such people who would be relevant to the economic and therefore health care realities of countries such as Tanzania. As has been made clear, the vast expansion of health manpower over the decade of the 1970's in Tanzania will be possible only because of the reliance upon primary school leavers for the bulk of these personnel. If primary school leavers were to be considered as unacceptable for health care training it would in effect mean a massive decrease in the number of health workers that it would otherwise be possible to train and employ. In this connection it is important to note that the vast majority of patients in Tanzanian health facilities are, and must continue for very many years to be seen by auxiliaries and not by medical doctors. Of the total of 53 million out-patient visits in 1970 some 40 million (75%) were conducted at dispensaries, which were mainly staffed by dispensary assistants.

Table 8 shows the costs attached to training and employing the three basic grades of Tanzanian medical practitioner; the R.M.A., the M.A., and the university qualified medical practitioner. From the data it is possible to calculate that at present it costs more than twice as much to educate and train an MA as an RMA, 15 times as much to educate and train a medical faculty graduate as an MA, and 24 times as much to educate and train a medical graduate as an RMA. In fact, these differentials are probably even greater because the clinical training costs attached to the programmes have not been included in the calculations and any such costs must be considerably greater for graduates of the medical faculty than auxiliaries. On the employment side it costs about twice as much to employ a medical graduate as an MA, and about twice as much to employ an MA as an RMA, therefore it is possible to employ four RMA's for each medical graduate. Of course the figures shown

79

Table 8 Education, Training and Employment Costs of Different Levels of Medical Practitioners Tanzania: 1971 (in £'s)

	Secondary Education	Training[1]	Employment Government Salary Scales
University qualified practitioner	450	14,250	975-1685[2]
Medical assistant	300	580	440- 830
Rural medical aid	0	425	220- 415

[1] Includes only the costs of the university or training schools and not those of the hospitals or other facilities where students do their clinical work. In the case of M.A.s and R.M.A.s these costs would be relatively small but in the case of students at the medical faculty they would be substantial.

[2] Medical officers only; does not include specialists or consultants.

represent the position at a given time and various changes could be effected that would alter the employment ratios in the different staff categories. It is also the case that wage differentials alone are not a complete guide to the additional employment and career expectations and requirements of such contrasting groups as rural medical aides and graduate medical doctors. Nonetheless the figures are such as to suggest that the benefits of auxiliaries would be even greater in other countries than Tanzania because wage differentials between auxiliaries and medical graduates are substantially greater in most other places.

At some point Tanzania will turn from the primary school to the secondary school leaver as a source of recruitment for basic medical practitioners: one important determinant of that point will be the supply of candidates from the secondary schools. Tanzanian educational policy is such that it only allows the expansion of secondary and higher education to planned manpower requirements. In principle, therefore, there ought not to be any over-supply of secondary school leavers relative to further training and employment possibilities, although one cannot be certain about future developments. In any event, the question of basing future RMA training upon primary school or secondary school leavers is more a matter of national policy than one determined primarily by the Ministry of Health. Obviously however, with the passage of time, it will become appropriate at some point to shift over from primary to secondary school leavers entirely, perhaps during the period of the fourth five year plan starting in 1980.

During recent years it has become apparent that the increase in supply of secondary school leavers is making a growing number of such people available for RMA training, in addition to those with science backgrounds who enter medical assistant training programmes. The number of such people is difficult to determine precisely and would in any event vary over time in keeping with other training and employment opportunities; however, it became necessary to take account of those secondary school leavers who wished to enter RMA training, as well as to anticipate the eventual shift of RMA training from a primary to a secondary school base. Tanzania may therefore have two sources of entry into RMA training courses of a somewhat different character. The existing three year training course for primary school leavers will continue, but in addition there could be an adjusted programme for those entering from secondary school. The exact number of the latter type of school would be determined in keeping with the volume of suitable applicants, although initially only one is likely. The intention would not be to create two sorts of rural medical aide, the cadre would remain unitary in terms of salaries, promotions, postings etc.

Most training curricula for medical auxiliaries need to be linked more closely to the problems of health and disease in the context of the countryside, and the realities of work possibilities as they exist there. Tanzania is taking some serious steps in this direction and curricula revision is being actively pursued; the creation of a division of manpower development within the Ministry of Health is helping to facilitate consideration of such questions. The need to switch the medium of instruction from English to Swahili, particularly for primary school leavers, is an urgent matter and is being put into effect. The fact that the medium of primary schooling in Tanzania is now Swahili (English is taught as a foreign language) means that the standard of English of primary school leavers is falling and it is no longer realistic to expect such people to enter into any form of further training in the English language. The major bottleneck to moving completely to Swahili has been the absence of sufficient written materials in that language, although it has been argued that the language of instruction could still be Swahili even if textbooks continue to be available for a time only in English. (Often those who argue most vehemently for the retention of English are older people who had relied heavily upon a good knowledge of English for their own career prospects.) The fact that an increasing proportion of all medical and nurse auxiliary training is being done by Tanzanians means that the problem of teachers not speaking Swahili is rapidly diminishing.

The production of an adequate volume of medical auxiliaries does not by itself guarantee a solution of all the problems connected with the supply of medical practitioners. There are still the questions of assuring an adequate level of training for the new practitioners and of their later appropriate utilisation. The training problem does not end with initial qualifications. As with graduate doctors, the medical auxiliary needs ongoing education. It is particularly important that both the initial curriculum and later education programmes recognise that the medical auxiliary is not a mini-doctor to be offered an abbreviated form of medical school training (or a subverted nursing curriculum). Although some parts of any medical training must be similar, even if geared to different groups, there must also be recognition of the differences in previous schooling as well as future job functions.

The question of continuing education for medical auxiliaries is likely to be even more important than for medical graduates. The graduate will almost certainly spend the bulk of his working life in the company of other health professionals with a similar background to his own and only a limited number will actually spend most of their careers as *leaders* of teams of health workers. The bulk of health team leaders in most Third World countries, on the other hand, will be the medical auxiliaries. Thus, in 1980 in Tanzania there will be perhaps 140 hospitals, all headed by medical graduates, but the 2,600 rural health centres and dispensaries plus many small urban units will all be run by a medical auxiliary. Of course these 3,000 or so units are all part of an organisational table that at some point in its hierarchy shows graduate doctors as having supervisory responsibility for their operation. The importance of strengthening this supervisory link, although primarily in the supportive and not policing sense cannot be overemphasised. However, even given the best of circumstances the medical auxiliaries in charge of rural units will probably continue to be substantially responsible for the efficient operation of these facilities.

All too often, medical auxiliaries are initially badly trained and then thrown into the 'bush' and forgotten. Twenty years later they are pointed to as a useless bunch that cannot be compared with the medical graduate who, of course, has had all sorts of advantages in the years since leaving medical school. To help change this pattern Tanzania is planning the construction of a postgraduate medical auxiliary seminar centre. This centre, plus ongoing curriculum revision, will go a long way towards assuring an appropriately trained medical auxiliary. Another important step has been the creation of an improved career structure for medical auxiliaries that will increase the possibilities for career advancement and upgrading, as well as their wage position relative to the medical graduate. It is probably fair to conclude that any country — as is the case with Tanzania — that shows sufficient concern to

82

produce large numbers of medical auxiliaries is also likely to show a similar concern for their training and proper utilisation.

The potential for the proper utilisation of medical auxiliaries often suffers as a result of the way in which most ministries of health are organised. Traditionally, especially within Commonwealth ministries. there are a number of 'chiefs' responsible for specified parts of the health services e.g. chief medical officer, chief nursing officer, chief pharmacist etc. Each of these chiefs (or sometimes directors) is responsible for all levels of personnel that fall within their own specialised areas. For example, the chief pharmacist is responsible not only for professional pharmacists but for auxiliary pharmaceutical staff as well. In the same way, the chief medical officer, in addition to his varied tasks as the chief technical officer in the ministry, has direct responsibility for medical graduates as well as, in some rather vague way, medical assistants and other medical auxiliaries; however, in practice it is usually difficult for a chief medical officer to find the time required to act on behalf of the needs of the medical auxiliaries. A sitution is then created in which there is in effect no 'chief' responsible for medical auxiliaries and therefore no one to look after their interests. The already ambivalent position of the medical auxiliary, i.e. needed but not really wanted, is thus exacerbated. As a result the medical auxiliary often exists in some sort of limbo. One way of insuring the production and proper utilisation of medical auxiliaries would be the creation in health ministries of a 'chief medical auxiliary'.

The massive expansion of medical auxiliary training in Tanzania has necessitated the building of many new schools which were designed within Tanzania by the buildings division of Comworks in cooperation with the Ministry of Health. The construction of so many new training institutions raised the question of the future of the buildings at the end of the period of very rapid manpower expansion. Some of the schools would then undoubtedly be utilised for the increased output of higher level medical auxiliaries, as well as for the training of several other categories of paramedicals that for many years will be in short supply in Tanzania, e.g. laboratory, pharmaceutical, and dental auxiliaries and technicians. There will also be other sorts of local training and inservice courses that would require additional facilities. In the end, if it is decided to close down a school completely, certain of the buildings could readily be converted into hospital wards and other similar facilities, although it might also be possible to convert them for other uses entirely outside the health services.

The Assistant Medical Officer

The Tanzanian doctor, the assistant medical officer (A.M.O.), had trained originally as a medical assistant and after some years of employment gone into an upgrading course of twelve to eighteen months duration. The A.M.O. is a good illustration of the usefulness of having a complete range of medical practitioners, beginning with those with no more than a few months of training and extending to others with very many years. Of course, it is necessary to consider specific employment and career prospects within any particular country before finally determining the variety and number of people to be trained at different levels. However, the basic criteria for this determination must be the disease and health care needs of the population rather than the priority to be given to the career requirements of any one particular group. The A.M.O. represents a particularly inexpensive way of training relatively highly qualified people capable of carrying out the great mass of medical work that needs to be done in the countryside. The fact that such groups have not been well utilised in the past is more the result of resistance to the idea of a 'second class' doctor than anything else.

Within the Commonwealth there are a number of countries that have in the past trained a cadre similar to the A.M.O., for example the licensed medical practitioner (L.M.P.) In contrast to university trained doctors this cadre was drawn from form 4 rather than form 6 and had a somewhat shorter period of training than that of medical graduates. In countries such as India and Pakistan this group is no longer being trained and the existing cadre is gradually being upgraded to the level of the 'fully qualified' doctor. The concept of the A.M.O. was first introduced into East Africa with the entry of these L.M.P.s from British India during the colonial period.

The first group of assistant medical officers were trained in Tanzania just prior to independence. After the initial training of a couple of dozen such people the programme was stopped, partly in response to the creation of the school of medicine, which was later to become the faculty of medicine, shortly after independence. There were strong feelings against the idea of the assistant medical officer on the part of most of the Tanzanian medical profession (indigenous and expatriate): in this they were in agreement with virtually all those who had considered such matters, in that LMP/AMO cadres were not considered to be viable just because they were too close to being 'proper' doctors and therefore confused too many issues. It is worth noting that even those who have favoured the creation of greater numbers of medical auxiliaries have usually argued that all categories of medical auxiliaries must be kept clearly distinct from that of medical doctors and, consequently, that such groups as assistant medical officers and licensed medical practitioners were not practicable. Such views may very well be correct, at least within situations in which there is little or no control over the licensed medical practitioner and they are therefore in a position to raise substantial (often political) demands for

84

upgrading to full professional status. Nonetheless, the more usual basis for opposition to such groups is the desire of the established medical profession, in its own interests, to keep very clear lines between itself and all other categories of health worker. However, in situations in which the needs of staff are not accepted as being paramount, but rather the health care requirements of the population, such considerations become relatively less important. It must be added that the re-establishment of AMO training in Tanzania in the late 1960's was more the result of political pressure by medical assistants wanting an extended career structure rather than any consciously thought out manpower policy on the part of the health ministry. However, the introduction in 1973 of a new career structure for auxiliary personnel (longer grades overlapping with next higher categories) is likely to reduce pressure of the type which originally led to the re-establishment of the training of A.M.O.s.

As a result of the current explicit recognition of the value of such personnel, the training of assistant medical officers will continue in Tanzania as a matter of deliberate policy. This overall policy view was established even while plans for the proper training and utilisation of the AMO were still under discussion. One school of thought held that this cadre was particularly well suited for the operation and supervision of rural services. It was suggested that as a goal for the 1980's it might not be unsuitable for Tanzania to have an assistant medical officer in charge of each rural health centre and its seven associated satellite dispensaries. Another possibility would be to train AMOs as specialists, especially in public and preventive health care areas but also in certain clinical ones e.g. anaesthesia, paediatrics or obstetrics. (There is some evidence that this specialist training would be comparable to the training of most Chinese specialists.) In any event virtually nowhere has serious thought been given to the utilisation of the experienced medical assistant for specialised medical work. The possibilities in this area would seem to be very great indeed.

Medical Graduates

In health manpower planning, no question is more sensitive than that of the setting of targets for the output of graduate doctors. There is unquestioned acceptance on the part of virtually the whole of the medical profession, and most of those involved with health service planning that the greater the number of doctors the better — even independently of the production of suitable numbers of other types of health workers. Thus the World Health Organisation has set a target for Africa of one medical doctor for each 10,000 of population. Although targets for other types of health workers may be set from time to time, the one for doctors is the only one that is commonly used as a point of reference. This figure does not take into account such factors as the accessibility of population to any given number of doctors, the number of paramedical or auxiliary staff to be trained, the number and type of facilities to be developed and, particularly, the trade off between the training and employment of doctors as compared to auxiliaries. There is too, in the context of newly independent countries, the feeling that the output of a 'sufficient' number of graduate doctors is a critical expression of independence; this feeling is likely to be aggravated if many expatriate doctors are in employment within the country. As indicated above, it has been conventional to measure the number of registered doctors against population and to conclude that the resultant ratio is of special relevance, even in the absence of related ratios of medical assistants or rural medical aids or nurses etc. The reality is that there exists a number of medical skills that need to be related to each other in order to determine balanced and effective health manpower priorities. The concentration of attention upon doctor/population ratios has resulted almost everywhere in Africa (and elsewhere too) in an over-investment in medical education as opposed to other forms of health manpower training. Not only does it make little sense to concentrate too much upon the output of medical doctors as such, but, in the absence of appropriate manpower pyramids and thus supporting staff, it is also the case that the work potentialities of the doctor are also severely diminished.

In the Tanzanian context it was agreed that by 1980 there should be 800 doctors in the country; that number would represent about half the number of medical assistants and a quarter of the rural medical aids. It was determined that such a medical practitioner pyramid would be more suitable than the one which had been in existence, which was shaped more like an hour glass than a pyramid (with more or less equivalent numbers of doctors and rural medical aids and a smaller number of medical assistants).

In the course of setting doctor targets consideration was also given to the national goal of manpower self-sufficiency by the year 1980. Self-sufficiency has been defined in Tanzania as requiring that any particular area of national activity should not collapse if all non-Tanzanians were suddenly to become unavailable. The target for 1980 having been set at 800 doctors, of whom about 700 would be citizens, meant that only about 100 to 150 expatriate doctors would remain in the country by 1980. This would represent a significant change from the 1973 situation in which of the 500 doctors in the country (excluding 70 to 80 Chinese doctors) less than 200 were citizens. It is worth noting that by 1980 the country will not only have largely Tanzanianised its medical cadre but will have a significantly larger number of doctors at work.

The question of the number of doctors to be employed in the country at the target date and the number of those doctors to be Tanzanians was also related to the question of the number of specialists planned for the country by 1980. In 1973 there were only about 75 medical doctors with specialist qualifications working in the country. Of that number only one-third were citizens, in addition to which another 25 citizen doctors were on overseas specialist courses. It is obvious that by 1980, even without any special efforts, the number of Tanzanian specialists will have outstripped the present total of specialists working in the country, therefore the question of self-sufficiency in relation to the output of medical doctors – and specialists in particular – does not arise in relation to the replacement of the 1973 stock of 50 expatriate specialists. The real question in this regard is the overall volume of medical doctors and specialists it is considered necessary to employ: if that figure is placed at a level that is higher than the national capacity to produce them, then it will become necessary to continue being dependent upon expatriates. It is quite possible to produce great numbers of medical graduates and still be dependent upon expatriates, in fact it is also possible to produce almost no medical graduates and still not be dependent upon foreigners, the relevant feature being the level of expectation of those fortunate enough to be able to enjoy the services of doctors, and particularly specialist doctors, should they become available. For example, Tanzania currently employs no expatriate as a regional or district medical officer, whereas neighbouring countries with a great many more registered doctors to population than Tanzania continue to employ expatriates in such posts.

A related problem that is becoming fairly common in Africa is for a country to lose some of its medical graduates to London or Paris, etc., at the same time as expatriates are being recruited to fill the jobs being left behind by the departing doctors. This situation relates to the training received by doctors almost everywhere, a training that leaves them unsuited for employment at any but the largest urban hospitals and the doctor's consequent unwillingness or inability to function in any other environment.

In 1972 it was necessary to decide the appropriate level of expansion for Tanzania's only medical faculty. Detailed calculations of the controlled 'demand' for citizen doctors in the year 1980 showed such demand to be no greater than the already planned output of 700 citizen doctors. In any event it was agreed that the cost of training doctors was such as to make it impossible to allow a major expansion of the faculty, although a very modest growth of doctor output was accepted. It should be borne in mind that it is assumed that virtually all medical graduates will enter into public sector employment. It has been agreed in Tanzania that it is not the business of government to produce medical doctors who will go into private practice/business. Of course this may happen, in fact a handful of Tanzanian doctors already are in private employment; however, the longer term conditions for private practice are not good, in spite of a continuing short term demand for private practitioners. The entire social ethic of Tanzania militates against the likelihood of further development of private medical practice and recent years have seen a very significant decrease in the number of such practitioners, although most of those were Asians, who emigrated from the country. Private practitioners cluster in the towns and give service primarily to relatively small middle class groups; as such groups are declining in Tanzania there would not seem to be much future for private practice.

There is also need to take into account the expectations of medical graduates with regard to post-graduate training and the relationship between those expectations and the possibility of graduates adjusting to a health care system that is increasingly being geared to the countryside. This question had become particularly important in Tanzania due to the fact that inherent in the decision to control the growth of hospital beds was the concomitant need for doctors able to function outside the hospital environment. It had become eminently sensible to control the output of those sorts of health workers who were primarily hospital based, including most registered doctors, in favour of those cadres which were to be concentrated at the rural facilities,e.g. medical auxiliaries, maternal and child health aids etc. It is not that doctors are unrelated to the needs of rural services, only that in such circumstances the number of doctors required is relatively less than if they were to continue to be mainly hospital based clinicians primarily engaged in curative activities in relation to existing numbers of beds and patients. By contrast, the rural based doctor, while continuing to have clinical duties, will in the first place have responsibility for the organisation and maintenance of the rural health infrastructure.

The question of the number of doctors to be trained, is basically dependent upon the nature of the product in relationship to the system into which it must fit. This is so not least of all because if that product was consistently being trained appropriately to typically Tanzanian conditions then training costs would fall far below the 1972 figure of £15,000 per graduate. In the first place staff/student ratios would depart sharply from those of the English speaking industrialised countries i.e. more than one academic for every three students. There would also be much more practical clinical training carried out in district and regional hospitals, as well as in rural health centres. In short, medical education would become geared to specific Tanzania requirements rather than to those established in keeping with totally different conditions.

There are very few countries in the world that have achieved inexpensive and practical methods for training doctors; where this has been achieved, primarily in the Socialist countries, it has been accomplished by turning the production of doctors over to those who are later primarily responsible for utilising the product, the ministries of health. In countries such as Tanzania the Ministry of Health is already responsible for the training of virtually all categories of health workers except the registered doctor. Of course it is the case that certain advantages attach to the training of professionals at independent institutions such as medical faculties; however, it is also certainly the case that a much more efficient method of producing doctors could be achieved than is presently the case without in any way diminishing the *relevant* quality of that product. A suitable approach might be for ministries of health to be given basic responsibilities for the financial management of the medical faculty at the same time as academic responsibility remains with the faculty. Such an arrangement could lead to certain problems, but might be more suitable as a compromise than to continue as at present or simply to place medical faculties completely into the hands of ministries of health.*

Medical Specialists

After agreement had been reached as to the number of Tanzanian doctors that would be trained by the year 1980 it was necessary to determine an appropriate programme of specialist training. Such a programme would have to be related to the future work possibilities for most Tanzanian doctors, the great bulk of whom must be employed as general duty doctors at district and regional level, if they are to provide for the needs of a population that will still be overwhelmingly rural. If it is actually the case that higher education in Tanzania is provided to the few only because the product is required by all, then the primary justification for producing graduate doctors would be their close and continuing relationship to the mass of the population who will continue to be accessible only at the district level. Implicit in this is the fact that the bulk of Tanzanian medical graduates will be spending all of their professional lives as general duty doctors. In other words, they will not merely be passing two or three or five years in district work waiting for their turn to undertake specialist training and practice, but from the beginning they would need to be specifically trained for a lifetime of general duty district level work. However, the

*In late 1974 Tanzania took the decision to stop all direct entry into the university. All secondary school leavers will first enter into employment and later selection for higher education will be based primarily upon their performance on the job.

philosophic cornerstone of medical education everywhere, except in a few Socialist countries, is based upon the expectation that the product of the medical schools will at some point 'move up' to specialist practice. This has certainly been the case with Dar es Salaam and Makerere graduates who have expected this opportunity as a matter of professional right. Just as primary schooling was previously seen as the stepping stone to secondary schooling, and secondary education as the bridge to higher education, so the medical faculty is only another milestone on the road to specialist training (President Nyerere has clearly pointed out the dangers inherent in such an educational system in his essay *Education for Self-reliance*). In any event, if most graduates were to continue on to specialisation it would quickly become impossible to find appropriate posts for them within the context of the health services envisioned for the country; that is, services based upon a rapidly expanding network of rural health centres and dispensaries linked to modest district and regional hospital centres. The rational choices then, would appear to be either a limited number of graduates who would primarily be trained for such specialist work as could be afforded, or a greater number of graduates trained in keeping with explicit recognition of the fact that the bulk of them would spend their entire working lives in general duty district work. It might be useful to point out that it is just this unwillingness to recognise the fact that most medical graduates, in all countries, will not be able to spend their lives as specialists, coupled with the continuation of training programmes that are largely geared to producing potential specialists, that is making for severe imbalances, malutilisation and a medical 'brain drain' in countries as dissimilar in other respects as are the United Kingdom, Ghana, Ceylon, etc.*

The entire problem of post-graduate training- in terms of numbers, types and potential employment — touches on the same sensibilities as does the more general question of the training of medical doctors. As pointed out earlier, the number of trained specialists in Tanzania is very small and until recently they had almost all been expatriates. For example, in June 1972 six of the 12 consultants in ministry of health employment were expatriates as were 19 of the 23 specialists. Realistic targets for specialist medical manpower can only be based upon correct assumptions being made about the nature of their training and later utilisation. Although it is usual in 'medical planning' to determine the need for specialists in relation to population, or per region or district, in practise this approach is unsuited to the realities of most countries, particularly the poorer ones. The primary obstacle to medical

*For more on this issue see the author's *Doctor Migration and World Health*,
G. Bell and Sons, London, 1971.

self-sufficiency in Tanzania, as in other poor countries, has been the continuing adherence to values and standards that are not derived from existing realities. Although such values and standards might be more or less related to the technological base of the countries in which they originate, they have the effect in countries such as Tanzania of furthering the medical poverty of the mass of the population by effectively denying them access to any sort of health care as scarce medical resources become more and more concentrated, both in terms of facilities and skills. In addition, the dependence of the nation upon expatriate skills is extended for many unnecessary years as people are sent abroad for 'certificates upon diplomas upon degrees' so that even when a national is finally judged from the point of view of international standards to be 'good enough' to replace an expatriate he is likely by that time to have completely accepted the value system of the international standard and may then very well turn out to be even 'more royalist than the king' thus, in effect, not making his country any more self-reliant. The sheer waste of manpower involved in this whole process is enormous; thus bright young Tanzanian doctors with a number of years of district and regional level experience have been sent abroad to places like Israel or Britain to learn all about public health in places like Tanzania (often from teachers with far less real experience than their students).

At the heart of the problem has been the continued acceptance of external qualifications and standards as the basis of recognition and advancement within the Tanzanian health care system. It follows that countries like Tanzania must create their own qualifications immediately, based upon their own standards. It needs to be stressed that such countries can only accomplish the creation of these programmes quickly if the nature of the programmes are adjusted to the possibilities of the countries themselves. It must be understood that such adjustments would produce a product that will be not less, but more useful even if, when judged by some abstract international standard, the product is held to be something less than that which is produced internationally. The question becomes essentially one of organising already existing resources with a view to assuring self-sufficiency in medical manpower, including the more specialised varieties.

Once it had been determined that there would be in Tanzania 700 registered citizen doctors by 1980 it became possible to set the number of specialists to be trained by that year as some percentage of the total volume of citizen doctors. Because the overall needs of the health service are so great and each specialist requires supporting medical staff, that figure was set at just over 30% of all registered citizen doctors, but only just over 20% of the combined total of registered doctors and assistant medical officers. Therefore, the maximum number of specialists that can be expected by the end of the decade in Tanzania is somewhat over 200. This figure represents a total of four times the number of specialists in the country in 1973. However, in spite of this substantially greater number of specialists it is likely that it would still be necessary for there to be a handful of expatriates at the medical faculty or engaged at the consultant hospitals in some of the more narrow areas of specialised practice.

To implement its targets for medical specialists Tanzania has initiated post-graduate training at the medical faculty in Dar es Salaam in the fields of medicine, surgery, obstetrics and gynaecology, paediatrics, community medicine and pathology. The majority of people to be trained in these specialities will be trained in Dar es Salaam. Overseas training will be needed for other specialisations requiring smaller numbers,e.g. opthamology, radiology, anaesthetics, psychiatry etc. If all goes according to plan, by 1980 there should be a specialist physician, surgeon, paediatrician and obstetrician in each of the country's regions; in addition, each regional medical officer should have a specialist diploma in community health. There will also be almost enough pathologists to cover all regions of the country. The medical faculty will also have been largely Tanzanianised.

Considerable progress has been made in Tanzania in coming to grips with the basic problems involved in determining the appropriate number of medical doctors and specialists required by a poor country: just how much progress, can be judged by contrasting the above with the report of a 'committee on specialist requirements in Tanzania in the year 1984' which recommended that of a total of just over 1,200 expected medical graduates by the year 1984 almost half should have specialist qualifications. However, this whole issue still poses questions within a Tanzanian situation that contains many paradoxes. A more radical position on the question of specialist training would hold that there is little need for specialist training of the sort under discussion and that the programme of post-graduate training which is going forward, in spite of its being modest when compared to most other African countries and what had been envisaged at an earlier point in Tanzanian experience, was still overly ambitious relative to the true health care priorities of the nation. The demand for bodies to fill the post-graduate training programmes being developed at the faculty of medicine can lead to considerable turmoil as medical graduates are moved too quickly through their district and regional postings and into post-graduate training. Perhaps this process is inevitable in the initial years of local post-graduate training, but it is a relatively high price that is being paid for the relatively swift expansion of the specialist cadres.

In any event, not all of those who influence events in Tanzania are of the same mind on all questions and decisions are of course the result of compromise; the final targets for numbers of doctors and post-graduate specialists represent an example of such compromise. It is important to bear in mind that the Tanzanian situation represents not a revolutionary solution to the whole question of specialist, or other health manpower training but rather a stretching of the possible in favour of the achievement of a minimally reasonable balance between the various categories and levels of health personnel. However, that which has been achieved is not negligible and might be compared with the recommendations made a few years ago by an eminent English professor of medicine, now retired, for the development of the medical faculty in one of the poorest countries of Africa. It was recommended that there be a basic six year curriculum, followed by a two to three year period of houseman/registrar work, followed by a two to three year period of overseas post-graduate training. The medical faculty would be constrained to an intake of around 35 per year, from amongst whom the least successful five to ten graduates would be sent off to meet the needs of the provinces while the other 25 went on to post-graduate training. The promise was held out that at the end of twenty years there would be perhaps 400 medical specialists within the country, who would then become the basis upon which to create a health service for the country as a whole. It must be stressed that this sort of approach to health service development is much closer to being the norm in Africa than what is happening in Tanzania.

D. Nurses, and Other Paramedicals and Auxiliaries

Nurses

In most countries nurses constitute the largest single group of health workers. In Tanzania nurses represent about half the total number of health workers in employment in the Ministry of Health and take close to 60% of the wages paid to staff. In 1972 there were about 1,000 A nurses and 2,000 B nurses in the country. (A nurses have had 11 years of education prior to four years of nursing education while B nurses have had only seven years of primary schooling prior to three years of nursing training, although most B nurses also do a fourth year of midwifery). About two-thirds of all the country's nurses were in Ministry of Health employment with virtually all the rest being employed in voluntary agency hospitals. There was also a third category of nursing staff in the country, the village midwife, primarily employed in health centres and dispensaries and drawn from primary school leavers who had on average about one year's training. Because the training of this cadre was not a national responsibility the programmes of training varied.

The training of B nurses has largely been left to the voluntary agencies (16 of the 20 schools) but the three A nursing schools are all government institutions. In 1972 intake into B nursing came to 530 and for A nursing 126, however, it is only in relatively recent years that the output of nurses has increased significantly. From 1962 through 1967 output was static at about 150 per year, but by 1973 that figure had more than doubled when it reached a total of 330. The increased output resulted both from increased intakes and a decrease in wastage from nursing training. During the early 1960's nurse training wastage was running to 40% to 50% of intake, however, there has been a steady decline in this figure since 1963 to less than 20% of the intake of 1970. It is worth noting that wastage rates from different nursing schools vary considerably, so that of the 1970 intake the wastage rate ranged from zero in the case of three schools to over 50% in the case of one.

In spite of the rising output of nurses the feeling of shortage continues, although the real problem may be more one of distribution and utilisation of nurses than that of absolute number. If the Tanzanian policy of not increasing nurse training intake above the present level is to be successful it will be necessary to assure their better distribution and utilisation. In addition to the more general problems relating to the proper utilisation of health manpower there is one aspect of the problem that is peculiar to nursing as a result of its being mainly a woman's profession; that is, the difficulties involved in posting women (arbitrarily) from one place to another as governments can generally do in the case of men – naturally enough women usually choose to move about with their husbands. In a situation of extreme shortage of nurses this has not mattered much, in that it was almost always possible for the nurse/wife to find an appointment at the particular place to which her husband had been posted, which was usually a district or a regional centre having a hospital. However, with increasing numbers of nurses and increasing need to assure the equal distribution of those nurses the matter has become more complex.

Tanzania has been attempting to broaden the perspective for locally trained nurses. For some years there has been the possibility for B nurses to go through an 18 month upgrading course and thereby qualify as A nurses. In future it is likely that this upgrading course will not simply train nurses to a higher level of hospital competence but will instead upgrade nurses into public health nursing. There are now only a handful of nurses with public health qualifications in the country, and all such training must now be undertaken outside of Tanzania. It is expected that an upgrading course in public health nursing would go a long way toward filling the gap for nurses with such training. In addition, training in two significant areas of nursing has recently been started in Tanzania: one is psychiatric nurse training, which began in 1973. This programme also takes the form of an upgrading course for B nurses who will, at the completion of their period of psychiatric nurse training, emerge as A nurses with a psychiatric specialisation. One particular area of nursing training that remains a problem in very many countries is that of nurse tutors; and in Tanzania it is the only significant area of nursing that is still heavily dependent upon expatriates. Of roughly 45 nurse tutors in the country in 1972 only eight were citizens (six others were in tutor training courses outside the country). A local nurse tutor course was begun in 1973 with an intake of about 15. Within a short time it can be expected that Tanzania will have produced enough nurse tutors to staff all the nursing schools in the country. One particular important aspect of this specific localisation process is that it will make it possible to transform nurse training entirely from English to Swahili. This is becoming a particularly pressing matter as the medium of instruction in the primary schools from which most nurses are drawn into training is now entirely in Swahili and English is only taught as a foreign language. Several other sorts of training for which nurses might be utilised were also under discussion e.g. physiotherapy and opthalmic nursing.

Maternal and Child Health Aids

With the decision to control the rate of expansion of hospital beds it followed that the growth in expansion of A and B nurses, being trained essentially for hospital work, should also be limited. At the same time the rapid development of the rural infrastructure required a new nursing type cadre, the maternal and child health aid (MCH Aid). For some years a category of health worker called the village midwife had been trained in Tanzania. The precise number of those that had been trained is not known but it is probably around 600. These midwives were locally trained, to no standard curriculum, generally over periods that varied between nine months and two years. The training schools were small and influenced primarily by the need for practical midwifery training. In spite of the previous lack of attention paid to this group there was a growing feeling that they could be a particularly valuable source of assistance to village women and children. In determining the staffing pattern of rural facilities, in keeping with expansion targets to the year 1980, it was agreed that there would be two key health workers at dispensary level – one being the rural medical aid and the other the maternal and child health aid. The new cadre although having its roots in the older village midwife group would be a much improved and standardised version. The target was the production of around 2,100 MCH Aids by the year 1980, plus the upgrading of the existing 600 or so village midwives. The resulting total of roughly 2,700

MCH Aids would allow for one to be posted at each of the 2,300 dispensaries and two to each of the 300 rural health centres scheduled to be functioning in the country by 1980.

The specific programme called for the construction of a training centre in each of the country's 19 regions; in addition there were to be 64 district 'outstations'. The young women, who would have completed their primary school education, would be recruited directly from their own districts to the regional centres. The trainees would spend twelve months at a regional centre before going for six months of additional supervised work at the smaller district outstations attached either to small district or voluntary agency hospitals or rural health centres, according to the situation in particular districts. The trainees would not be required to leave their own regions during training and after having completed their eighteen months would be posted to a dispensary or rural health centre within their own district.

It is intended that having been posted to dispensaries and health centres the MCH Aids should be capable of organising and maintaining maternal and child health services; including, ante-natal and post-natal care, conducting normal deliveries and recognising abnormalities of labour, providing newborn and baby care, organising and conducting child health clinics, offering health education, teaching practical nutrition, and providing family planning services. The MCH Aid's primary function will be educational with regard to desirable MCH and promotive and preventive health care practices. They will not take primary responsibility for those health services requiring more advanced training when more highly trained personnel are readily available. However, as the demand for some services is likely to exceed the capacity of other health workers to provide them, responsibility for their delivery may be taken by the MCH Aid. Current demand for routine prenatal, perinatal and postnatal services already exceeds the service capability of the existing health cadres, so such services will be a part of the responsibilities of MCH Aids. Difficult prenatal cases, abnormal deliveries, and postnatal complications will be referred to a nurse-midwife or other appropriate professional as required. It is expected that the MCH Aid will represent a particularly important departure in favour of the health care requirements of Tanzania's women and young children. The fact of local training for these young women and the attendant totally rural orientation of the training could make them a particularly significant cadre.

Paramedicals and Paramedical Auxiliaries

Before closing this manpower chapter a few words will be added about some of the other groups being trained in Tanzania. Earlier it was indicated that there were several levels of personnel being trained in the various categories of dentistry, pharmacy etc. In dentistry, although fully qualified dentists continue to be trained outside of Tanzania, there is already one school for dental assistants and a second one is under development. There is also a training course for dental technicians. Pharmacists are also educated outside the country, but within Tanzania there is training for both pharmaceutical assistants and pharmaceutical auxiliaries. By 1980 it is expected that there will be 35 qualified citizen dentists in the country and over 100 dental assistants as well as a couple of dozen dental technicians. In the area of pharmacy there were also expected to be 75 trained citizen pharmacists, in addition to around 300 pharmaceutical assistants and auxiliaries. Laboratory technician training is proceeding within the country and it is planned for there to be over 300 such people in employment by 1980, supported by 500 laboratory auxiliaries. There will also be 45 radiographers and they will be supported by 100 radiographic auxiliaries. All of these figures represent a substantial increase in these various cadres. Particularly important are the ratios and relationships between the professional and technician and auxiliary levels. In the case of dentists there will be over three dental assistants to each dentist; for pharmaceutical personnel there will be five assistants and auxiliaries to each pharmacists; for radiographers, two auxiliaries to one radiographer; and in the case of laboratory workers there will be two auxiliaries for each technician.

Another important area of training is that of health officers (the former sanitary/public health inspectors) and the auxiliary of this cadre, the health auxiliary. The primary duties of the old sanitary inspector had been that of inspecting hygienic conditions at public markets, restaurants, and other public places and buildings, as well as being responsible for the collection of rubbish in urban centres. In practice their responsibilities virtually ended at the gates of the towns, although the health auxiliary did move somewhat further into the districts. The historical limitations of these groups is coming to be recognised in Tanzania and ways are being sought to make their activities more relevant to the whole of the population of the country which is, of course, primarily rural. The current intake into sanitarian/health officer training has been somewhat slowed although it is still expected that they will number 240 by 1980, however, the training of the health auxiliary will be expanded and the target for the year 1980 is 800.

There are several other categories of people receiving training in Tanzania; for example, there is a course for nutrition instructors which draws people from both inside and outside the health services. Also under discussion is the training of various sorts of opthalmic health workers, including refractionists and ocular technicians. The importance of the training of hospital secretaries, administrators and records assistants has been recognised and is likely to be expanded fairly quickly.

In concluding this discussion of manpower it should be stressed again that specific output targets had been decided upon in keeping with the financial and economic possibilities of extending the health services to the whole of the Tanzanian population. Also, that the targets represent a very substantial expansion of the rural health cadres and such planned expansion was possible primarily because of the constraint that had been placed upon the growth of hospital beds and their related staff. Of course, it was also made possible by the expected expansion of the Ministry of Health budget by roughly 6% to 7% per annum in real terms. The entire process has been facilitated by the fact that wages in Tanzania for those few fortunate enough to be in wage employment are reasonably well controlled, thereby making it possible for the Ministry of Health to employ a greater number of persons than might otherwise have been the case. The greatest danger to the successful implementation of the manpower plans discussed above would be the further expansion of output of some cadres, in the absence of a cutting back on others. Because the entire volume of manpower output was determined in keeping with overall economic possibilities, any expansion of one cadre would have to be compensated for from another group — if the overall balance of the plan were to be retained.

5. HEALTH SERVICE FACILITIES

Although there is general agreement that a much greater proportion of
health services should be brought to the population, particularly in
the form of preventive and promotive health activities, a very
substantial part of all services will continue to be offered from within
the confines of health service buildings, and the construction of these
will take the greatest part of the development budget of a health
ministry. Most Third World countries have three basic levels of health
facility — the hospital, the health centre and (what is called in
Tanzania) the dispensary. The hospitals in turn are divided into district
or rural hospitals, regional or provincial or state hospitals, and
national/referral/consultant hospitals (in addition there are certain
types of long stay hospitals e.g. psychiatric or T.B.). In principle each
of these various facilities has a particular function to perform and
is related in a hierarchical way to the others, so that more difficult
illnesses can be referred to the larger and more sophisticated institutions.
The somewhat startling fact is that size of building has relatively little
to do with the size of the catchment area it is serving. In practice the
dispensary may serve reasonably well the population living within
three to five miles, the health centre the population within five to ten
miles, and the hospital the population within ten to twenty-five
miles; that is, each facility may serve an area twice as distant as the
next smaller one. In Tanzania the costs of building and running the
three different levels of institution (dispensary, health centre and
regional hospital) had a relationship of one to ten to a hundred for
capital expenditures, and one to six to forty for recurrent costs.
Critical decisions have to be taken about the choice of appropriate
sized buildings, in some combination of the three basic levels
mentioned above, as well as their allocation and siting throughout the
whole of a country. It should be stressed that such health service
development must be based upon realistic possibilities for the
referral of patients rather than merely the abstract desirability of such
referral. In practice this means that lower level institutions must be
strengthened almost everywhere, so as to be more capable of providing
adequate services in the absence of extensive referral possibilities.

A. Construction
Some of the organisational problems of health service construction
have been touched upon earlier. At this point some questions relating
to the actual construction of health service buildings will be discussed.

The issues relating to construction techniques are important, but exist as problems primarily for ministries of construction and public works departments, and not for ministries of health. Although health ministries are unlikely to be able to determine, for example, the materials from which their health facilities are to be constructed, they can play an important role in the development of appropriate designs for health service facilities. The primary considerations in choosing appropriate designs would be those that would affect the future recurrent costs and efficient operation of the institutions. For example, hospital wards built on a fairly open plan can be more efficiently run with less nursing staff; and single storey construction with extensive veranda space will more easily allow patients to sit outdoors, which people generally prefer to do in warm climates. Single storey buildings also mean cheaper construction, improved chances for the use of local materials and contractors, less maintenance difficulties (particularly as no lifts will be required), and easier future extension or alteration of the hospital. The main arguments against single storey buildings are the potential losses of staff time and increased difficulty of guarding against pilferage. It might also be the case that sufficient land area is not readily available for single storey construction. It is also worth noting that annual costs of maintenance for most buildings seldom exceed one or two per cent of the capital cost so that emphasis on materials and designs which are justified solely on the basis of a reduction in maintenance costs is not usually economically justified.

Even cursory examination of most new hospital designs shows significant possibilities for savings. There appears to exist a great deal of confusion between that which is necessary for good medical care on the one hand, and hotel keeping standards and staff interests on the other. It is not unusual to find, for example, several offices being allocated to the same doctor, or large and multiple areas being made available to nursing and other staff. Special teaching and meeting rooms also have a way of multiplying themselves. In fact, in many hospital designs the fraction of space available directly to patients is extremely limited relative to the total area of the hospital complex.

Some parts of hospitals seem invariably to be constructed too small to meet future requirements. This is particularly the case for out-patient departments, perhaps because hospitals are primarily designed with in-patient requirements in mind, and the fact that hospital architects in Third World countries (Africa particularly) are often expatriates with little experience of out-patient conditions in such countries' hospitals. It is difficult for such architects to imagine the very large crowds that will present themselves at a typical Third World hospital out-patient department (at least in the absence of fees): it is certainly not uncommon to have well over 1,000 out-patients per day, primarily women and children, attending a typical regional hospital in a relatively small African town. The general underestimation of out-patient requirements extends to waiting areas in rural health centres and other small rural facilities. It might also be noted that the need for stores space is also often underestimated.

Some hospital and health service planners have laid great emphasis on the need to construct every dispensary in such a way as to make it possible for it to be expanded into a health centre at some future date and, in turn, each health centre to be constructed in such a way as to make it possible to later be turned into a hospital. This emphasis has often contributed to awkward and initially overly large buildings being constructed. When dispensaries can be put up for no more than two or three thousand pounds each (which is an appropriate cost) there would seem to be little point in worrying about their future expansion into hospitals which would occur, if at all, only at a very much later date. Dispensaries and other small institutions should be designed for the work they will be doing for many years to come and if they later turn out to be inappropriate for expansion there is hardly likely to be any serious loss. In the case of health centres there may be somewhat more justification in considering their later expansion. But, here again, such considerations should not be allowed to detract from the ability of health centres to function as efficiently as possible in keeping with their current requirements.

It is important that the recurrent costs arising out of particular construction choices be borne in mind, especially because health service development is likely to be appropriate just to the degree that it is labour rather than capital intensive (although this labour intensity will be reflected more in the recurrent than the capital budget). In practice the ratio of (recurrent) labour costs to capital expenditure is greater in smaller rather than larger buildings. In a Tanzanian dispensary the annual cost of employing the staff will be about one-quarter of the cost of constructing the dispensary 'complex', for a health centre the comparable figure will be only one-fifth or one-sixth, at a district hospital perhaps one-eighth, and at larger hospitals still less. The preference for labour intensive health service development follows from the fact that the additional construction costs of larger buildings do not offer a commensurate gain in services, as these are essentially determined by the volume of available manpower and not the size of the building (although a larger staff will probably require a larger building). In any event, in the building of large facilities there is the usual confusion between hotel keeping and medical care and careful analysis of the construction plans of most large hospitals would show that a very substantial part of the construction cost has to do more with hotel standards than medical care as such. Some of these issues will be touched upon again.

B. The Hospital Alternative

The key questions in the development of health service facilities are the relationships between the different level institutions i.e. the smallest unit (the dispensary or health station or sub centre etc.), the middle level unit (the health centre), and the hospitals; and, the most appropriate way to allocate across the country those different level facilities due for development. One intervening problem is the fact that the already existing hospitals are often so badly overcrowded that it is considered necessary to construct additional hospitals and/or more wards to relieve that overcrowding. However, the overcrowding itself is largely the result of the supply of an ever greater number of beds; that is, the supply of health services creates its own demand. This happens not only because potential patients have easier access to such services, but because medical doctors largely determine the volume and length of stay of hospital inpatients, and the number of such patients to be found in any given hospital at a particular time will be very much related to the medical professional's view of illness and its appropriate treatment. Thus the rigorous belief of the doctor in the efficacy of hospital based treatment will guarantee that all available hospital beds will inevitably be filled (at least in the absence of fee charging) and the more beds available the greater the number of admissions and the lower the rate of discharge. Conversely, in situations of extreme bed shortage fewer patients will be admitted and the average length of stay will decline. Actually, the number of beds available to the ill in Third World countries is small, although the number may not be quite so extreme as appears at first glance. In Tanzania, for example, the total of 17,000 hospital beds makes for a ratio of one hospital bed for each 750 people. However, if the 10,500 rural health centre and dispensary beds are included that ratio changes to one to 470. Although the ratio of beds to population is often as much as one to 100 in an industrialised country, as many as half of those beds will be in long stay (primarily psychiatric) institutions. In Tanzania long stay beds amount to only about 3,000 of a total of over 17,000 hospital beds. In all, in an industrialised country there will be about one general hospital bed for 200 people, while in Tanzania there is one general bed (at either a hospital, RHC, or dispensary) for each 530 of population. Such comparisons are difficult, not least of all because of the different volume and type of diseases that exist in industrialised and poor countries. In any case, the bed situation in Third World countries is not so extreme in comparison to industrialised ones as is usually thought to be the case. The real challenge does not lie in constructing more hospital beds, but in improving the level of medical care available at simpler institutions such as health centres and dispensaries and in improving the-efficient use of the relatively few hospital beds that are already available.

Nonetheless hospitals in most Third World countries, and certainly in Tanzania, are very crowded and there is need to establish in some rational way just how many (and which) patients shall be admitted to hospital and for how long. What is crucial is recognition of the fact that the overall answer to this question is not basically medical but economic; that is, firstly, to correctly determine the volume of resources to be made available to the health sector and, secondly, to allocate those resources in such a way (as between the hospitals and other activities) so as to bring about a maximum health care return. Thus, an intensive care unit will return a much smaller volume of health care when compared with the expenditure of an equal volume of resources on, say, a dozen or more dispensaries. While the case of the intensive care unit is quite obvious (to all but some doctors and parts of the urban elite) the choice between, say, additional paediatric wards at a large urban centre and a number of rural or even urban outpatient centres is not nearly so clear. As an example, in 1961 several new paediatric wards were built at Muhimbili Hospital in Dar es Salaam. As a result it became possible to double the volume of paediatric admissions over the succeeding two years. Although it was certainly true that the children admitted to the new wards were in fact ill, it is not necessarily true that these particular children most needed hospital admission (or other medical care) when compared with the children in most of the rural areas of Tanzania. It can be expected that as greater numbers of patients are admitted to hospital particularly in the urban areas, a smaller proportion will absolutely require hospitalisation. Thus, as the number of children admitted to hospital in Dar es Salaam doubled over the two years 1969-71 (from 6,181 to 12,691) the number of deaths as a percentage of admissions dropped from 9.8% to 3.2%.* Although some (small) part of that decrease might be accredited to improved care, the very greatest part of this declining death rate could only have resulted from the fact that more children who were less ill were being admitted, due to the increased supply of paediatric beds in Dar es Salaam.

The Tanzanian experience of an increased supply of beds bringing forth a greater volume of inpatients is quite striking. Until recently these were in Tanzania 47 government hospitals of more than 60 beds

---

*Data provided by Dr. M. Segall, formerly Professor of Paediatrics, Faculty of Medicine, Dar es Salaam.

each (20 others with 60 or less beds — an average of 41 — are not considered here as they are subject to too many special factors to be representative). Of those 47 hospitals 26 had their bed numbers increased, over the years 1967-1970, by an average of 52 per cent. All but two of these 26 hospitals experienced an increase of inpatients that was greater than the national average of 15 per cent over those same years (for the 26 as a whole their average increase was 58 per cent). Of the 21 hospitals that did not have their bed numbers increased only six had an increase of inpatients that was greater than the 15 per cent national average (and three of those six were not much above the average). Although some of the data are probably subject to a certain amount of error the picture that emerges is quite clear, an increase of inpatient numbers that is roughly proportional to the increase in the number of beds — even to the specific years in which the beds were added (as more detailed data show).

It can be said that doctors will generally admit in relation to available bed space; although there may be special factors at work at a particular time or place the overriding consideration, over time, will be the availability of the bed itself. It can be stated with some confidence than an increase in bed numbers will almost certainly lead to an increase in the number of patients (other things, e.g. fees, being kept equal) and, conversely, in the absence of such an increase in beds it is probable that inpatient numbers will increase but slowly, if at all. Because the provision of additional hospital beds of the conventional type must produce more inpatients and thereby make more difficult the allocation of more resources for the preventive and rural health services it is necessary to avoid the extension of conventional hospital services except in the most desperate circumstances. However, in keeping with a policy of postponing as long as possible the building of additional beds there is need to develop suitable alternatives to conventional hospital wards (see later discussion) and, of course, to quickly expand the preventive services.

The discussion will now consider, in turn, the different levels/ types of health service facilities/buildings to be found in countries such as Tanzania.

C. The Dispensary

In Tanzania the dispensary represented the lowest level of permanently staffed, fixed health facility. Most countries in the Third World have such small facilities (although often bearing different titles e.g. health station or sub-centre), and frequently in substantial numbers as evidenced by the fact that there are roughly 1500 of them in Tanzania (about 1200 government and 300 voluntary agency). It is almost always the case that these facilities are badly staffed and supplied and function primarily as minor curative centres distinguished by the absence of any preventive and promotive health activities. Some of these problems stem from the fact that these facilities are often financed out of very scarce local or district authority funds while the hospitals are financed at a significantly higher level by relatively wealthier central government ministries. In addition, in situations in which central government ministries are not directly responsible for the dispensaries they are less likely to be particularly concerned over the training of appropriate personnel to man these small facilities. It is usually the case that, in Africa at any event, these dispensaries are staffed by the 'descendants' of the rather casually trained cadre of tribal dressers created during the colonial period. In the post-independence period the number of dispensaries has grown in many countries and the tribal dresser has gradually evolved into what is called in Tanzania, the dispensary assistant. In practice, however, there is little to distinguish the new dispensary assistant from the old tribal dresser; if anything the current version may be trained even more haphazardly than the previous one. Very often the dispensary assistant is someone who had been connected with the health services in some way, often as a sweeper or nursing assistant at an urban hospital, before striking off on his own and finding employment with a local authority as a dispensary assistant.

In recent years the establishment of the health centre concept, which was intended to be helpful to the proper functioning of dispensaries, has had the net effect of turning attention away from the dispensary in favour of this next higher/larger unit of service. Although health centres are generally supposed to function in conjunction with some half dozen satellite dispensaries, in practice they often have very little to do with them. One of the reasons for this, in some countries at least, being that health centres may be the responsibility of central government while dispensaries are the responsibility of the local authorities. However, more fundamental has been the fact that they have seldom functioned as the intended centre of preventive and promotive health care activity which would have been capable of offering proper support to the work of the (satellite) dispensaries. The overwhelmingly curative orientation of the health services has spread to the health centres and they tend, in spite of some exceptions, to operate as little more than either large dispensaries or small hospitals.

Many of the problems involved in the running of dispensaries and health centres have been recognised in Tanzania and steps are being taken to guarantee their improved operation. As part of the decentralisation of government certain responsibilities that had

105

formerly been held by the local authorities have been transferred to the new regional authorities, along with many of the activities that previously had been carried out directly by central government ministries. Thus all the dispensaries, health centres, and district and regional hospitals are now operated by the regional and district authorities, for the first time bringing all of these institutions together under the same management. Consequently, the District and Regional Medical Officers now have direct authority over the dispensaries. It is expected that these changes will strengthen the dispensary network, and that this strengthening will have an important effect not only upon the level of curative health care available in the countryside but, even more importantly, will facilitiate the development of a broad range of preventive activities.

It is important to note that experience has shown that it is often difficult to separate preventive health care programmes from *appropriate* curative facilities; in fact while some diseases may be prevented in the absence of any curative measures there are others which absolutely require a combined approach. In any event, many of the difficulties which have arisen with regard to curative services have been caused by the fact that these services have been of the wrong sort,i.e. concentration upon (usually large) hospital development. It is the case that Third World health care programmes are likely to be more appropriately measured by the rurality of their content than any other single factor, and it is extremely difficult to imagine a successful rural health care programme which is not substantially built upon preventive practice. The expanded rural health care programme in Tanzania very much involves the dispensaries in a programme of improved management and staffing. The new situation offers both a substantial challenge as well as opportunity: a challenge because of the current difficult situation of most of the existing dispensaries, and an opportunity in that if these units could be made to function properly they would make a major contribution to the health of Tanzania's rural population. The main functions of a dispensary should be:—

1. Treatment of simple diseases and short illnesses by outpatient care.
2. Initial treatment of serious illness pending referral to a rural health centre or hospital.
3. After care, if required, of patients discharged from hospital.
4. Participation in immunisation and community health programmes, including control schemes for communicable diseases by mass treatment e.g. tuberculosis, leprosy etc.
5. Maternal and child health work, including ante-natal, delivery and post-natal care.

In 1972 only about a third of the Tanzanian dispensaries were staffed with rural medical aids, the rest were in the charge of a dispensary assistant. As discussed earlier, the establishment in 1972-74 of 11 additional rural medical schools (to a total of 16) will result in sufficient output so as to have such an aid at each of the country's 2300 dispensaries by 1980. It must be stressed that the rural medical aid will function as the Tanzanian general practitioner, the health worker who will offer first medical contact to the bulk of Tanzanians when they fall sick, or assist in the preventive and promotive work intended to keep them from becoming ill. In addition to a rural medical aid each dispensary will have at least one maternal and child health aid who will be particularly responsible for the needs of women and children. The dispensary staff is likely to include at least one other person, although the precise functions of this third person are not yet precisely defined. The operating costs of a fully staffed and properly functioning dispensary should come to around £1,300 per annum, of which about half will be for salaries and most of the balance for drugs and other supplies. The planned expansion of dispensaries for the rest of this decade is 100 per annum. This figure is based upon the overall size of the recurrent health budget, the possibilities of manpower output to staff the dispensaries, and the balance between the dispensaries and the other types of health facilities to be constructed during the decade. It is also the case that ujamaa village development is proving to be helpful for the location of new dispensaries; as population is gathered together it becomes possible to better serve a greater number of people from any one new dispensary, and especially so if they are sited with care.

The standard dispensary now being constructed in Tanzania was only recently designed. The dispensary 'complex' includes a basic service building of two rooms — a clinic for the rural medical aid and an examination/meeting room for the maternal and child health aid, a two bed delivery hut built of traditional materials, a house for the rural medical aid, and two pit latrines. The clinic is used for consultation, examination, injections, dressings and the dispensing of drugs. There is also a small corner for a laboratory. The maternal and child health room is used for patient examination and meetings. The estimated cost of the fully equipped dispensary complex was roughly £2,000. Actual construction should in most cases include an element of self-help labour, particularly for the delivery hut and the pit latrines.

In Tanzania, as elsewhere, there has existed a tendency to escalate the size and activity of the dispensary in the direction of more inpatients and other hospital type activity. For example, one dispensary built in the Tabora region of Tanzania consists of a three room outpatient clinic, a nine bed maternity unit and two staff quarters.

The estimated construction cost came to about three times that of the new standard dispensary plan. There were six staff employed at this dispensary, including two dispensary assistants, two village midwives (now MCH aids) and two sweepers. The number of deliveries averaged about 25 per month which, therefore, left seven of the nine beds generally unoccupied. The number of outpatients numbered less than 50 per day (small by Tanzanian standards). This particular dispensary was approximately twice as large as it need have been and was employing about twice as many staff as would be appropriate if the whole of the country were to be able to meet its dispensary manpower requirements. It so happened that the overly large dispensary described above resulted from misplaced political (over) support given to a new ujamaa village. Although it is right that special support be given to all such efforts there had been a tendency in some cases to ask for and grant even more than was necessary. The same type of situation can also develop in relationship to dispensaries being built for special groups, including industrial and plantation estate workers whose health care needs may be met from the budget of their employing (private or governmental) organisations.

D. The Rural Health Centre

The concept of the rural health centre represented a significant departure from the curative orientation of the previously existing hospitals and dispensaries. It was hoped that these centres would play an ever increasing role in raising the general standard of health of the majority of people, particularly those residing in the rural areas. The accent of work in the rural health centres was to be on improving standards of health rather than the treatment of disease. It was hoped that in time dispensaries would increasingly take on the same functions as the rural health centres. It was intended that a vehicle should be available at all times to be used by the rural health centre staff, although it was considered quite feasible for staff to go visiting locally on foot or by bicycle: it was considered essential that the medical assistant, the rural sanitarian and other key staff should spend rather more time out of the centre than in it. Within the centre the staff would provide:—

1. Simple outpatient care; including examinations, diagnosis, basic laboratory investigations and treatment.
2. Comprehensive maternal and child welfare services; including ante-natal examinations, health education for mothers, delivery facilities and post-natal care, and child welfare clinics.
3. The health officer (rural sanitarian) and his staff should provide continuous services for education of all kinds, but particularly in environmental hygiene.

108

4. A limited inpatient service for illnesses lasting two or three days; only a very few beds should be provided for this as it would be a relatively minor function of the health centre.

The work to be performed outside the health centre was to be even more significant than that to be done inside, as follows:—

1. Working with the staff at five or six of the nearest dispensaries for a day at least once a fortnight, giving advice and teaching new techniques, training staff in standard methods, organising immunization schemes with the staff, and generally giving more skilled advice than is normally available at a dispensary.
2. Spending time searching for infective diseases, examining local water supplies, and giving lectures on health education.
3. Involvement in disease surveys and the collection of accurate statistics, particularly with regard to nutrition and malnutrition and such diseases as malaria, bilharzia, tuberculosis, leprosy, hookworm, tetanus and other locally important conditions.
4. Building up a complete picture of the living conditions and customs of the people of the area.
5. Helping to put into practice whole aspects of environmental sanitation.
6. Provide a health service in all the surrounding schools. This involves physical and laboratory examinations of apparently healthy school children, including dental examinations and eye-testing. Immunization schemes and health education should form a part of this service.
7. Working in conjunction with other agencies and groups functioning in the area of the health centre.

Examination of the actual work of rural health centres almost anywhere would show a substantial departure from the idealised picture presented above. The reasons for this situation are many, starting with the curative orientation of the health services into which the health centres have been fitted. This orientation means, among other things, that the resources being made available for specifically preventive work are very limited and that the training of health centre staff is usually inappropriate for the sort of work they are supposed to be doing. In any event, it is usually the case that staffing is extremely limited because enough resources are not being made available for the training and employment of a sufficient number of rural health workers. Health centres are usually grossly understaffed, consequently the staff are severely overworked (or would be if they always attended to their duties) and faced daily with a huge demand for curative attention. It is also the case that if a medical assistant in charge of a health centre were to wish to spend more time out of the centre than in it he might quickly find himself in opposition to local political personages who see the health centre as serving the people living in its immediate proximity through the provision virtually only of curative services. In addition, the population living near the health centre also demand that their 'doctor' be in attendance whenever they require his services.

The general lack of attention given to the development of the rural health services by the administration at the centre (Ministry of Health) exacerbates all of the problems under discussion. Given the shortages of staff, and particularly of medical assistants, usually means their being posted from health centre to health centre in response to emergency conditions, so that they seldom stay long enough at any one place to develop the local knowledge required to properly serve the community. In addition, medical assistants and others are trained and then thrown out into the 'bush' and left with no further possibility of refreshing their skills. It is not surprising that all too often the medical assistant and other rural health staff become corrupted and begin to charge illegally for their services, or turn to drink as they become both corrupt and drunken. It must be stressed that all this need not be and is the result of the general neglect and lack of interest in rural development and rural health services that is so often the case in so many countries.

The rural health centre concept has also suffered from medical attention. Initially the centres were seen as being quite modest and certainly not intended for any significant level of inpatient care. Over time, however, the combination of certain of the factors discussed above i.e. the popular demand for inpatient care and local political influences, added to the suspicions of those medical doctors who felt that health centres were simply inadequate to accomplish the tasks expected of proper medical institutions. It therefore became necessary to increase the scale of the health centre so that it began to look more like a rural hospital than the institution originally envisaged. A combination of wanting the health centre to be a larger structure, in fact a rural hospital, coupled with the general constraint on funds being made available for health centre development meant that increasingly fewer health centres were being developed. In spite of their larger size the relatively few centres that did get built had very limited catchment areas, at least partly because they continued to function basically as dispensaries i.e. as minor curative centres with little outreach into the community. Thus, the health centres became increasingly inefficient in relationship to their originally intended function, and ability to provide services relative to their increasing cost. It would not be unfair to conclude that there is hardly any justification for the continued development of rural health centres if they are to continue to be nothing much more than large dispensaries or small hospitals. If that is what they are to be and

110

it is judged that there is indeed need for more large dispensaries or small hospitals then, accordingly, they should be so properly labelled and planned.

The health centre is capable under a range of East African conditions of serving directly some 10,000 to 25,000 people, and if its six or seven satellite dispensaries were properly run they would increase the total catchment area of the centre to perhaps 35,000 to 60,000 persons. However, such figures assume more efficient working capacity than is now usually the case as well as significantly more mobility on the part of the staff. One of the critical factors preventing more mobility and the better functioning of rural health centres is the ever increasing number of inpatient beds to be found in many of them. The general belief of the medical profession, as well as the public, in the efficiency of inpatient care had led in Tanzania, as elsewhere, to the construction of larger health centres containing greater numbers of beds. The earlier health centres, built by generally impoverished district councils, were initially relatively modest institutions. However, it was often possible for a district council to provide the relatively small amounts needed for the later addition of very simple wards containing an additional eight or ten or twelve beds. In 1975 the 100 or so rural health centres in Tanzania averaged about 30 beds each, which is roughly double the appropriate number.

When the Tanzanian rural health centres came under the management of the Ministry of Health a new design for them was brought into effect. This plan formalised what had already been happening in the district council rural health centres in that it was designed along the lines of a small hospital containing 56 beds. Fortunately only a few of these centres were actually constructed. The emphasis on hospital type beds coupled with increasing costs had led to a reduction in the floor area being made available to outpatients, and the possibility of the centre carrying out much mobile and village work. In such small hospital-like health centres it is almost invariably the case that many beds will either not be occupied if there is accessibility to a hospital or they are likely to be taken up by social welfare rather than medical cases, i.e. people who are kept in a health centre bed more because there is no other place for them to go rather than for any particular medical reason; by contrast, the maternity beds in such centres will often overflow. It is important to bear in mind that the provision of so many beds requires that there be present most of the facilities of a hospital e.g. kitchen, laundry, more staff quarters than would otherwise be the case, etc.

For various reasons it proved virtually impossible to construct more than a very few of these centres and after long discussion a more modest plan was introduced. In this plan it was intended that the number of

111

beds should be standardised at twenty, but that to serve these beds there would still be a separate (hospital type) service block, relatively expensive staff housing and several trained nurses to care for inpatients. This rural health centre complex would have cost, at 1972 prices, about £50,000. After another intensive discussion about the nature of an appropriate rural health centre this plan was in turn replaced by a still simpler one costing (then) less than £25,000. The overall area of the new centre was very similar to the old (except that the area allowed for staff quarters was substantially reduced) although the distribution of floor space within the centre was very significantly changed. Thus, the new design allowed for 24 per cent more space for outpatients and 25 per cent more for public health activities; while the area for inpatients was reduced by 40 per cent.

The new rural health centre plan includes four buildings. The largest of these is the outpatient facility, which was particularly designed from the point of view of smooth outpatient flows. A second structure is intended for maternal and child health and other public health activities. A third building is made up of three inpatient 'wards', one of six beds for maternity and two others of four 'holding' beds each for males and females. A fourth building includes a workshop and storage space for a rural sanitarian, cooking and washing areas based upon traditional usage, and additional storage space. It was intended that patients and their families would do the cooking and laundry at the health centre. There are two other small structures, one being an extremely simple relative's hostel and the other a small mortuary necessary for cultural and religious reasons.

The changed rural health centre design, and expected consequent change in its functions, also meant a substantial savings in likely recurrent costs. The old design called for 28 staff, but the new one only 16. The major manpower reductions were in the number of trained (bedside) nurses and hotel keeping staff. These reductions resulted partly from the decrease, from 20 to 14, in the number of beds at the health centre. The estimated capital cost of the new centre was less than half that of the old, and the recurrent costs about two-thirds. The decrease in the number of staff required at the new health centre, which resulted in a one-third reduction in operating costs, was considered to be of even greater importance than the decrease in capital costs of one-half. It is especially worth noting that the decrease of staff from 28 to 16 took place almost entirely amongst those who were involved with inpatient care. It was expected that the staff cuts would not affect in any significant way the functioning of that part of the health centre which carried the highest priority, the outpatient and mobile work; that is, primary care. Of course the design and staffing changes indicated above do not by themselves

112

guarantee that the new rural health centres will function properly, although it does at least assure that a much greater number will be built than would otherwise have been the case (about double in fact).

The need to devise standard health facility plans and guarantee that they are not exceeded, particularly as to bed numbers, is a difficult and important question. If additional beds are made available at a health centre it is likely they will be occupied, except that if the centre is easily accessible to a hospital these beds will often be found to be empty. This problem can be well illustrated by reference to a rural health centre located just several miles from one of the larger Tanzanian towns (in the centre of one of the most developed areas of the country) which is also the location of one of the country's largest and most sophisticated hospitals. The centre was built in 1968 at a cost of about £15,000 and included three twelve bed wards, one male, one general female, and one maternity. The male and female wards were often completely empty because anyone having a problem requiring inpatient care went on to the town for treatment. The maternity ward, on the other hand, was being intensively utilised. This particular health centre had 35 almost completely immobile staff, from whose point of view this was a very desirable posting in that it was just a few miles from an attractive town in one of the most pleasant areas of the country. However, even this large number of staff could not ensure the efficient working of the health centre as they were almost completely immobile, even in the absence of any significant number of inpatients, in spite of the fact that many thousands of people lived within very easy reach of the centre. What had become the case was that the health centre programme of Tanzania, as virtually everywhere, was to a significant degree bogged down by a hospital (curative) and bureaucratic mentality which required that all its potential clientele come to the health centre while staff remained carefully protected within their own environment.

E. Hospitals

Government general hospitals in Third World countries fall basically into the two categories of district and regional (or provincial etc.) institutions, and the national referral/consultant centres. In addition, there are special long stay institutions mostly for tuberculosis, leprosy and mental illness. The district and regional hospitals are located in the smaller urban centres while the national referral centres will be found in the largest cities. The voluntary agency hospitals are generally located in the rural areas or smaller urban centres. In addition to the above there are usually some hospitals associated with the occupational and insurance supported health schemes, as well as a number of private, commercial institutions. The medical faculty may also have its own teaching institution. In many countries the management and finance for government district and regional institutions are separate from, and subject to different conditions than the national referral centres. In most countries however, they remain nominally within the same system and draw their finance from the budget of the Ministry of Health, although in practice it is often the case that different criteria are applied to the development of the two sets of hospitals. In African countries there often may be no more than one or two or three hospitals that fall into the special category of national referral centres, with the one in the capital city being designated the teaching hospital for the only medical faculty in the country. In principle all the hospitals at district, regional and national level are part of a referral hierarchy, with the larger and more specialised institutions being justified on the basis of their serving not only the immediate population but the whole nation through the medium of the referral system. As has been discussed earlier, these referral systems seldom work and the hospitals tend to serve virtually only the population having immediate access to them. Much has already been said about hospital development in relationship to the overall development of the health services and here the discussion will focus upon a number of more specific problems concerning the hospitals as such.

Buildings

It has already been indicated that Tanzania had managed to develop relatively inexpensive standards of hospital building, and in the last several years new designs have been developed for district hospitals and their component parts. It is estimated that a 26 bed ward for example, can be added to an existing hospital at a cost of roughly £400 per bed. To build a new 80 bed district hospital to a standard design will cost about £100,000, or about £1,250 per bed. To add beds to existing national referral centres or to build such centres costs considerably more. For example, a 156 bed maternity block was added to Muhimbili Hospital in Dar es Salaam in 1970 at a cost of almost £2,000 per bed, and the cost of two new referral hospitals (the second and third in the country) came to in one case almost £4,000 per bed and in the other £7,000 per bed.

Relatively little attention has been paid to the question of organising the physical improvement and expansion of existing hospitals, as compared to the construction of new facilities, and yet often a relatively significant part of all hospital construction costs in any one financial year will be spent on already existing institutions. Very many smaller and older district and regional institutions could be significantly improved if relatively minor investments were made at these facilities. In Tanzania it was found that quite a number of the older hospitals were lacking even in electricity and one of the more

114

significant aspects of hospital improvement in recent years has been to electrify all those hospitals not previously supplied. Other useful improvements included the extension of stores space in many hospitals, the building of extensions to outpatient waiting areas, the addition of water storage tanks, improvements to kitchen and other similar equipment, and so on. All of these are relatively inexpensive improvements and can make a significant difference to the running of a hospital. It is also useful for health ministries to conduct organised surveys of the physical conditions of their hospitals with a view toward their planned improvement. Information should be gathered about the state and volume of work of the laboratories, X-ray facilities, and kitchens and laundries, as well as about the supplies of water and electricity, the sufficiency of stores and pharmacy space, the condition of hospital transport and the state of staff housing.

Equipment

The problems connected with hospital equipment are often serious, and generally start with a sheer lack of information at the centre about the state of the equipment scattered around a country (or region etc.). In fact it is often virtually impossible to find out just which equipment exists, as well as its age and condition. In Tanzania steps are being taken to meet some of these problems by creating a hospital equipment maintenance unit responsible for the upkeep of most of the hospital, health centre and dispensary equipment in the country. An effective maintenance unit would lead not only to the more efficient use of equipment, but to savings on the importation of an unnecessarily large volume of additional equipment. The unit should be concerned not only with medical type hospital equipment but that of the laundries and kitchens as well. The Tanzanian unit is likely to be placed somewhere near the geographic centre of the country, thus making it easier for equipment and skills to move between it and the rest of the country. The unit should have a major responsibility for artisan training, both for those who will remain at the centre and maintenance personnel at regional and district level. The national centre could become a model for other, smaller regional centres. In time the unit should be able to help formulate policy on the purchase of hospital equipment as well as keeping a schedule for the planned replacement of all equipment stocks. This would represent a major improvement over the present ad hoc methods of maintaining, replacing and purchasing equipment.

The setting of appropriate equipment standards for health service facilities is complicated by the fact that such standards are often set in relationship to some (hoped for) level of staffing which is unlikely to be fulfilled. It would be usual for a health ministry to ask, say, a senior radiologist to advise on the X-ray equipment necessary

115

for a district hospital. However because such specialists often have little real knowledge of actual situations at such small hospitals their recommendations can often be out of touch with reality. What is needed are determinations of the *minimum* equipment requirements of district and regional hospitals which have been defined in keeping with the overall volume of resources (especially manpower) that is likely to be made available to the hospital under consideration.

Organisation

There are a number of widely accepted principles for improving the efficiency of hospitals that, although fairly well known, are not very often put into practice. One important example is that of progressive patient care which would, in the context of most Third World countries, mean the utilisation of existing hospital beds only for the most seriously ill, coupled with the construction of simple hostels to house those who require relatively little medical attention and yet cannot be sent to their homes. At present hospitals are being built to only one standard which assumes an equal degree of illness on the part of each patient (except possibly for a small intensive care unit), thus per patient unit costs become substantially higher than they otherwise might be. The patient hostel could cater for the estimated third or more of hospital inpatients who spend all or part of their time in hospital more for social than medical reasons, and are basically able to care for themselves. A great many T.B. and leprosy bed days fall into this category as well as cases of tropical ulcers, burns etc. Such hostels might or might not supply food to patients, who would in any event prepare it for themselves. Patients could also be responsible for their own laundry. The staff requirements of such hostels would be negligible. Another similar innovation would be the maternity delivery unit which would make use of staff only for assistance at the time of delivery: the mothers would be responsible for the preparation of their own food, washing of laundry etc.

Because district and regional hospitals are located in towns the volume of outpatient service demanded of them is likely to be very large indeed, at least in the absence of any deterrent such as the charging of fees. One way of approaching this question is through the provision of urban outpatient/health centres that would operate as screening points, so that hospital congestion could be eased and patients relieved of travelling and waiting time. A relatively complete outpatient service could be provided in the larger towns, although in smaller population centres, it would be sufficient for only the more basic services to be provided. These units should be seen as a substitute for some of the existing hospital outpatient services and not simply as additions. Where these facilities have been built in Tanzania they have succeeded in reducing the volume of outpatients

116

coming to the hospitals, although they have also stimulated the overall volume of urban outpatient attendances. There is a certain contradiction inherent in the situation, in that by making services more efficient through decentralisation, the demand for them is also likely to be stimulated.

As presently organised most hospitals have relatively little contact with the outside world. Patients come to the hospital, but the hospital staff does not go to the people. It would be appropriate for some set percentage of hospital staff (not excluding the most senior) always to be on duty at satellite health facilities on some sort of rotational basis. Also, a greater investment in transport is necessary to improve the mobility of all hospital staff and services. In this connection, more flexibility should be shown in vehicle choice which should include as appropriate two wheeled and perhaps animal transport. (Mobile services will be discussed in some detail in the next chapter.)

Planning

Many of the most pressing problems of the hospitals are of a non-medical character and can only be solved by administrators and planners. (Training schemes for such people have been discussed elsewhere.) It is particularly important to strengthen the administrative cadres at district level and that they be given more executive responsibility, thus freeing the District Medical Officer for more direct medical tasks. As a matter of fact, making the annual investment necessary to employ such improved staff would in the short run probably do more to improve the management and efficiency of the hospital and other health services than any other single action. Such people could not only make the services more efficient but also provide the statistical base for improved, decentralised health planning.

Long term hospital planning is not common in Third World countries. More often than not there appears to be a policy of merely adding more beds to the larger national referral institutions, with little reference to the real priority or actual need for those beds or even the possibility of managing them efficiently. The resistance to proper hospital planning reflects the same general attitude as to overall health service planning. The question of utilising already existing hospital beds more efficiently has already been touched upon. This question becomes even more pressing in circumstances such as exist in Tanzania where agreement has been reached to control the growth in the number of hospital beds. The problem of using efficiently all the hospital beds in the country is complicated by the fact that almost 40 per cent of them are run by the voluntary agencies. Although in many ways there is excellent cooperation in Tanzania between the government and voluntary agency hospitals it is still sometimes difficult to plan properly for the development of such separate services. Some of the problems involved in coordinating voluntary agency and government institutions will be discussed in a later chapter. However, it might be useful to present here an example of a hospital planning issue which arose in Tanzania in connection with the development of a new regional hospital intended to replace a very old institution that could not by any standards have been considered to be in acceptable condition. As background it is important to note that the regional capital in which the hospital was located held only one to two per cent of the over one million people in the region. Although a new hospital had been promised in both the first and second five year plans nothing had as yet been done, the basic obstacle being the cost of the new institution which was estimated at around £300,000. Not surprisingly the local leadership was pressing very hard for an entirely new hospital (to be built on one of the hills at the edge of town). Although the Ministry of Health was finding it difficult to justify the allocation of the large sum necessary to build a completely new hospital it was conceded that something had to be done about the unacceptable state of the old institution, even though it would have been relatively easy to explain away the need for any hospital improvement at all by pointing to the even greater need for a network of rural health services spread through the whole of the region. In this connection it is worth noting that a survey of the inpatients making use of the existing regional hospital showed that 38 per cent came from within five miles of the town, 27 per cent from 5 to 25 miles away and 35 per cent from more than 25 miles. However, the hospital's effective catchment area might have been somewhat greater if its facilities were better, although improved transport and staff would probably be more important in this respect than better physical facilities.

The alternatives involved appeared to be the following:—

(a) Construction of a new two to three hundred bed regional hospital at a cost of around £300,000, even though no rational economic and/or health case could be made for such a level of expenditure for what would be a hospital primarily to serve one small town.

(b) A new core hospital of about eighty to one hundred beds to be developed at a cost of perhaps £100,000, which would utilise another hundred or so of the beds at the old institution.

Some of the local leadership involved would have favoured such a solution, not least of all because of the probably correct belief that it would become possible to expand the hospital at a later date on the basis of the core structure. The major objection to any new hospital, even a smaller one, was that it would merely continue the pattern

118

of inefficient use of medical resources to be seen in the immediate area of the regional centre. Already there are in existence three hospitals, all under different management, within a few miles of the town. Aside from the government institution under discussion there is a voluntary agency hospital and one belonging to a mining company. Although the population of the town constitutes less than 2 per cent of the regional total the three hospitals in and around the town hold over 60 per cent of all the hospital beds in the region.

(c) Reorganisation of the hospital system to include the regional hospital, the voluntary agency hospital and mining company hospital. Although a very clear case, in both economic and medical terms could be made for such a rationalisation of the already existing services the decision that would have to be taken would be essentially of a political character, perhaps especially with regard to the mining company hospital. One major obstacle to the reorganisation of the three hospitals would be the cost to government of the £50,000 per annum being spent for the operation of the voluntary agency hospital (as well as some unknown sum for the mine hospital) that would have to be met in the absence of any fees to patients, which would have been the situation if it had become a government institution. It is also probable that in the absence of fees there would be a considerable increase in the volume of patients, thus raising even further the cost to government of running the institution, although this factor might to some degree have been offset by the more rational use of the two hospitals after integration.

(d) Reconstruction of selected portions of the old regional hospital. The most practical short-run solution to the problem was the replacement of key sections of the government hospital in conjunction with greater use of the voluntary agency facility. The parts of the old regional hospital that most needed rebuilding included the operating theatre, laboratory, laundry, kitchen and administrative block. The existing outpatient facilities were also extremely unsatisfactory. It was estimated that the essential transformation of the hospital could be accomplished for approximately £50,000.

The desire of the leadership in the region under discussion for a completely new hospital was perfectly understandable, particularly when faced with the glaring inequality between the three existing Tanzanian referral hospitals located in other parts of the country and their own unsatisfactory institution. The regional leaders could not see the justice in the existing situation. However, it is also quite clear that it would have been equally unjust to repeat the error of building another large referral type hospital in this (or any other) particular small town. Although this might have decreased the level of inequality, with respect to Dar es Salaam, it could only have done so at the expense of increasing the disparity between the regional town and the rest of the region. It should be noted that the question of building new hospitals to replace old ones is less important that that of the construction of totally new institutions, which add to the total number of hospital beds and therefore will have a much greater influence on the recurrent budget: although it is also possible to significantly increase the size of the recurrent budget of a rebuilt hospital even in the absence of an increase in bed numbers.

Specialist Services

Although specialist medical services ought not to be given high priority in poor countries it should be possible to extend their outreach by following the principle of carrying health services to the populace to the greatest extent possible. The fact that the growth of large hospital and conventional specialist services must be strictly controlled does not necessarily mean that those that now exist need continue to be run relatively inefficiently or in keeping with most past practice. It would be useful to experiment with specialist services intended to reach out to the rural populace with some of the benefits of quality health care that do not carry with them all the costs of large, expensive and isolated consultant hospitals. For example, a team of specialist doctors could be based at one or more relatively nearby district or regional hospitals with only limited specific hospital departments of their own. Their main task would be the upgrading in the region as a whole of paediatric, or obstetric, or surgical services. The specialists would inevitably perform a certain amount of direct curative work, but, their primary task would be to act as consultants to all those engaged in any aspect of the work of their own medical speciality. A major responsibility of these 'mobile specialists' should be the teaching of young doctors and auxiliaries in community paediatrics, or community surgery etc. It would also be possible for students from the medical faculty to spend some training period within this type of specialist service. Most important to the success of such projects would be the national replication of their experiences, therefore no aspect of such an effort could be allowed to develop in such a way as to be too expensive to be duplicated in most other regions of a country.

F. Distribution of Facilities

The existing distribution of health facilities in Tanzania still shows a significant level of inequality. For example, the bed population ratio in Dar es Salaam is close to one bed for each 300 of population, but in one district of the country the ratio was only one to 3,500. Inequality of health centre distribution is not as great as for hospital beds, and for dispensaries it is relatively small. The significance of such variations in distribution is very great for district populations; for

120

example, although 80 per cent of the population of Tanzania lives within six miles of either a hospital, health centre or dispensary only 25 per cent are within 6 miles of a hospital. Ease of access to any health facility varies widely from district to district. In only five districts is less than 2 per cent of the population located further than 6 miles from some sort of health facility, but in twelve others over 40 per cent of the population lives further than 6 miles away. Excepting the capital city, in only two districts does more than half the population live within 6 miles of a hospital, and in only twelve districts does one-third.* It is important to note that 6 miles is likely to represent, in practical terms, the catchment area of a dispensary or a rural health centre, as well as a substantial part of that of hospitals. It takes a healthy adult approximately two hours to walk 6 miles; it takes twice as long for a sick person or a child to walk such a distance. It is interesting to note that in some industrialised countries such as Sweden two hours travel time to a health facility is taken as the maximum acceptable limit for purposes of planning. In determining the distribution of additional health facilities the major Tanzanian objective is to decrease existing levels of inequality. In the actual distribution of additional beds, health centres and dispensaries the following criteria were utilised. In the case of hospital beds it was determined that the 300 or so additional beds needed to keep up with annual population growth were to be spread primarily across those districts having the worst bed population ratios. In the case of health centres the pattern of distribution being followed is that which had been decided as part of the second five-year plan. Although this does not precisely follow population ratios no district would be allowed to exceed its quota of one health centre per 50,000 of population, and overall adjustments would be made during the forthcoming (third) five year plan. The criteria developed for the distribution of dispensaries were slightly more complex. The long standing national target of one dispensary per 10,000 of district population has already been exceeded by most of the country's districts. Although it is clear that those districts that have not yet reached the national standard ought to be given a certain priority, there are other considerations that also have to be brought to bear in the distribution of these smallest, and perhaps most important of all units. Thus, in addition to district dispensary — population ratios extra weighting was given to those districts whose population had least overall accessibility to health care facilities, and to those districts with the highest percentages of population organised into ujamaa villages. Each district is weighted according to each of these three variables, which are

*Thomas, I.D. and Mascarenhas, A.C. Health Facilities and Population in Tanzania. Bureau of Resource Assessment and Land Use Planning, University of Dar es Salaam, Research Paper No. 21.1.1973.

121

then combined to become the basis for the distribution of the 100 dispensaries to be constructed annually. In 1973/74 this system of distribution resulted in just under half of all Tanzania's districts having at least one dispensary allocated to it.

G. Utilisation of Facilities

By 1971 the total of all health institution inpatient days in Tanzania had reached just about seven million, which was ten times the 700,000 institutional admissions. The following table shows the distribution of those inpatient days and admissions by different type of health institution.

Table 9 Total inpatient days and admissions: 1971 (000's)[1]

Type of Institution	Inpatient Days	Admissions
Consultant Hospitals	704	72
Regional Hospitals	1,080	108
District Hospitals	1,119	98
Special Hospitals[2]	532	4
Sub-District Hospitals	154	17
Voluntary Agency Hospitals	1,200	167
Rural Health Centres	596	74
Local Authority Dispensaries[3]	600	57
Central Government Dispensaries	97	11
Voluntary Agency Dispensaries	864	80
	6,946	688

Source: Unpublished data of the Ministry of Health, Dar es Salaam

1. Does not include occupational health service institutions.
2. Mostly psychiatric and T.B.
3. Calculated on the basis of assumed similar utilisation as rural health centres.

Just under a third of all admissions and almost a quarter of all inpatient days were at health centres and dispensaries. The voluntary agency hospitals with almost 40 per cent of all hospital beds accounted for only 25 per cent of all admissions, although 36 per cent of inpatient days.

Detailed hospital attendance figures show that in Tanzania the urban population (six per cent of the total) produces almost 30 per cent of all government hospital inpatients and at least half the outpatients. Dar es Salaam produces at *government* institutions almost eight times as many inpatients relative to population as does the rural population and more than 15 times as many outpatients. The figures for the other urban centres show similar ratios for inpatients and even greater ones for

122

outpatients. In all, the urban population annually produces one inpatient for each nine people and about 10 outpatient contacts per capita. Under Tanzanian conditions the catchment areas of health facilities are extremely limited. Figures from the national referral hospital in Dar es Salaam show that 91 per cent of all inpatients admitted in 1971 were normally resident within 10 miles of the capital, and another 6 per cent came from within the region in which Dar es Salaam is located. These figures are almost identical with those resulting from a survey conducted at the national referral hospital in Uganda (Mulago) some years earlier.* Data from another Tanzanian referral centre (at Moshi) show that 94 per cent of all inpatients come from within the region in which the hospital is located, another 3 per cent from the adjacent region, and only 3 per cent from the rest of the country. Similar data have also been developed for a number of regional hospitals within Tanzania. At four of these hospitals it was found that in 1971 around 40 per cent of all inpatients had come from within five miles of the town in which the hospital was located, about 30 per cent from five to 25 miles away, and a similar percentage from further than 25 miles. One of these hospitals was located in a town (Musoma) with a population in 1971 of not quite 25,000. The district and region in which the town is located had total populations of just over 400,000 and 600,000, respectively. In 1971 a total of 43 per cent of the hospital's 4,600 inpatients came from within five miles of the town. Therefore the town had produced one inpatient for each 12.5 of population, but for the rest of the district the comparable figure was only one inpatient to each 150 people and for the region only one to almost 250 people. Of course there are other hospitals in the region accepting inpatients (one other government institution and two voluntary agency hospitals), but from the data the justification of regional and other larger hospitals as centres providing specialised care for the whole of a region can be seen to have little basis in practice. Even the figures for small district hospitals show very limited catchment areas. For example, one survey of a small district hospital showed that one-third of all attending outpatients were drawn from the less than 1 per cent of the district population that lived in the town itself (really a large village of about 3,000).** Other data for a district hospital near Lake Nyasa show 55 per cent of inpatients being drawn from within five miles of the town, another 35 per cent from five to 25 miles away and only 10 per cent from further than 25 miles.

*P.J.S. Hamilton and A. Anderson, An Analysis of Basic Data on Admissions in 1963 and 1964 to Mulago Hospital, Kampala, mimeo.
**Van Etten, G. Towards Research on Health Development in Tanzania. *Social Science and Medicine*, Vol. 6, (1972), pp.335-52.

The catchment areas of rural health centres seem generally to be limited to an effective maximum of 10 miles (80 per cent of all attendance). One survey showed that over half of all outpatients came from within five miles of the health centre, another 30 per cent from five to 10 miles away, 10 per cent from a distance of 10 to 15 miles, and a final 10 per cent from beyond 15 miles. The particular study cited here was carried out at a quite well developed site in a relatively advanced area (Kibaha rural health centre, only forty minutes by road from Dar es Salaam). Another rural health centre survey done near Lake Victoria concluded that 50 per cent to 60 per cent of attending outpatients had travelled less than four miles and 80 per cent less than 10 miles. *

From the above it can be seen that utilisation of health facilities is directly related to geographic accessability. Other evidence is available from the Tanzanian data on hospitalisation, cited earlier, which show that although the overall annual rate of hospitalisation in Tanzania is 35 per 1,000 of population district averages range from as little as seven per 1,000 to over 100 in Dar es Salaam. In all, in Tanzania, there is one inpatient admission per year for each 20 of the rural population as compared to one admission for each nine of the urban population. For outpatients, the results range from 3.7 visits per annum for rural dwellers to about 10 for the urban population. One significant difference is that the urban population makes use almost entirely of government institutions (although there is also some additional use of private practitioners and industrial health services) thereby avoiding the necessity of paying fees. By contrast, although the rural population also enjoys the use of free services at available government institutions a substantial part of their utilisation of health services is at voluntary agency institutions, where charges are generally imposed. It is also important to stress that urban dwellers not only make greater use of health facilities, but also enjoy a substantially more expensive level of care at the institutions they frequent.

It should be apparent that in countries such as Tanzania a correct health development strategy will allow for the widest possible spread of services based upon the simplest level of facility. While a referral system in which patients can be moved along to higher levels of care is very desirable, it does not follow that the health planning process must continue at this time to provide for the expansion of referral care as a precondition or even accompaniment to the development of more basic facilities such as the health centre and dispensary. The

*Van Etten, G. Towards Research on Health Development in Tanzania. Social *Science and Medicine*, Vol. 6, (1972), pp.335-52.

fact is that the much vaunted referral system rarely functions effectively in developing countries. And yet the undoubted desirability of referral leads many to favour the expansion of that now virtually nonexistent upper end of the health care system. In addition, medical planners often set up idealised district and regional plans that include everything from clinics/dispensaries to national referral hospitals. There is then said to be a plan that allows for the expansion of the nation's referral hospitals, even if it is not possible as yet to fulfil those parts of the plan that call for a greater number of dispensaries and health centres, even though these constitute the area of greatest need. The net effect is a deepening of the health care resources available to the urban few, who always have easy access to the referral centres and the consequent denial of resources to the rural masses.

The preference for referral centres is actively supported, of course, by the organised medical profession virtually everywhere in the name of improved patient care. The problem, however, is that most members of the profession see only those patients presenting at urban facilities which claim the presence of most of the doctors in Third World countries and virtually all the eminent clinical specialists who play a critical role in influencing resource allocation in the health sector. Those who insist on ignoring the realities of health care delivery in poor countries because they are not familiar with them, and who favour expansion of large hospital services which supposedly are the peak of a referral system, are a major obstacle to the formulation of more realistic priorities.

Table 10. Financial Input and Curative Service Outputs of Different Grades of Medical Facilities

| Facility | Average No. of Beds | Financial Input per year | | Curative Service Output per year | | |
		Capital	Recurrent	Inpatients per bed	Outpatients Total	New
Dispensary	2.5	2,000	1,300	21	22,000	11,000
Rural Health Centre	30.0	25,000	7,500	28	65,000	30,000
District Hospital	95.0	1,250	275	32	140,000	52,000
Regional Hospital	185.0	2,500	500	45	380,000	158,000
National Hospital	675.0	5,000	950	36	not comparable	

Source: Unpublished data of the Ministry of Health, Dar es Salaam

As shown in Table 10, the capital cost of a dispensary complex in Tanzania is £2,000 and the planned recurrent cost is approximately £1,300 per annum. The comparable figures for a rural health centre are £25,000 and £7,500. At the district level, hospital beds cost close to

125

£1,250 each to construct and £275 to run; at regional level both capital and recurrent costs are about double; and the figures double again at the level of the national referral centre. It must be emphasised that these Tanzanian hospital figures are exceedingly low by comparison with other African countries. Hospitals in Africa often cost several times as much per bed as the figures shown in the table.

On the services (output) side a typical government dispensary in Tanzania has 2–3 beds; to each of these an average of 21 patients per year are admitted for a stay of about 10 days each. The dispensary also services over 20,000 outpatients per year (just half being new cases). The existing 100 or so rural health centres average 30 beds each; to each of these 28 patients per year are admitted for an average stay of eight days. These rural centres accommodate 60,000 to 70,000 outpatient visits in a year (a little less than half being new cases). District hospitals average close to 100 beds each; to each of these 32 patients per year are admitted for an average length of stay of 11 days. There are a total of 140,000 outpatient visits (only 37 per cent of them being new cases). The comparable figures for a regional hospital are: 185 beds and 45 admissions per bed with an average length of stay of eight days, and 380,000 outpatients visits of which 42 per cent are new cases. For the three national consultant hospitals the comparable data are: 674 beds and 36 admissions per bed with an average length of stay of 10 days (outpatient data are not comparable with those cited above).

Investment in an additional hospital bed is not divisible, and can benefit only those with access to that bed. For example, an extremely modest 200 bed regional hospital could cost at least £300,000 in Tanzania. For the same volume of expenditure it would be possible to build 15 fully equipped rural health centres, including staff housing. With 15 such centres it would be possible to meet most of the curative health care needs of approximately 300,000 to 500,000 people, and to launch a wide variety of preventive health care activities. In Tanzania at 15 such centres there are close to 15,000 admissions and one million outpatient visits per annum. At the regional hospital, by contrast, it would be possible in a year to admit about 9,000 inpatients, a great majority of whom − at least potentially − could be treated as well at a health centre (15 centres would contain more beds than the regional hospital), and a total of close to 400,000 outpatients, virtually all of whom could be provided for as well at a health centre. The running costs for 15 rural health centres in Tanzania are virtually the same as for one 200 bed regional hospital. An even greater advantage than the larger volume of services offered by the 15 rural health centres, as compared with the hospital, is their much broader coverage. The health centres could provide virtually all the health needs of about half the population of an average Tanzanian region of 750,000. The regional hospital would serve well the 10, 20 or 30,000 people in the urban area in which it was located. This relatively small group would absorb about half of the available inpatient care, and most of the outpatient. The rest of the region would share 4,000 to 5,000 admissions and a very small number of outpatient visits.

The advantages that would result from correcting the present overdevelopment of the hospital sector relative both to its service possibilities (especially in the realities of Third World countries) and the underdevelopment of the rural and preventive health infrastructure are so clear that further opposition to the concept can be judged to be based more upon narrow class, professional and personal interests than any serious examination of the realities of the present situation in most parts of the world.

6. VILLAGE AND MOBILE SERVICES

A. Village Services

It is clear that to a greater or lesser degree the work of hospitals, health centres, and dispensaries will reach into and affect the population living in rural villages. At the same time these are not the same as village services as such, which would primarily comprise the training of a villager, probably with a continuing village occupation, for selected health care activities. Such training schemes have not often been successful. The basic reason being that the village health workers are generally not salaried and are expected to serve within their village context out of a sense of duty. Unfortunately, in the conditions of most Third World countries, where there is such competition for wage employment, it often proves impossible to retain the village health worker on such a basis. As a matter of fact, where there is a shortage of health workers willing and able to work in rural communities these village aids are often able to go to other parts of their own country and find salaried employment. In general, the situation with regard to these people varies widely and relatively little information is available on a cross-country basis about such types of health workers.

In any event, the training of these kinds of village health aids has in most places been perfunctory and relatively small numbers have actually been produced, with the obvious exception of China's 'barefoot' doctors; the reasons being basically the same as those that have led to the general lack of the proper development of rural health services almost everywhere. However, it is possible to train such people and some success has been met with in some schemes. The training should generally be of a short-term character, probably not more than three to six months long. The candidates must be selected from their own villages and must return to them. The training should emphasise the preventive and promotive side of healthwork with only limited attention being paid to the curative aspects. The trainees, however, must be able to treat minor illnesses, offer first aid to more serious ones and do what they can to refer such cases to more skilled practitioners. If the national rural health services are reasonably well organised and mobile teams reach the villages in which the village medical helpers are located it would be possible to increase their skills with each visit of the mobile team. The village medical helpers should also be brought back for further training on a regular basis, thus laying the basis for an upgrading of their skills.

128

In Tanzania, too, there is an ongoing effort to train village medical helpers, primarily for work in ujamaa villages. After recruitment the young people are sent to district or regional hospitals where they receive training that varies in length from one to several months, after which they return to their villages and take their place within the community. The village medical helpers are trained to be able to assist the community primarily through health education — especially about environmental sanitation — as well as with a certain amount of first aid and the dispensing of some elementary drugs. The overall number of those that have been trained is growing, especially in the case of those districts in which special ujamaa development operations have taken place. Because these people always remain within their district context — including recruitment and training — the Ministry of Health has had relatively little information in the past about their numbers and utilisation. The preparation of these medical helpers tended to be rather haphazard, as in most other countries that have experimented with such training. The reasons relate to the basic inability of most ministries of health function well at village level. In Tanzania it is likely that if something of a more serious nature is to be accomplished with regard to the training of 'non-professional' health workers — that is people who are not in the salaried employment of the Ministry of Health — the issue will be carried not by the health ministry but by the national political party, although the decentralisation of government does offer new opportunities to the Ministry of Health in this respect. Although it is obvious that present efforts in this direction should, and will, continue, it will probably require that a higher level of political consciousness come to exist in Tanzania before it will be possible to train and utilise successfully the many thousands of part-time unpaid village level workers needed to lead their own communities in preventive and promotive health campaigns.

B. Mobile Services

Another way through which Ministries of Health could spread their services from fixed health facilities into a greater number of villages is by the extensive use of mobile services. Just as village level services are not usually well worked out by ministries of health so it is with the appropriate use of vehicles and mobile services in general. Most commonly the discussion of mobile services tends to focus upon the use of expensive motorised vehicles, often of the four wheel drive variety. However, when such vehicles do become the basis of mobile services they are often too expensive for typical health ministry budgets to support, and the vote for petrol and other operating costs of transport will have run out long before the end of the fiscal year. This was in fact a usual situation in Tanzania, where the Ministry of Health had about 400 vehicles in operation. Although the number of vehicles in use in Tanzania and elsewhere is likely to be relatively small, when measured against their duties, the inefficient ways in which the vehicles are utilised constitute at present at least as great a problem as their limited number. Not only are many off the road at any particular time but they are often being used for other than their intended purposes. In practice no objective standards are applied in determining the proper number and type of vehicles to be in operation by a ministry of health at any particular time. It appears to be a matter of bargaining between the ministry and the treasury (or other financial authority). It is doubtful whether any ministry of health, in Africa in any event, has worked out and applied standards for judging the appropriate number and type of vehicles to be used within its health services.

The proper organisation and staffing of mobile health teams is a particularly difficult problem. In many places there has been a tendency to set up specialised mobile services concerned only with, say, nutrition or tuberculosis activities; this process has been encouraged by donors who offer vehicles only for one or another specified purpose. For example, UNICEF has in the past given vehicles that were to be used only for nutrition work, and national tuberculosis associations in Europe still give vehicles to be used for tuberculosis related activities only. These donors do not realise that such specific activities are usually far too expensive for poor countries to support. In any event, recipient countries will often wisely deviate from the instruction to use the vehicle for a single purpose only and instead utilise them for integrated preventive and curative services. However, even when vehicles are used for a broader set of activities they often become too expensive for countries such as Tanzania to support. For example, mobile teams working in the area of maternal and child health in a pilot scheme in Tanzania found that the average cost of each visit to a child, over the course of a year, came to £0.18. Such cost levels automatically rule out the use of mobile teams, at least to the level of staffing of this particular pilot project.

Although there is growing agreement that mobile teams must be of an integrated nature, offering a wide range of both preventive and curative services, many problems connected with the efficient operation of these services still remain. In practice most of these matters can only be worked out in detail at local level because they depend upon the specifics of population density, local terrain, the number and location of fixed health facilities, the availability of staff and vehicles etc. Central ministries of health could, however, offer guidelines about such questions. One broad area of choice concerns the operation of a vehicle over a large area whereby the mobile team remains in a different place each night and returns to its home base perhaps only at the end of the week, or having daily journeys from district hospitals, or other points that return to headquarters each night. The weekly round is likely to reduce the amount of time the team spends in travelling, thus assisting them to become more mobile than if located at one base to which they must return each evening. With this system, it is also less likely that the mobile team's vehicle will be usurped by base staff for uses unconnected with the operation of the mobile-team. However, if the team travels for the whole of the week, or other overnight periods, some increased costs are likely to result from the staff's entitlement to night allowances or other special remuneration.

The question of mobile services goes much beyond that of the relatively high powered team travelling the countryside in a four wheel drive vehicle. Because mobile teams of this type must cover relatively large areas, they cannot pay frequent visits to each village; however, it is also possible for health centre and dispensary staff to travel extensively to surrounding villages. In Tanzania one District Medical Officer described the development of mobile services from the dispensaries in his district, as follows. "This is a system established together with the public health team with the aim of making maximum use of the meagre medical manpower we have for the maximum benefit of every individual in the District. By this system the conventional function of dispensaries as first aid treatment centres was smashed. The unevenness and inadequacy of dispensary services due to remoteness from most villagers has ceased. Medical services have been moved from their confinement at the dispensaries and [have been] sent out to reach every villager in a well worked out system. Three days a week almost all dispensaries close down, and staff and equipment move to the villages where all the specified medical and health services are offered to the villagers by the staff. Village leaders and villagers act as hosts to the visiting dispensary teams and provide them with free accommodation, food and other necessary living aids in addition to helping in the movement of equipment from village to village. Apart from minor inconveniences in transport and food, for most distances are covered on foot, and minor complaints from those living near dispensaries and used to easy access to medical care, the whole system is extremely popular and effective. In addition the health education and other public health services are now truly practical and are carried out at the village and family level where the problems actually are. The other point in this system is that it is rapidly effective, boosts the villagers' morale and confidence in living and working in communal ujamaa villages and is in keeping with socialist aspirations. In some respects even the curative services at the

131•

village level benefit the patient more as, for example, in the case where a seriously ill patient needs better observation while awaiting transport to the hospital. Villagers offer the extra help not available at the dispensaries, and bed rest and feeding in addition to the continuous presence of the medical staff near him are fully available in the villages while most dispensaries lack these facilities."

In general mobile services should exist at several levels, although the essence of them all will remain the taking of health services to the people rather than waiting for patients to come to the fixed health facilities; and of course, continual training activities for lower level staff. A mobile team based at the district centre might operate 'continuously' or for some period of time, or it might return each night to the district headquarters depending on the density of population and distances that need to be travelled in particular districts. At the sub-centre (dispensary) level the most efficient method of operation has been described above, although possibly bicycles could be added to such a service. Between the hospital and the dispensary there is the health centre, where it is possible to combine the hospital and dispensary approaches with mobile activities in various ways.

The staffing of mobile teams will depend on the alternatives available within specific contexts. In Tanzania the larger district teams are generally led by a medical assistant, assisted by nurse-midwives, maternal and child health aids, nutritionists, sanitarians and perhaps such non-health ministry staff as agriculturists. The team moving out from the Tanzanian health centre or dispensary should include the person in charge of the health centre or dispensary. A typical rural health centre team might include either a medical assistant or rural medical aid, a rural sanitary officer and a nurse midwife or MCH aid. The dispensary team should consist of an RMA and an MCH aid. At each visit to a village the district team holds a mass health education session about the various health related problems affecting the villagers, followed by activities that centre on MCH needs, for example, nutrition demonstrations and practical instructions about hygiene and sanitation. Immunisations are a standard part of the work, and curative services are provided as required. The health centre and dispensary staff carry out similar programmes to those indicated for the district teams, although at a somewhat simpler level.

The successful operation of such schemes is dependent more upon the work of the local political and administrative machinery than the health ministry itself. Local health committees should be organised and participate fully in arranging the programme of village visits, including the functions of the teams once they reach the village. In Tanzania the actual working out of these schemes is found to correlate very closely to the general level of political awareness and organisation

132

in a particular district or region. In those parts of the country where the conception of ujamaa and cooperative development had already reached a high level these schemes tended to work well; in other parts of the country with relatively low levels of political development the schemes tended to work much less well.

The whole question of appropriate mobile services is often confused by what may be termed extremist positions. There are those health workers who resist any efforts directed toward the development of mobile activities on the basis of the anticipated professional difficulties involved in village level work in the absence of the support provided by the accustomed health centre or hospital. Of course, certain of the personal discomforts arising from mobile work are not unrelated to the argument. At the other extreme there are those who would travel any distance, at any cost in order to reach the very last villager. Such an approach is not practical and, in any event has been found to be economically impossible. On balance, however, it is probably quite safe to argue that mobile services need to be very much encouraged and strengthened, in relation to their present status, in just about all countries. One problem is that the appropriate development of mobile services is an area in which little relevant research has been carried out, so that even where there is the desire to extend such services there is relatively little practical knowledge at hand. Much of the research that has been done has taken the form of pilot projects, often set up with funding from expatriate medical sources. One of the major difficulties of such schemes has been their inability to accept a level of staffing for the mobile teams which would allow them to be reproduced on a national scale. Usually this happens because the pattern of staffing that could be reproduced nationally is not up to that minimum level of medical qualification which the supporters of the scheme feel able to accept. As a result the schemes that are set up prove to be too costly even to be maintained — much less extended — once the foreign donors have withdrawn. It may also be the case that the individual expatriate involved in the scheme is connected with a home agency, perhaps a department of Community Medicine at a medical facility, which is operating the particular scheme in conjunction with some other work in other parts of the world. In the interests of the comparative study, the scheme may turn out to be inappropriate for some countries. Tanzania has experienced more than a few such experimental programmes.

One other related question is the use of radio communications and the airplane in the health services. The radio systems being used in some advanced countries, e.g. Australia, are based upon regular communication from outlying stations to a central base where there is a medical doctor. Although the radio is mainly used for exchanging information and general communication, it is best known for those dramatic cases of emergency intervention in which it is used to call a flying doctor to help someone who is extremely ill. Such flying doctors are now operating in a number of African and other countries. It is claimed, and rightly, that it is possible to fly a patient in a small plane for a distance of 500 miles to emergency care at no greater cost than transporting the patient the same distance by road. Although this is indeed the case, it is equally true that a poor country's health services would not be transporting a patient 500 miles for care, except in the most unusual circumstances.

Although the comparison between the airplane and the land vehicle for use in emergency care situations might not be helpful there are other purposes to which the airplane might be put in the context of the health services of Third World countries. For example, if a specialist team of obstetricians or paediatricians were to be flown round from hospital to health centres, spending a day or so at each conducting staff seminars and other educational activities, the use of the airplane might then be justified in saving travel time. In keeping with such educational activities the airplane could also be used to fly specialists from hospital to health centre on a regularly scheduled basis to carry out selected curative duties. There is little doubt that such specialists, particularly the surgeons, are able in these circumstances to carry out a significant volume of useful work and it may be that such activities can be justified economically. Nonetheless, the use of the airplane in health service development is likely to be rather limited and is certainly not to be linked in the first instance to the needs of the emergency case.

There is an experimental scheme under development in one region of Tanzania whereby about 15 rural health centres will be linked by radio to the regional hospital. The primary purpose will be to communicate on a regular basis about the problems of staff and patient movement, supplies, organisation and administration etc., and not particularly for purposes of discussing emergency care of patients – although there is no reason why such cases could not be discussed as they arise. If the scheme works well it may be extended so that all the country's health centres would be linked by radio to district or regional hospitals.

7. PREVENTIVE SERVICES

The case for preventive medicine is overwhelming, and yet very few ministries of health spend more than a fraction of their total budget on preventive or promotive health care activities. This state of affairs stems, in the first place, from the overwhelming pressure for curative services which does not allow attention to be paid to the more important, if seemingly less urgent, preventive activities: this occurs both at the highest level of government decision-making for the health sector as well as in the day-to-day work of health workers. Doctors and other health cadres faced with long queues of patients find it virtually impossible to organise the time necessary for preventive health work.

Much of the discussion until now has taken as its point of departure the necessity of providing health services to rural populations, an issue posed in terms of rural versus urban services, rather than in terms of the more common argument of preventive as opposed to curative care. These arguments, however, are closely connected. It is virtually impossible to mount effective preventive health campaigns in rural areas in the absence of a rural health infrastructure. Moreover, the technological requirements of eliminating or seriously reducing the incidence of many diseases requires a combined curative and preventive approach. It is as difficult to imagine that rural — or other — populations would accept preventive health care activities in the absence of curative work as it is to imagine a society that can do well with preventive health care activities without reorientating its curative health services toward the mass of population living in the countryside. Finally, any number of preventive activities are already built into the functions of a properly operating and staffed dispensary or, to an even greater degree, a rural health centre. This is not to suggest that preventive activities should be allowed to wait until the rural infrastructure has reached a particular level of development. The development of preventive programmes must go hand-in-hand with the growth of rural services, but for purposes of analysis, and of political and administrative action, as well as for the reasons offered above, a planning approach specifically directed toward the rural sector is more likely to be fruitful than concentration on the more specialised and narrow concept of preventive versus curative services.

A. Organisation, Administration and Planning

Although the correctness of giving priority to preventive health care programming is widely recognised, it is also seen that such activities will require concommitant activities that are beyond the competence of any set of individual health workers; that is, activities usually carried out by ministries of water, education, agriculture, etc. In fact, much of the preventive activity of health ministries is not only best carried out in conjunction with other ministerial work but is basically dependent for success upon the work of other ministries and overall government policies. This is most clear in the case of such broad based activities as nutrition, health education and environmental sanitation. However, the organised health services will have the key role to play with regard to certain communicable diseases that are amenable to control or eradication through special national campaigns. For example, smallpox campaigns have now been completed in most of the Third World and, given minimum attention, this disease need not again occur to any significant degree in these countries. Some other diseases that have also been attacked through special vaccination campaigns e.g. measles, have proved to be more difficult to control. Other insect borne diseases may be eliminated or decreased through control of the vector. For example the incidence of malaria has been significantly decreased and even eliminated in parts of the Third World, although it remains a major and difficult problem (in fact in some countries there has been an increase of malaria after early successes in the fight against the disease). The critical difference in the success or failure of certain of these preventive campaigns seems to be whether or not the disease can be eradicated through centrally organised activity on a more or less once and for all basis. If there is a need for continuing localised activity in controlling the disease, thus requiring a well-established local/rural health infrastructure, the problem becomes more difficult. It appears to be considerably easier for ministries of health to organise centrally run campaigns successfully than to create rural infrastructures capable of carrying on day to day preventive activities. In addition some preventive health care activity incorporates a curative as well as preventive element, for example tuberculosis which requires treatment of those carrying the disease as well as mass vaccination and elimination of the conditions that help it to flourish. In addition a wide range of preventive health care activities, essentially of an educational type, require a continuing relationship between health workers and the general population: maternal and child health activities are a prime example of this sort of work. It may be the case that substantial successes in most of these areas cannot be expected in the absence of the development of political structures capable of drawing the mass of the population into the struggle to improve its own health status, at least in conditions in

136

which the resources available for health care are very limited.

There appear to be two 'ideal' models for the development of preventive health care activities leading to a substantial improvement in the prevailing health status of the mass of the population. On the one hand, is a rising standard of living coupled with technological innovation in the health sector, symbolised by the history of the western industrialised nations, and on the other, health work leadership given by a political structure capable of organising the mass of the population into a front for the defence of its own health, symbolised by Chinese experience. The socialist countries of Eastern Europe appear to represent some middle ground between these two ideal types; that is, an improved standard of living and technological innovation has been coupled with higher levels of political participation and organisation, although primarily through the medium of ministries of public health rather than the political structure as such. It may be argued that the higher resource level of European socialist countries has allowed for a different model of social development than that experienced by China.

The low level of the resource base of Tanzania would make it appear that the Chinese model of health development would be most appropriate i.e. the mass of the population must be organised through the political structure for the defence of their own health. Of course, the political structure of Tanzania is not that of China and although much progress is being made in terms of lifting the political consciousness of the population there is still a very long way to go before any very significant level is reached. At this point the best way forward would appear to be concentration upon the strengthening of the organised public health services at the same time as they are increasingly being made responsible to the developing people's organisations, especially at local level. In general this is in fact the road being travelled by Tanzania, although it is a road along which only the first few steps have been taken.

In Tanzania as in most former British colonies there is, in principle, an integrated curative and preventive health care structure, although some health workers are specifically responsible for preventive work e.g. public health inspectors. In practice, this integrated structure has tended to lead to the submersion of preventive work in favour of curative activities. This has occurred not because of any weakness inherent in the structure itself but because of the biases of the particular political and social environments into which it has been set. As such, it might have been more appropriate to have created entirely separate preventive structures, although it could be argued that any sort of structure would have fallen victim to the same biases as have the present ones.

Reference has already been made to the question of the most

137

appropriate way of approaching the problem of the development of preventive and promotive health care; that is, either through the more traditional approach of preventive 'versus' curative services, or the concept of rural 'versus' urban services. (Of course it is not really a question of 'versus' although the debate often seems to take that shape.) Reasons for preferring the rural/urban approach rather than the preventive/curative one have been offered earlier. However, even if agreement is reached on the need for a massive expansion of the rural services there are still many problems left to be solved. The development and substantial expansion of a rural infrastructure, both in terms of facilities and, more importantly, staff, creates the possibility of carrying out the preventive work that needs to be done but does not by itself guarantee that the work actually will be carried out. Although there are no easy ways of assuring that necessary preventive health work is done, steps toward that end can be taken at every stage in the planning process. For example, not only must the necessary resources be made available for the construction and quantitative staffing of rural facilities but the development of curriculum and appropriate training of staff must also be assured, as must supporting supervision of the rural health units, especially through close cooperation with community organisations whose leaders, especially at local level, must be educated to understand more clearly that it is only through promotive and preventive health activities that the great volume of illness can ever be reduced.

A critical prerequisite for the planning of preventive services are quantifiable targets. It is generally the case that the introductory sections of national health plans will describe highly laudable goals for the development of the preventive side of the health services, however, the specific sections of the plan document, which set out projects and costings, will be dominated by the development of curative institutions. The preventive programmes will seldom have specific targets attached to them, one of the reasons being that in very many countries there is no clear picture of the availability or utilisation of already existing preventive services. For example, if the number of children being vaccinated against measles is not known it will be impossible to set precise targets over the course of a forthcoming five year plan for the growth in the number of such children. More precise knowledge of existing preventive activities must be obtained and precise quantification of targets for the growth of these activities must be set forth in each annual or multi-annual plan.

The question of the appropriate organisation and administration of preventive work requires much consideration. Although ministries of health usually include a preventive section its administration and staffing is often severely limited relative to that part of the ministry

138

which is responsible for the work of the curative services. Such a situation is particularly unfortunate just because the preventive side of health work requires considerably more expertise and a wider diversity of skills than the running of hospitals and other such institutions. In addition, the level of epidemiological work being done by preventive sections within ministries of health is often very low. Nonetheless, the main problem may not be the lack of conventional epidemiological expertise but the fact that such work as is being done, is often unrelated to the real possibilities of the ministry for the actual carrying out of campaigns directed towards the control of disease. Too often the work of epidemiologists within ministries of health is limited to the creation and running of surveillance units. Such units are capable of monitoring the disease situation within the country fairly satisfactorily, but the real requirement is for plans of attack through which the incidence of preventable diseases can be decreased. In many countries there are public health institutes or other university related bodies that could be of some assistance in this area; however, these institutions are all too often divorced from the work of ministries of health and too narrowly devoted to conventional teaching and research. One way of solving this problem would be for health ministries to develop their own public health 'institutes', having as their primary responsibility the development and implementation of practical preventive programmes.

Tanzania had long felt the need for a public health centre capable of planning and implementing preventive health care programmes. The basis for such a centre had been included in the second five year plan, but nothing had been developed during the early years of the plan. A major obstacle had been the difficulties involved in formulating the precise role of such an institution within the still relatively undeveloped framework of preventive and public health care activities existing in Tanzania. Although many valuable preventive health care programmes had been in operation, it was the case that one of the primary difficulties was the very proliferation of those programmes and their relative lack of coordination. For example, in the field of nutrition there were activities being organised by the Ministries of Health, Agriculture and Education as well as various other non-ministerial bodies. Environmental sanitation work was being carried out by the Ministries of Health, Agriculture and Water and other governmental groupings as well. On the research side there were the activities of several ministries, the medical faculty of the university, the East African Medical Research Council and WHO.

The 1973 reorganisation of the Ministry of Health created three divisions within the ministry; the divisions of manpower development, curative services, and preventive services. The type of public health institute being envisaged would become, in effect, the operational arm

139

of the preventive services division of the health ministry, although it needs to be emphasised that the activities of such an institute, if they were to be successful, would extend beyond the confines and requirements of any one ministry. The nucleus of such a centre already exists within Tanzania in the special groups responsible for health education, nutrition and environmental sanitation that function within the Ministry of Health. There is also a group of WHO personnel who act in effect as a communicable disease control unit. A major step forward in the development of such a public health centre has been taken with the opening of negotiations with an external donor for necessary support. The centre would group together the various units and activities mentioned above (and others) in a new building having adequate laboratory and library facilities, as well as statistical and publishing services. The institute would carry the basic responsibilities for organizing disease control programmes, and undertaking a substantial volume of training for all levels of Ministry of Health staff. It might also add to the medical faculty's capacity for the training of medical students. The creation of such a centre would be a significant step forward in the development of preventive health care work in the country. It must be stressed that the idea of the institute is not to create a research orientated, university linked body but rather one capable of having an immediate impact upon the nation's capacity to develop and implement preventive health care programmes. Although the institute will include a research component it is intended for it to be linked, in the first place, to the nation's capacity to act on the results of that research.

It is not the intention of the succeeding sections to cover the gamut of preventive health services. Rather, some of the more important issues in some of the more significant areas will be touched upon with a view to illustrating the broader issues involved.

B. Nutrition

The primary thrust of ministry of health nutritional activity is too often in practice directed toward the discovery of those who are sufficiently malnourished as to justify hospitalisation. This orientation is a reflection of the commonly held medical view of malnutrition as a disease amenable to normal, curative medical care. Of course malnutrition can result in physical, and perhaps mental incapacity and in its extreme forms leads to conditions that are medically classifiable e.g. kwashiorkor, marasmus, anaemias etc. Although it is possible for health care systems to rehabilitate those who suffer from such nutritionally classifiable diseases there is relatively little to be found in the conventional work of ministries of health that can alleviate general malnutrition among a substantial part of a population. In the absence of other more significant governmental activity it is highly unlikely that any particular set of activities undertaken by ministries of health alone can contribute very importantly to the ending of nutrition. As that may be, ministries of health can incorporate nutritionally related programmes within the context of such other ministerial activities as health education and, especially, maternal and child health programmes. They might also be producing technical materials and running nutrition training programmes, hopefully under the aegis of some sort of national nutrition centre.

The nutrition unit of the Tanzanian Ministry of Health has carried out a significant number of surveys, is involved in nutrition training for health workers and maintains personnel in most districts of the country. The work of the personnel was being merged with the activities of broader mobile health teams, in keeping with the policy of integration of public health work. Other nutrition related activities were being carried out by several ministries (agriculture, education, Prime Minister's office) and other bodies.

The country has long been involved in a discussion about the nature of an appropriate nutrition policy, and consequent nutritional activities, that would go beyond the conventional work of any one ministry. This discussion included consideration of the nutrition related aid programme expected to be forthcoming from Sweden. An initial team of consultants had proposed the foundation of a sophisticated research institute that would concentrate almost entirely on technological problems (it was to be called The National Food Science and Nutrition Institute). The proposed institute provided for no social scientific staff except for two economic planners, who were to join only several years after its founding. While isolating itself with relatively narrow scientific pursuits the institute was only to have a very limited relationship to the ministries and other bodies actually responsible for carrying out nutritional work; in addition, the institute was to carry relatively little responsibility for nutrition training. It would also have been expensive to operate, especially as it was to have been dependent upon expatriate staff for a relatively long period of time.

Nutrition activity must be seen in the first place as an overall part of planned development rather than as an agricultural question or health problem. It follows that the organisation of nutrition activities is best coordinated by a national centre with the capability of bringing together representatives of ministries of agriculture, education, health and others that have a contribution to make to the work in this area. As such the proposed Tanzanian institute could only have been a retrograde step, as it was gradually seen to be, and after several years the question was reopened with the arrival of another and differently orientated consultant misson. This

141

group held the view that the basic nutritional problem was more socio-political than technological, and a fresh definition of the functions of the proposed institute in this light, was considered to be particularly important, especially in its relationship to those ministries and other bodies already involved in nutrition activities.

The broad objectives of the new overall programme are likely to be the reduction of mortality and morbidity due to malnutrition especially amongst young children, increased food production including improved quality and availability, increased labour productivity through improved nutrition, and the provision of improved training and education in food and nutrition. The principle functions of the new centre, in keeping with its broad objectives will cover such areas as the planning of food and nutrition programmes, relevant training and education, advisory and information services, and the setting up of further research activities. The programme will include a central headquarters building and structure (the Tanzanian Food and Nutrition Centre), but will be linked to the development of a Tanzanian food and nutrition programme and to the bodies having ongoing nutrition related responsibilities.

In spite of the progress being made in the development of a Tanzanian food and nutrition programme there remains much underlying doubt about the effectiveness of nutrition activities as such. In point of fact it is not really clear just how much governments can affect overall nutritional status through the pursuit of more or less conventional 'nutritional activities'. Tanzania is less prepared than most to accept the ready made solutions which foreign consultants are prepared to dispense in this area, and is trying to develop a nutrition policy suitable to its own special way of development. Although it is likely that the nutritional centre and programme discussed above will proceed satisfactorily, just because of its importance it is also probable that during its development the programme will see very many changes indeed!

C. Health Education

Ministries of health usually have their own health education units. Such units should be responsible for the production of technical materials to be used by all those groups in the country which have widespread links with the population as a whole e.g. teachers, health workers, political leaders etc. These units also generally operate training programmes for those with these widespread population links. Although health ministries can make particularly important technical contributions to national health education activities they need not be the major health educators in the country. For example, the prevention of disease is one very suitable subject for mass literacy campaigns, and although the health education units of ministries of health should be in a position to

142

produce much of the teaching material needed for such campaigns. It is clear that health education activity should constitute a major part of the ministry's maternal and child health work.

A major problem for the work of ministries of health in this field is that they are primarily in touch with that part of the population which is already suffering from disease. In practice it therefore follows that health education on the part of ministries of health tends to be conducted amongst hospital and health centre patients. Although this constitutes valuable work in itself, health education activity must stretch far beyond the usual reach of the ministry's curative network.

The health education unit of Tanzania's Ministry of Health has its headquarters within the confines of the Muhimbili Hospital complex in Dar es Salaam. It is fair to point out that its geographic range has been extremely limited. The work of the unit is primarily directed toward the production of teaching materials. It is debatable whether a national health education unit should be located within the administrative structure of a ministry of health at all, rather than in the Ministry of Education or perhaps even Information. In addition to the work of this unit there are other health education activities being carried out in Tanzania, especially within the schools.

A very good example of a successful health education campaign was carried out in Tanzania in 1972/73 as part of adult literacy work. The campaign, 'Mtu Ni Afya' (Man is Health), was conducted by the ministry of national education through the Institute of Adult Education of the University of Dar es Salaam with the support of the ministry of health and other relevant government and party organisations. Financial support was provided by Sweden for the production of a million copies of the teaching brochure, as well as costs connected with the training of roughly 75,000 study group leaders. The teaching materials were entirely concerned with preventive health activities and written so as to be suitable for teaching literacy. The campaign began with the participation of a handful of people and gradually expanded until the 75,000 group leaders had been trained. It was intended that the group leaders should reach approximately a million people. Preliminary reports indicated that the campaign had met with great enthusiasm and success.

D. Environmental Sanitation

The problems of environmental sanitation in African and other Third World countries are immense. They can broadly be classified as falling into the following areas: provision of safe water supplies, removal of waste and refuse, food hygiene, housing, and certain measures related to the control of communicable diseases.

In most ministries of health, environmental sanitation activities tend to be heavily urban biased. The public health inspectors spend the bulk of their time in the towns inspecting the water supply, cleanliness in restaurants, the freshness of food at markets, and so on. Although all of this is undoubtedly important work, it is extremely limited in scope and does not touch upon the lives of the majority of the population who continue to live in the countryside. One particular problem is that public health inspectors continue to be dominated by the concept of policing and punishing those who violate the public health statutes.

Because 95% of the Tanzanian population is rural it is necessary to single out for special attention those particular sanitary problems that are most related to the rural environment, i.e. the supply of safe water and the removal of human waste, both of which are related to many fly and water borne diseases. In Tanzania the Ministry of Water and Power has primary responsibility for the supply of water, although the Ministry of Health retains an interest in the quality of the water being supplied. It should be emphasised that in Tanzania in any event, the problem of the quality of water is far less significant than its actual provision. The minimum quality standards to be set e.g. levels of fluoride, must recognise the cost and difficulty of always obtaining the most pure water and thereby become more relevant to particular national possibilities.

Encouraging the use of latrines is a responsibility of the health ministry in Tanzania, but for many reasons relatively few additional latrines are constructed each year. With the intensification of ujamaa village development it has now become a matter of even greater urgency to guarantee the provision of basic sanitary facilities to these and other villages. It will be especially important to demonstrate the construction and desirability of using protected, well made pit latrines. The current overall expansion of rural health services creates the possibility of a significant growth in rural environmental sanitation activities. What is particularly lacking in Tanzania, as elsewhere, are specific programmes that ministries of health could actually carry out in these fields including, of course, schedules for the planned implementation of the proposed programmes.

The very weak data base in the area of rural hygiene constitutes an important block to progress in this area. The following 'community sanitary survey', under discussion in Tanzania, could be a way of approaching the problem. As a starting point the survey, to be carried out in appropriately selected locations, would: (1) create baseline data about rural sanitary conditions, (2) devise the most suitable techniques for meeting rural sanitary needs, (3) improve the sanitary conditions of the survey areas through the use of techniques that will be capable of being reproduced throughout the country, (4) assist in the training of rural sanitation workers, (5) based upon the survey data and other accumulated experiences, develop a long term plan for the creation of sanitary conditions for the whole of the country. The sort of data that the survey would set out to gather would concern: (a) latrines (number, types, physical condition, distribution, and utilisation), (b) waste disposal places and treatment facilities, (c) waste collection equipment and their maintenance, (d) manpower (types, distribution and utilisation), (e) health and sanitary administration (organisation and finance). Such a survey would be undertaken by the ministry of health, mostly by utilising the existing staff of rural sanitarians; including the planning period, it should be possible to complete such surveys and the general recommendations for long term rural sanitation plans over a period of less than two years.

E. Tuberculosis

Tuberculosis is one of the major debilitating and fatal diseases of poor countries. The volume of health care resources directed toward the treatment of T.B. patients is substantial. During the years 1956-1964 in Tanzania's hospitals there was an average of about 5,000 tuberculosis admissions. In 1965 that figure rose to over 9,000 and has since remained at around that mark. The volume of tuberculosis out-patients had risen relatively regularly from 4,000 in 1956 to 8,000 in 1968. In 1969 that figure rose to over 12,000, largely as the result of a special effort in one region of Tanzania which turned up an additional 4,000 cases for out-patient care. The figure rose to 13,000 in 1970, again largely as the result of a special effort in one region which increased its number of T.B. out-patients by almost 5,000 (thereby replacing the previous year's 'special' region). In 1971 the total national figure of T.B. out-patients rose to over 23,000, almost entirely as a result of continued special case-finding campaigns being carried out in the Coast region of Tanzania (14,000 cases). It is estimated that there are roughly 150,000 people suffering from tuberculosis in Tanzania, with the annual incidence estimated at about 30,000 per year.

Tuberculosis presents, in many ways, the classic choice between in-patient and out-patient care. It has been well established that the long periods of hospitalisation for T.B. care that were common in past years are now no longer required. A period of in-patient care of 6 to 10 weeks is considered to be acceptable, and many T.B. specialists contend that even shorter stays would be sufficient. It is clear that tuberculosis in-patients are often kept longer than necessary in hospital, more for the lack of proper out-patient services than the intrinsic need for hospitalisation. The essence of the problem is to guarantee the attendance of tuberculosis out-patients at dispensaries and other local institutions on a regular basis so that they receive the daily drug they require.

In Tanzania, in 1971, about 2,200 beds were designated for tuberculosis in-patients. It is estimated that the average annual cost of these beds is somewhat over £350,000. A significant number of beds were connected with localised tuberculosis control schemes. The Lake Victoria Tuberculosis Scheme was a notable example, although it has since been integrated into the overall health services of the country (as have many other special disease schemes). In general it can be said that tuberculosis work in Tanzania, as virtually everywhere in the Third World, tends to be significantly more in-patient orientated than is strictly necessary. The major reason for this, apart from the often advanced stage of the disease at the time of initial treatment, is the lack of follow-up facilities for out-patient care. For example, one survey* of 445 tuberculosis in-patients at a district hospital in the south of Tanzania found that 56% lived within 5 kilometres and 85% within 10 kilometres of a dispensary or other health facility. Thus if these facilities were able adequately to care for T.B. patients on an out-patient basis most of the existing 52 T.B. beds at the hospital where the survey was conducted could be used for other purposes. In these circumstances what is clearly necessary is the integration of tuberculosis control activities into an expanding network of rural facilities capable of dealing properly with the disease, which means vaccination, case finding, following up contacts and treatment. This would require improved administration, staffing and transport possibilities at these rural institutions. Such improvements are especially necessary because of the mass campaign of B.C.G. vaccination (anti-T.B.) carried out in conjunction with the smallpox eradication campaign completed in Tanzania in 1973. During this campaign all children under the age of 15 should have received B.C.G. vaccinations, and these are scheduled to continue as part of the maintenance phase of the smallpox eradication campaign through the regular immunisation programmes of the health services.

It might be unrealistic to expect all T.B. patients to come faithfully to a dispensary or health centre for their drugs or to take them regularly at home, and therefore dispensary, health centre and hospital mobile teams should have special responsibilities with regard to such people. In certain areas where there is an extremely high density of tuberculosis (and leprosy) patients it might be economical to utilise the services of 'T.B. (and leprosy) home visitors' who would visit such patients with the necessary drugs and assure the attendance of others for treatment at dispensaries and health centres. Although it is theoretically possible to phase out almost immediately the bulk of tuberculosis beds in favour of ambulatory out-patient care at dispensaries and health centres, in practice it is probable that a number of

---

*By Dr. David Gill, former District Medical Officer, Masasi; personal communication.

intermediate and complimentary actions need to be taken to facilitate this basic change. For example, hospital beds now being occupied by T.B. patients would best be replaced by patient hostels that would cost little to build and run. In keeping with other such hostels these would be places where patients could look after their own day-to-day requirements.

F. Mental Health

There is in Tanzania great concern about the potentially deleterious effects upon mental health of the process of very rapid social change. Justification for that concern can be found in the results of one survey of Muhimbili hospital out-patients* which showed that exactly one-half of those sampled were not suffering from any discernible organic disease. Better management/care of the large numbers of such patients is a matter of urgency.

Extreme financial constraints have made it difficult for Tanzania to accomplish what is even minimally required in the field of mental health. However, the planned expansion of rural health services will create a basic network in the rural areas upon which could be built substantially improved mental health services. One important development which will facilitate the expansion of mental health services has been the starting in 1973 of psychiatric nurse training. This training is in the process of creating a cadre capable of staffing the increased number of mental health centres that are due for development in Tanzania over the rest of this decade.

Throughout East Africa during the colonial period the pattern of care of the mentally ill was based upon the need to protect society from those who were violent or aggressive by keeping them in remand prisons or mental hospitals.** Each territory had one such hospital. In Tanzania this hospital was located near Dodoma at the geographic centre of the country. Until recently the care provided was primarily custodial and the number of patients steadily rose until it reached a high point of 1,350 in 1968. There are now about 750 patients at this mental hospital. In 1965 the first psychiatric unit apart from the National Mental Hospital was opened in Dar es Salaam. In 1968 the Ministry of Health adopted the policy of regionalisation, as far as mental health programming and psychiatric care was concerned. Five units attached to the regional hospitals were opened between 1969 and 1973.

---

*By Dr. N. Speight, formerly of the Dar es Salaam medical school.
**Much of this discussion is based upon: Swift, C. R. Mental Health Programming In A Developing Country: Any Relevance Elsewhere?, *American Journal of Orthopsychiatry*, vol.42, No.3 April 1972 pp.517-526; and discussion with Dr. Swift who was professor of psychiatry in Dar es Salaam.

A village for 50 or 60 convalescent psychiatric patients (built by the patients themselves) is developed in conjunction with each regional unit. These villages provide a 'halfway house' for selected patients, where they may work in a fairly normal setting under minimal supervision. The Ministry of Health has adopted the following principles as guidelines for the national mental health and psychiatric programmes:

1. Much psychiatric illness can be prevented. Basic to this concept is educating citizens in the principles of strengthening mental health. Such educational efforts can be most productively directed at groups in the community who naturally have contact with individuals in times of special stress (death in the family, physical illness, separation, adolescence, moving from village to town). Such key groups include various cadres of medical workers, teachers, religious leaders, welfare officers, police and party workers.

2. All psychiatric illness is treatable (though not necessarily curable). Treatment should be instituted promptly and as near the patient's home as possible. For this to be carried out properly, early case finding must take place through the cooperation of dispensary workers, teachers and parents. It follows that these groups must know which problems to refer and which to manage themselves. Again, this emphasises the need for education.

3. When hospitalisation is necessary, it should be as brief as possible. The presence of a village for convalescent patients makes this easier. Most people in Tanzania requiring psychiatric hospitalisation improve quickly, especially if treatment is begun promptly. This principle reduces hospital costs and enables the patient to return home without long absence.

4. Mental health services should be integrated with existing and developing health and welfare services. This principle applies equally for preventive and curative services. With proper orientation and training the several medical and welfare cadres are strategically situated to carry out mental health programmes.

In line with the above cited mental health principles, as well as the nation's policy of decentralisation it is expected that mental health centres will be developed in those regions of the country (12 or 13) where none now exist. Such centres would include meeting rooms and offices for educational sessions, consultations and out-patient treatment. They would also include a limited number of beds and appropriate courtyards for patients' day activities. These centres would be an integral part of the regional hospital to facilitate mutual consultation between medical staff. Some of the existing units are likely to serve as models for those still to be built. A village for convalescing psychiatric patients will be developed in conjunction with each of the units (as with those that already exist) so that selected patients could leave the hospital more quickly and benefit by residence in the therapeutic community of the village. The goal of these villages is to become basically self-supporting, except for salaries for the relatively few staff to be attached to them. It is likely that most regions of the country will have one such mental health centre with its related village by the end of the next five-year plan (1980).

8. MATERNAL AND CHILD HEALTH SERVICES

Women, and children under the age of 15 total almost three-quarters of the population of Third World countries, while women of child bearing age plus children under the age of five comprise almost 40% of the total population. These large numbers mean that the health services need largely to be directed towards the requirements of women and children. In practice it would be artificial to attempt to separate the health needs of the mothers from those of their young children, and both groups must be considered together.

The volume of morbidity and mortality amongst children is very high. Infant mortality can easily reach 200 per 1,000 live births and childhood mortality (ages 1-4) can claim another 100 of those who survive the first year of life. In addition, of every 1,000 conceptions over 100 are unlikely to result in a live birth. The children die overwhelmingly of the 'disease of poverty', the most important manifestation being malnutrition coupled with diarrhoea, pneumonia, measles etc. Although a child may be strong enough to live through any one of these diseases, when malnourished and attacked by, say, measles and malaria at the same time it becomes very difficult to survive.

A. Maternity Services

The following table shows the development of maternal and child health services in Tanzania between independence and 1970.

The 1970 figure of 470,000 antenatal first attendances covers perhaps two-thirds of all pregnancies: the comparable figure in 1961 was one-third. The total number of confinements in 1970 represented close to one-third of all pregnancies: the comparable figure in 1961 was about one-tenth. Although the number of children attending child welfare clinics as a percentage of the total number of children is indicated as having increased from only 7% at independence to 16% in 1970, the functional percentage is greater as these data include only those children attending clinics specifically organised for them. Although the figure for maternal mortality has decreased substantially from 4.7 per thousand confinements to 2.7, in industrialised countries the comparable figure is around 0.4 per thousand live births. It can be seen that although some important progress has been made in Tanzania in the development of maternal and child health services very much still remains to be done. Figures have been cited earlier which indicate that perhaps 350 to 400 out of every thousand conceptions does not result in a living five-year old child.

150

Table 11. Maternal and Child Health Services: 1961-1970

	1961	1970
No. of antenatal clinics	412	627
No. of antenatal first attendances	176,800	469,900
No. of antenatal total attendances	671,900[1]	1,785,500[1]
No. of institutional confinements	67,500[2]	212,100[2]
No. of child welfare clinics	454	578
No. of child welfare first attendances	136,500[3]	362,400[3]
No. of child welfare total attendances	737,100[4]	1,853,400[4]

[1] An average of 3.8 attendances per pregnant woman in each case.
[2] In 1961 there were 4.7 maternal deaths per 1,000 confinement, 50.9 abortions and 44.8 still births: the comparable figures in 1970 were 2.7, 40.0 and 24.2
[3] Representing an estimated 7.4% of the 1961 child population and 15.6% in 1970.
[4] An average attendance of 5.4 per child in 1961 and 5.1 in 1970.

The demands made upon the health services by children and women in their child-bearing ages is very great indeed. Figures for one district in Tanzania show that just under 40% of all first attendances at dispensaries were children under the age of six. A very substantial part of all hospital services are devoted to maternity services; of the total admissions to government hospitals 22% were maternity cases. The comparable figure at rural health centres was 36%.

The question of appropriate maternity services in Third World countries is a particularly important one, not least of all because maternity beds take up such a significant proportion of all hospital beds. The recent history of maternity service development in Tanzania had been to a significant degree dominated by the debate over a new maternity block hospital for Dar es Salaam. In many ways the issues raised were representative of much of the broader debate over hospital building and the role of specialist services; as such, it might be instructive to examine the question in some detail. The old maternity hospital in Dar es Salaam, Ocean Road Hospital, goes back to the German period, predating the construction of the city's general hospital, Muhimbili. In late 1967 the Ministry of Works recommended an expenditure of approximately £50,000 for necessary renovations to Ocean Road Hospital. Within a year suggestions were being made for the building of a new 250 bed obstetric block within the Muhimbili complex costing almost £200,000. This was argued to be a more economic proposition than the expenditure of £50,000 for the repair

151

of the old Ocean Road structure. Agreement was then reached on the construction of a new 250-bed block at a proposed cost of something less than £250,000. It was then further proposed to expand to a 350-bed block, at an estimated cost of almost £300,000. The first phase of the 350-bed institution was basically completed by late 1971. This first phase comprised a 156 bed block and cost £250,000. A new estimate for the completion of the maternity hospital was made to cover a second, 200-bed block as well as the main service building intended to house an operating theatre, X-ray and pharmacy. This additional estimate came to a total of almost £850,000. What had begun as a less than £200,000 project had increased to a cost of £1.1 million, although there were now to be 350 beds instead of the originally proposed 250. As the funds needed to complete the building were not available, the whole 'second phase' had to be postponed.

The initial error in all this was the idea of building a large general obstetric hospital in the middle of a very crowded referral hospital such as Muhimbili. The potential conflict between the need for some specialist services and the general maternity hospital requirements of an urban population is very clear. The basic justification of a referral hospital is the need for some specialist care, but the maternity requirements of a city such as Dar es Salaam, where about 20,000 deliveries a year take place at Ocean Road Hospital, means that any new obstetric facility located within the referral hospital would inevitably become the general maternity hospital for the city and thus could not fulfil its supposed specialist role for a substantial part of the country. The uneven development of Muhimbili, as with other African urban hospitals, has been encouraged by its dual function as a national referral centre and a general hospital for Dar es Salaam: if Muhimbili was only the district hospital for Dar es Salaam there would be little justification for much of the expenditure which goes into the development of such projects as the one under discussion. However, if this type of hospital are truly to be specialist referral centres there can be no justification for adding to them large institutions for the delivery of perfectly normal births. It is important to note that the major problem of Ocean Road Hospital with its 250 beds, that of overcrowding, would not be solved by moving to a new 350 bed block within Muhimbili, and in fact the situation might even be made worse as increased health service supply created its own demand. In 1971 in Tanzania urban confinements were equal to only three-quarters of new antenatal attendances (but 116% in Dar es Salaam) and it is not uncommon for babies to be born before arrival at hospital or for mothers to arrive unduly early for the fear of being too late. In other words, women will come to hospital rather early to deliver in increasing numbers (at least until all deliveries are at hospital) and will

152

stay rather longer, in keeping with the capacity of the new maternity hospital.

The way out of this seeming impasse is through the creation of decentralised maternity services. The Tanzanian decision to constrain the growth of hospital beds to that of population increase means using those beds which already exist more efficiently. It also means that the regional urban centres, which already enjoy relatively good bed population ratios, are unlikely to have very many beds added to the hospitals located there. It is just in these urban centres that it is most possible to develop decentralized maternity services. The largest single group of hospital in-patients are expectant mothers. As stated above, maternity now accounts for almost one-quarter of all government hospital admissions. Naturally enough the great bulk of these deliveries are of the perfectly normal variety. Available data show that some 13% of all medically supervised deliveries in Tanzania entailed some form of complication, but 87% did not. Although the maternal mortality rate for government hospital admissions of 0.3% is certainly not low by international standards, in absolute terms relative to other types of hospital admissions, the figure of less than 200 deaths out of almost 70,000 maternity admissions is not great. Therefore, it would be appropriate to remove the bulk of maternity work from the hospitals, thus freeing the resulting beds for other more pressing needs. In contrast to the concept of having virtually all deliveries at one central establishment (which starts from a concentration on the abnormal delivery and its specialist requirements) what is needed is a structure which recognizes that the vast majority of deliveries are perfectly normal and require hospitalisation more for social than for purely medical reasons; that is, if Tanzanian homes were equipped more like those in industrialised countries it would be perfectly acceptable for most women to be delivered there. In any event, given the critical shortage of health care resources in a country like Tanzania, this means that those scarce resources must be spread thinly for those not requiring in-depth care e.g. the normal delivery, so that more can be available for those requiring a greater level of attention, e.g. the abnormal delivery.

Overcrowding in maternity institutions can be overcome by the development of a maternity service capable of screening all pregnant women and directing them to the level of care which they require; so that those for whom no medical problems are anticipated, and it is usually possible in maternity cases to predict possible complications, can be directed to normal delivery centres, while others can be channelled into hospitals. In some abstract sense it is right that every delivery be carried out at a specialist centre, just as in an ideal world with unlimited resources any and all illnesses requiring medical care would be seen first by a highly qualified medical doctor and then referred to a specialist. Unfortunately, Tanzania is not blessed with unlimited resources and so it becomes necessary to choose deliberately just where to put resources for maternity services. Data for Ocean Road Hospital show that of all admissions in 1970, 3% required surgical intervention. The total number of those with delivery problems has been estimated at 13% of those admitted. In order to reach all of this group and ensure that they receive the best possible care it is necessary for the whole of the urban population making use of the maternity services to be screened and channelled into institutions appropriate to their requirements.

The advantages of a decentralized system are numerous. Not only will the cost per delivery be lessened but the women will enjoy a broader, more efficient service located closer to their homes. An urban maternity unit containing, say, 15 beds would have the capacity of providing a complete maternity service, including antenatal and postnatal care as well as delivery, for a population of at least 25,000 to 50,000, depending upon location, density, etc. The total cost of such a complete urban service in Tanzania would be less than is presently being spent for urban delivery services alone. The urban maternity units could be properly staffed by well qualified nurse-midwives who would be in immediate contact by vehicle or telephone with the town hospital should an emergency arise.

These urban maternity services need to be managed by trained administrators in conjunction with more specialised medical advice. It is necessary to break with the tradition which attempts to suspend entire sections of the health service from specialist institutions. This tendency is not unrelated to the fact that medical specialists are usually called upon to organise the various parts of the health service, and given the nature of specialist training it is not surprising that their starting point is, more often than not, the specialised requirements of the few.

In 1971 the fifteen Tanzanian towns (all those having urban councils) contained a total population of about three-quarters of a million. From among that population there was recorded almost 70,000 new antenatal attendances and just over 50,000 confinements. The average length of hospital stay for each confinement was four days. In Dar es Salaam alone there were 18,000 new antenatal attendances, and 21,000 confinements of an average of 4.6 days each. A rough estimate shows the average cost of one confinement (4 hospital days) to be £5 or £250,000 for the total of 50,000 confinements at hospitals located in the fifteen towns. One of the major reasons for the relatively high average of 4 days per confinement is that many women come early to hospital because of the difficulty of transport from their homes. If urban delivery units were to be

154

conveniently located throughout the towns it should be possible to reduce the average length of stay to two or three days per maternity case. Given this assumption and the present volume of maternity it can be estimated that the requirements for urban delivery units at the 18 Tanzanian regional centres (which now contain regional hospitals) is at most 30 units of 15 beds each. All of the 18 regional centres except Dar es Salaam would require only one or two units while Dar es Salaam would require eight. The per unit recurrent cost should not be greater than £7,500 per annum. On that basis the annual cost of running the required thirty units would total about £225,000. This figure is somewhat less than the present estimated costs for the 50,000 annual confinements alone taking place at 15 of the 18 hospitals located in the regional towns. Therefore, it is possible to provide complete and improved urban maternity services, including delivery, for what is now being spent for urban deliveries alone.

The major possible objection to the development of a decentralised maternity service is that doctors would not normally be available within the delivery centres. However, this need not be a serious objection provided the urban maternity units are properly integrated into the overall health care system of the towns to which they would be allocated. One of the most significant advantages of a decentralised service is that it would relieve the hospitals of the burden of normal deliveries so that a greater level of care could be made available to those requiring such a specialised service. However, the entire system could be made to work properly only if each expectant mother were to be adequately screened so as to insure that difficult cases would be hospitalised at the time of delivery. In practice a well organised decentralised system would be more likely to assure complete antenatal screening for the whole of the population as well as such normal postnatal services as family planning than a conventional one.

The services that have been described here would represent one significant way of improving urban health services without at the same time drawing more resources into the urban areas where the population has become accustomed to a greater level of health services than exist in the rest of the country. The need to make more efficient use of existing urban hospital beds under situations of constraint upon the expansion of their number is obvious and immediate, as shown by the following figures and later discussion.

Although the data provided in the table are far from perfect some important increase in mortality, particularly maternal, is indicated, even if allowance is made for under-reporting in the figures shown for 1971. The difference in mortality between Grades 1 (higher) and 4 (lower) especially for infants is more likely to be a reflection of the nutritional and general health status of the two groups than of the care

155

Table 12. Maternal and Infant Mortality at Ocean Road Hospital, Dar es Salaam 1971 – 1973

| | 1971 | | | 1972 | | | Jan - June 1973 | | |
| | Admissions | Mortality | | Admissions | Mortality | | Admissions | Mortality | |
		Maternal	Infants		Maternal	Infants		Maternal	Infants
Grade 1	1,397	0	14	1,492	1	12	664	2	8
Grade 4	17,023	7*	319*	17,924	17	542	9,306	33	248

Source: Unpublished data of the Ministry of Health, Dar es Salaam.

*These figures are probably under reported.

obtained while in hospital. In this connection it should also be noted that a significant proportion of those admitted to Grade I are Asians and Europeans. There were virtually no deaths of mothers admitted to Grade I; however, for mothers admitted to Grade 4 the figure rose from one per 1,000 in 1972, and probably a similar level in 1971 if under-reporting is accepted, to almost four per 1,000 in the first half of 1973. (The 1970 figure was one per 1,000 in Dar es Salaam but almost three per 1,000 nationally.) Though it is not possible to know all the reasons for the increased death rates in 1973, there are good reasons to suspect that the figures do reflect worsened hospital care. An editorial in the Dar es Salaam Sunday News of 22 July, 1973 stated that: "What emerges from the figure is a horrifying picture of mounting casualties. If this is the pattern at our best maternity hospital, one can only be depressed at the imagination of deaths in the rural areas where only grandmotherly experience is available to expectant mothers. . . Yet account must be also taken of the standard of services at the Ocean Road Maternity Hospital. As many letters to the Press have pointed out, and notwithstanding the complaisance of the Women's Organisation, the nurses' association Tarena and the Medical Association, the services there are appalling." The Editorial goes on to say that this "is by no means the whole perspective. But it is part of the total perspective. And it gives weight to the public fear or impressions of negligence or unconcern about the services rendered at Ocean Road Maternity Hospital. Clearly the situation demands immediate attention. It is necessary that (health improvement) involves significant improvement in the standard of health services rendered in public hospitals. Otherwise the rhetoric will only intensify the public's dissatisfaction with these services".

Such editorials, complaining about the health workers in Tanzanian hospitals, are not uncommon although in this case the attack was particularly bitter. Because these complaints appear in the national press they have an important political significance. It is quite clear that in the absence of improved services and work habits on the part of staff, and the implementation of the sort of schemes discussed above for urban maternity services that such political 'health care crises' can only get worse, in Tanzania and elsewhere. It is expected that urban maternity units will be an important feature of the next Tanzanian five-year plan.

The urban maternity or, preferably maternal and child health units are analogous to the urban health centres that are often proposed in conjunction with 'site and service' schemes for expanding urban areas. Such urban centres can provide virtually all of the needed health services for anywhere up to 100,000 persons, especially if they are constructed in conjunction with several small outlying dispensaries or

157

clinics. In the planning of such centres it should be assumed that there will be annually at least five attendances per person, so that 100,000 people would provide at least a half a million attendances a year — or 1,600 out-patients per day (between the main centre and the outlying clinics). Maternal and child welfare clinics would also be held daily. A population of 100,000 in Tanzania would produce up to 5,000 maternal deliveries a year although probably less in the urban areas, of which total 10% to 15% should be delivered in hospital, and perhaps 4,000 at a smaller unit (requiring 30 maternity beds.) The operating costs of such centres in Tanzania would come to the quite acceptable figure of £0.50 per head. Again, it must be stressed that the success of such units would depend largely upon their management and integration into the health services of the whole of the town, they must be seen as part of the total structure and operated in conjunction with the existing hospital services. If the units are seen to be offering a second-class service and there is no control over movement into hospital it would be inevitable for patients to press into the hospitals and to resist the idea of services offered at subsidiary centres.

B. The Family Planning 'Issue'

Before turning to a discussion of the family planning 'issue' some demographic data will be presented as background.

The Demographic Background

Tanzania's population has been enumerated in 1948, 1957 and 1967. The 1967 census showed a population of 12.3 million, a rise of 3.2 million over the 1957 enumeration and an annual growth rate of over 3%. However, further analysis showed the inter-censal annual growth rate to have been about 2.6%. The crude birth rate was estimated at 47 per thousand, the crude death rate 21 per thousand, infant mortality 160-170 per thousand live births, life expectancy at birth 40-45 years, and a total fertility of 6.5 births. By 1980 the mainland population of Tanzania is expected to be around 17 million, based upon a steadily rising rate of growth of population.

Population density in Tanzania rose from 22 per square mile in 1948 to 35 in 1967. About a third of the country's 18 regions has a population density that exceeds the national average. The urban population of perhaps 800,000 (compared to 200,000 in 1948) constitutes only about 6% of the whole. Although the urban population has been growing at a rate that is more than twice the national average only about one-sixth of the total population growth is accounted for by the towns. In 1967, of Tanzania's total population, 44% were under the age of 15, and 18% were less than five. As a consequence of the present age distribution, the country's dependency ratio will become even greater in succeeding years.

The Family Planning Issue in Tanzania

In his introduction to the second five year plan President Nyerere said
the following:

> "The thing I want to say is this. It is very good to increase our
> population, because our country is large and there is plenty of
> unused land. But it is necessary to remember that these 350,000
> extra people every year will be babies in arms, not workers. They
> will have to be fed, clothed, given medical attention, schooling, and
> many other services for very many years before they will be able to
> contribute to the economy of the country through their work. This
> is right and proper and is in accordance with the teachings of the
> Arusha Declaration. But it is obvious that just as the number of our
> children is increasing, so the burden on the adults – the workers – is
> also increasing. Giving birth is something in which mankind and
> animals are equal but rearing the young, and specially educating
> them for many years, is something which is a unique gift and
> responsibility of men. It is for this reason that it is important for
> human beings to put emphasis on caring for children and the ability
> to look after them properly, rather than thinking only about the
> numbers of children and the ability to give birth. For it often
> happens that men's ability to give birth is greater than their ability
> to bring up the children in a proper manner."

President Nyerere spoke again on this issue in his report to the party
Conference in September 1973.*

> "In assessing our progress, however, it must always be
> remembered that whatsoever we produce has to be divided between
> an increasing number of people every year. An extra 380,000
> mouths are calling for food this year as against last year; it was the
> same the year before that and it will be the same next year. This means
> that before any of us can improve our standard of living, we as a
> nation have to increase our output by nearly 3 per cent every year
> even to maintain the standard of living we had in the past! If we do
> not increase our production of goods by at least 3 per cent a year
> the living conditions of every one of us will get worse; we shall have
> less food to eat, and a lower proportion of our children will go to
> school, and there will be more people waiting for the help of every
> medical worker. It is no use saying that these extra 380,000 people

*President's Report to the TANU Conference, Sept. 1973, pp.1 and 2).

have hands as well as mouths. For the first ten years of their life, at the very least, children eat without producing; we as adults have therefore to increase our production accordingly.

"That is a very relevant and important fact. If our national output increases by 3 per cent in a year then our annual income per head remains the same — it goes neither up nor down. If our output increases by 6 per cent in a year in real terms (that is in terms of goods produced), then we can, taken together, increase our consumption by only 3 per cent. Half of our extra efforts will have had to be devoted to the well-being of the extra population."

The concern of the Tanzanian government about the implications of its demographic structure should be clear from the above statements by President Nyerere: this concern is an important part of the background of the events which will be described below.

The Family Planning Association of Dar es Salaam was founded in 1959, and seven years later became the Family Planning Association of Tanzania. The Association is affiliated with the International Planned Parenthood Federation from whom it derived over 80% of its income. Although its personnel are basically Tanzanian, until quite recently the influence of expatriates in the management of the organisation was considerable. Although the Association receives no direct support from government, it utilises government medical premises and personnel: it is basically a service organisation that works through government and voluntary agency medical institutions; it operates a significant number of clinics throughout the country and is expanding the number of these with the expectation of soon reaching every district town in the nation. Family planning services are free at government institutions but require a small payment when supplied through the voluntary agencies. During the first half of 1970 there were almost 13,000 new visits and almost 5,000 revisits to Dar es Salaam family planning clinics. The total for the rest of the country was about equal to that of Dar es Salaam. Of the 3,500 family planning recipients in 1969 almost 2,000 chose oral contraceptives and 1,300 the IUD.

The position of the Ministry of Health with regard to family planning is that it is to be promoted on a voluntary basis as part of the improvement of maternal and child health services. The position of the Ministry with regard to the 'population question' is equally clear. Although it recognises the obvious advantages to individual families of family planning built around the concept of appropriate child spacing, the question of the formulation of a population policy is a totally different matter that can only be decided at another and higher governmental level than the Ministry itself.

In Tanzania, as in most other African countries, there has been

160

intense discussion of the questions involved in the concept of population control and family planning, and extreme positions have been taken on all sides of the question. One extreme considers that the growth of population is the most serious problem facing Tanzania and the root cause of the country's underdevelopment, as in the rest of the Third World. At the other extreme there are those who see family planning and population control as nothing more than an imperialist plot intended to reduce the number of, mostly poor, non-whites coming into the world because they constitute an increasing threat to the domination of the Third World by western capitalist powers. These extremist positions appear to offer a choice between a 'hard sell' in favour of technological solutions to the problem of over rapid population growth — even in the absence of other economic, social and political changes, and those who see decreasing rates of population growth as being possible only after the achievement of a state of 'development'. Most responsible opinion in Tanzania does see the dangers inherent in uncontrolled population growth, dangers both to individual mothers and families and to the nation as a whole. It also understands that such population growth is not the cause of underdevelopment and that the present situation cannot be altered in the absence of other necessary changes in the pattern of existence of most people in the Third World. Basically the problem is that of achieving a 'rational' rural life within the context of relatively low per capita incomes; this requires the proper utilisation and distribution of such income as is being generated within a poor country such as Tanzania. It would seem obvious that there are no easy ways of changing peoples' attitudes about family size while all other things around them remain basically as they were, at least insofar as they effect the possibility of the family benefitting from decreasing family size. In any event, in Tanzania, it is the case that responsible and official thinking is not opposed to appropriate types of family planning activities. This is so in spite of the view of many involved in international family planning efforts that Tanzania, unlike its neighbour Kenya, has been violently opposed to family planning as such and would not permit any expansion of family planning activities within the country. What has been the case is that Tanzania was reluctant to accept some of the more vulgar manifestations of family planning activity that can be seen in so many countries which start with a philosophy that sees population growth as the root cause of underdevelopment and appears to be concerned only with decreasing the number of births in Third World countries.

The fact that expatriates had for a long while played a very prominent role in family planning activities within Tanzania had been a special focal point for discontent, especially on the part of those who might have been in any event opposed to family planning activities within the country. However, in mid-1972 the Minister of Labour and Social Welfare was named Chairman of the Family Planning Association of Tanzania. The employment of a Tanzanian minister to head the Association, coupled with other steps intended to organise the country's family planning activities, was helpful in quietening some of the more extremist anti-family planning sentiment. One of the first actions of the revised Family Planning Association was to direct that externally supported family planning activities be channelled either through the Association itself or the Ministry of Health. In other words, family planning activities were not to be brought into the country from outside without the proper knowledge of appropriately designated groups, as had sometimes happened in the past.

From this point until mid-1973 the general tone of the discussions about family planning gradually took on a more balanced and rational character. For example, in November 1972, in the National Assembly a Member of Parliament asked "how many officials were in the Family Planning Association of Tanzania and if it was necessary to have family planning in Tanzania, as there was enough land to accommodate many people."* In reply, the junior minister of health informed the members of parliament that the Family Planning Association "had 180 officials which included executive committee members and branch officials. There were only 49 paid officials". And that "the aim of the association was not to decrease the population of the country but to have healthy mothers and children. The aims of family planning were not against our socialist policies". The Prime Minister entered the debate with the following remarks "the government believes that the association will not accept any advice which is against the country's traditions on family planning . . . the association was being run by Tanzanians [who] would not allow any foreign country to undermine its work which agreed with our traditions . . . family planning was aimed at educating people to have healthy children and thus have a healthy nation." The entrance of the Prime Minister into this parliamentary debate was of particular significance as many had thought him to be at least a potential opponent of family planning activities.

In February 1973 the English language newspaper in Dar es Salaam published a long interview with the Executive Secretary of the Family Planning Association.** The tone of the interview is reflected in most of the questions that were asked. A representative sample follows:

"In the press and in conversations lately your association has been a

---

*Reported in the *Daily News* (Dar es Salaam) 16 Nov. 1972 under the headline "AIM of family planning is healthy nation".
***Sunday News* 18 February, 1973.

subject of controversy — mainly on its origin and international links. Just what and who was the inspiration behind the Family Planning Association of Tanzania?"

"When was it founded and with what funds?"

"Is it therefore the case that you are controlled by the financial purse strings of people in Britain and America who do not have the interests of Tanzanians at heart?"

"How is your association autonomous and how does it insure that the International Parental Association does not interfere in the running of it?"

"One of the reasons why your association arouses such deep emotions is that it is associated with birth control. Is your association a birth control organisation?"

"But is it not true that to plan the size of your family you must control births in the family?"

"What of the charge that you want to control the population growth?"

"Opponents of the association say that the whole notion of family planning is alien to the African tradition and culture. What is your reply to this?"

"Yet other people complain that your activities benefit only those with ample incomes who have therefore no pressing need to have small families. What is the association's answer to this complaint?"

The final question and reply were particularly interesting. The question: "Why do you think your association has been so misunderstood, and what do you think can be done to put its activities in proper public perspective?"

The reply: "There are many reasons why the association has been misunderstood and some of them have already been covered in our discussion — such as people's ignorance about our aims and their suspicion about our links with outside countries and organisations. Such ignorance and suspicions can be removed by mounting intensive publicity through various channels of communication especially the mass media. However, there is one disturbing feature about this misunderstanding. It involves a few vocal people with vested interests who, although they understand everything about the association and in private do avail themselves of the family planning services, yet in public they vehemently try to discredit it. Also there are in the country some individuals in institutions and agencies currently indulging in some family planning activities which are not in line with the policy of our association or of our government."

The public debate about family planning continued throughout the first half of 1973. In general, its tone tended to be moderate although it was still possible for the following to appear in the press:

UMATI Must Go

You call them family planning methods!
You call it a family planning association!
You lie, I'll tell the truth.
It's birth control, nay, it's family destroying.
They are birth control drugs, these family destroyers.
It's a birth control clique, it destroys families.

Who are the addicts?
Married mothers?
Very few, ignorant of the dangers.
Unmarried mothers?
Yes, once bitten twice shy.
Schoolgirls, working girls with no families.
What do they plan?
Prostitution, destroying harmonious families,
Selling themselves to every man, the so-called girls;
Big men, small men, married men, unmarried men.
When wives know run away from husbands.
You call this family planning?

These drugs are evil, they spoil the female lot.
Un-African, unsocialist, inhuman, reactionary.
Complicated pregnancies, births of deformed babies, sterility,
Venereal diseases, like in America.
Where they spread incurable gonorrhoea,
Have they found the cure?
STC* order it now we'll need it in five years.
Alternatively UMATI must be assassinated.

Women, girls of Tanzania, women, girls of Africa,
Look where you came from, look where you are going.
Plan for Tanzania's socialist transformation,
Plan for the African Revolution.
Ladies, we need your constructive ideas,
Not new-colonialist ones from imperialist nations.
Father Tanu, mother UWT,+
For Africa's sake, wipe out UMATI.

UMATI, you've done enough harm,
Should we wait till you drain us,
Of foreign exchange, manpower, ideology, culture, morals . . .
No! I demand total ban,
On importation of the evil drugs.
UMATI you've done enough harm,

*State Trading Corporation,
+United Women of Tanzania.

UMATI, You're the people's enemy,
Traitor of Africa, You must go.+

In July 1973 a tremendous uproar broke out over the activities of the
Family Planning Association. The Association had employed a new
senior Tanzanian medical consultant who recommended that the use of
the contraceptive drug depo provera be discontinued. The basis of the
recommendation was that not enough was known about the drug's
potential side effects and that in any event it was still in its experimental
stages. The wide publicity given to the banning of a drug being used by
the Family Planning Association once again exploded the family
planning/birth control issue. Long articles appeared in the Tanzanian
press under such headings as 'The pill scandal uncovered'* and
'Family planning should be state controlled'**. In at least one region
of the country all the activities of the Family Planning Association
were temporarily suspended. The whole issue was summed up in an
editorial appearing in the *Daily News* on 16 July 1973, which
said:

"Many parents in Tanzania agree with the idea of family planning
for better health and development of their families. This idea is not
new. Even in days gone by, the idea that children had to be spaced
prevailed. But in recent years this process of family planning has
almost wholly been usurped by the Family Planning Association of
Tanzania and the emphasis has almost been entirely on the use of
imported drugs [rather] than other methods. Readers of this and
other newspapers discerned the dangers of this emphasis long ago
and have been writing and advising against it as long as half a decade
ago. Many times our readers in particular and Tanzanians in general
have advised that the crucial undertaking of family planning should
be incorporated under the Ministry of Health". The editorial also
criticised the lack of expertise and experience of those running the
F.P.A. and concluded that, "Under these circumstances is there any.
wonder that our Family Planning Organisation can be hoodwinked and
turn our women into guinea-pigs to be experimented on by
international drug manufacturers and suppliers? The case of recent
withdrawal of the family planning drug "Depo Provera" is a telling
proof of the vulnerability of the Family Planning Organisation in
Tanzania. The drug in question has been used in Tanzania for some

+*Daily News* 11 March 1973. The author is D. Rwehikira Bashome whose address
was given as the University of Dar es Salaam.

**Daily News* 21 and 22 July 1973.

***Daily News* 21 and 22 July 1973.

years. There is only one other country in the whole world where it has been used — Thailand. That in the countries where this drug is manufactured it is still being experimented on rats, mice and rabbits is, to say the least a terrible blow to the Tanzanian women who were misled into using it by the Family Planning Association of Tanzania. No one knows the number of these victims. No one can tell their future. What can be said is that they are suffering from all sorts of dislocations and abnormalities. What a pity! There are still various elements in our society. One of them is the reactionary petty bourgeoise. This is the most dangerous element in our midst today. As long as international capitalist organisations are prepared, directly or indirectly, to bribe this element with money, or to offer it the niceties of air travels here and there, this particular opportunistic and parasitic element will champion even a road to the very death of its sisters and brothers! Now even the United Women of Tanzania comes to lament when it is almost too late. But can we continue lamenting in the face of an organisation whose activities if not controlled and given direction can betray our nation. We say NO".

Although there is very much that is open to dispute in the editorial quoted above, there is much to be learned from its very publication and the entire incident of which it was part. Family planning techniques cannot be brought surreptitiously to a nation; not by its citizens and certainly not by foreigners. Especially in places such as Tanzania, where the nation and the people take the question of development seriously family planning activities can only be introduced in keeping with the broader aspirations of the nation and its people. There must be open discussion about the nature of family planning activities, the source of its funding, and its purpose. Deviation from a policy of openness can only lead to the sort of difficulties that have arisen in Tanzania.

Initially at least family planning activities are probably best spread through the services offered by ministries of health which, however, is not to argue that family planning activities need always be confined to such services. As a matter of fact it is probably the case that truly national coverage by family planning services can only be achieved when they are organised in ways that reach much beyond the usual activities of ministries of health. However, to begin with it is the organised health services that are best equipped to introduce family planning in keeping with the development of appropriate health services capable of reaching out to the mass of the population. As with other key health inputs it is the case that ministries of health have only a partial role to play in relationship to family planning services; nonetheless, the traditional role of health workers in this regard, coupled with their close contact with pregnant women, assuming there is a service capable of reaching most of the pregnant women, gives the relevant health workers particular opportunities in this regard. The problem of creating a changed family view about the desirable number of pregnancies is, of course, complex; it is probably the case that from the family point of view the key variable is the survival rate of children. In conditions of uncertainty about child survival, it is the better part of wisdom for individual families to have a greater number of births than they might otherwise have considered to be necessary. Considering that in many parts of the Third World a third or more of all conceptions do not result in a living five year old child, it is not surprising that many families take steps to provide against their being left with fewer survivors than they consider to be optimal. Survival rates will in fact vary considerably between urban and rural areas and from one rural area to another, so much so that in some villages certain families will even see the majority of their children die. Families living in such villages will consider such events to be much more significant in relation to the planning of their own families than the fact that there is a generally increasing rate of population growth in the nation as a whole.

Although national policy may be such as to stimulate the use of contraceptive devices and to make them available through any one of a variety of sources, including commercial ones, the role of ministries of health in increasing the demand for contraception will be almost entirely limited to two particular areas, although these two are probably the most crucial ones. The first is contributing towards decreased infant and childhood mortality so that families are in a better position to plan and control completed family size effectively. The other is through proper postnatal maternity care; that is, postnatal care that stresses from the point of view of the mother, the most recently born child and the family as a whole the desirability of postponing the next pregnancy for some 3 to 4 years. If a typical Third World health ministry could accomplish these two major goals i.e. increased survival rates for children and longer spacing between pregnancies, it would have made a major contribution towards changing the prevailing demographic pattern.

The specific question of just which contraceptive devices particular health workers should be allowed to prescribe or deliver can only be determined within the context of given national political, social, economic and health conditions. It is probably fair to assume that almost everywhere the major constraint at this time is not the unavailability of contraceptive supplies or health workers to make them available to the existing level of demand, but the lack of greater demand for those contraceptive devices. There are very few countries which do not make family planning services available, at least to the level of existing demand, which is growing fairly significantly in urban

167

areas but only to a much lesser degree in the rural parts of most countries. It is of course important that nations continue to train health workers in keeping with the expected increasing demand for family planning services. But the basic problem remains the reality of the situation in which most rural families live, which is itself the major barrier to the idea and practice of family planning.

9. PHARMACEUTICALS, AND OTHER ANCILLARY SERVICES

This chapter will touch briefly on some major questions with regard to the supply of pharmaceutical products, and the organisation of laboratories and other ancillary health services.

A. Laboratory Services

In very many Third World countries the hospital laboratories are better developed than the public health labs are. Although this pattern of development has placed the 'cart before the horse' it has been in keeping with the overall emphasis that has been put on the development of the curative health services. Tanzania too has a large new central medical laboratory, located at Muhimbili Hospital in Dar es Salaam. In principle this lab is intended to serve the whole of the country, or a large part of it in any event, on the referral principle. In practice, however, the work of this Central Pathology Laboratory is largely restricted to serving the needs of Dar es Salaam, except that it also acts as a training centre for lab technicians and is responsible for the distribution of vaccines throughout the country. Apart from this laboratory there are those located at the regional and district hospitals. The quality of the equipment, manpower and work of these labs varies considerably, but generally there is a vast gap between their capabilities and the one in Dar es Salaam (except for the two new referral hospitals at Mwanza and Moshi).

The same general neglect of lower level institutions as exists in other aspects of hospital and health service development is to be found in the laboratories, in that the state of these labs in terms of their buildings and equipment is usually no better than that of the hospital in which they are located. In this respect the question of equipment is rather more important than that of buildings, in that labs must have a minimum level of equipment if they are to be able to function at all, although the problem is more likely to be one of maintenance than of procurement (not that there usually is sufficient equipment but one of the major constraints to the purchase of more is the doubtful ability of the regional and district labs to keep it functioning). The problem in Tanzania is similar to that of other hospital equipment problems, and the planned hospital equipment maintenance unit (discussed earlier) might be able to solve some of the problems involved, at least insofar as the simpler laboratory equipment is concerned.

The staffing of the labs varies considerably, although there is a reasonable expectation that the standard of staffing will rise significantly in the near future as a result of the continuing outflow from training of lab technicians and laboratory auxiliaries. Between 1972 and 1980 the number of laboratory technicians and auxiliaries will have almost tripled in each case, to a total of over 300 technicians and 500 auxiliaries. Although an improved staffing pattern will go a long way towards guaranteeing the proper functioning of regional and district labs there still remains the question of practical supervision and guidance for these additional laboratory workers, especially by pathologists. Although the number of Tanzanian pathologists will grow through the decade of the 70's, by 1980 there is still expected to be only about 20. Perhaps even more important than the absolute number of pathologists will be the question of their orientation and capability of organising laboratory work outside the largest hospital centres. What is needed in countries like Tanzania are pathologists capable of helping to improve the quality of work being performed by middle level laboratory personnel, in small district and regional laboratories. This need must be met both in the training of pathologists and their later employment situations. The relatively few pathologists cannot continue to be tied to laboratories in the few large hospitals of a country but must be linked to the work of district and regional hospital labs, including actually spending a substantial proportion of their time at the smaller institutions.

B. Dental Services

Dental services have not been one of the higher priority areas for health service development in poor countries. In Tanzania, in 1972, there were only about two dozen dentists and a similar number of dental assistants. Fully qualified dentists were located only at the three national referral hospitals, but dental assistants could be found at most of the regional hospitals. The present expansion of dental assistant training means that there will be 90 in the country by 1980 (about twice the number of dentists), so that it will become possible to post at least one to each of the government regional and district hospitals. About two dozen dental technicians will also have been trained by 1980. Of course, the services offered will still be relatively minimal, and available primarily to those living in the towns.

The problem of reaching greater numbers of people with dental care, and most particularly with preventive and promotive dental services, is a difficult one. On the one hand it might be possible under Tanzanian conditions to have the equivalent of a rural medical aid at each rural health centre, thus raising the annual recurrent costs of each centre. In principle, these staff would spend most of their time in dental health education activities. On the other hand, it might be more

170

efficient instead, or as well, to include additional material about dental health education within the curriculum of rural medical aids and other health workers, so that all would be better equipped to discuss and deal with the problem. At this time in Tanzania the goal is to achieve coverage of all districts in the country with at least one dental assistant by the end of the next five year plan. The training of qualified dentists also proceeds, thus increasing the possibility of setting up broader preventive dental health programmes — presuming that these additional dentists and dental assistants are used for wider activities than simply the provision of curative dental services.

C. Optical Services

Serious eye diseases such as trachoma are widespread in Third World countries — including Tanzania, particularly in the drier central areas of the country — and the resulting incidence of blindness is considerable. Trachoma and other similar diseases are mainly caused by poverty leading to a lack of adequate sanitary standards, and could be drastically reduced by improved hygienic and living standards, particularly for rural populations. However, it is not the intention here to discuss eye diseases but rather the question of optical services and the provision of spectacles. The need for spectacles hardly arises in preliterate societies, and it is only with increasing literacy that the question of glasses becomes important. In most of Africa the number of opthalmic and dispensing opticians is extremely limited and they can usually only be found in the larger towns. In addition most countries have to import frames and lenses for the assembly of spectacles. In fact, it could be argued that in Africa most countries remain without the benefit of such services. This has been the situation in Tanzania also, at least until fairly recently; however, with the growth of the literacy campaigns of recent years the need for spectacles has taken on a new significance.

Spectacles are made up of two component parts, frames and lenses. It appears that only a relatively small number — perhaps a dozen — standard lens types are required for the production of spectacles suitable for the great mass of those requiring them, at least for the limited needs of (even literate) rural populations. The basic manpower requirement for the fitting of spectacles is not very complex, calling for one person capable of judging the spectacle required (a refractionist) and another able to either grind a lens or fit already ground lenses into spectacles. It is possible to purchase, if need be from abroad, frames and blank lenses in bulk and then to assemble them for distribution through, say, adult literacy campaigns. The actual workshop and equipment required are relatively simple matters, as is the training of an optical technician. The other and more significant question is the training of refractionists. Overseas training for such people generally takes about

171

three years from form 4 or form 6; however, the basic requirements
for such people could probably be met under local conditions in from
six months to one year. The costs of the basic equipment required by a
refractionist in order to practice are also not significant. The problem is
essentially one of training an appropriate auxiliary without specific
regard to the training requirements and curricula developed in the more
industrialised parts of the world. The question is one of recognising the
difference in requirements, in this case for refractionists, that result
from differing conditions in poor countries as compared to
industrialised ones. The same principles would hold true for all other
categories of paramedical health workers e.g. physiotherapists,
physiotherapy auxiliaries, x-ray technicians etc.

D. Pharmaceuticals

In most African countries the supply of pharmaceutical products will
consume around a quarter of the total budget of the Ministry of Health.
These products also constitute one of the major import items for Third
World nations as a whole. The pharmaceutical market in Third World
countries is also expanding very quickly, so much so that it usually
represents the most rapidly growing portion of all health expenditure.
Most countries, including Tanzania, have 'central medical stores'
responsible for the purchase, receipt, storage and distribution of medical
supplies and equipment. The volume of work of such central medical
depots is expanding rapidly for the following reasons: one, the
widening network of health services to be found in most countries
means that more people have accessability to pharmaceutical products;
two, the dispensing of drugs is seen as the major road to better health
and thus the primary activity of health facilities and health workers; and
three, there is often insufficient financial control operated over the
purchase, distribution and utilisation of drugs. While it is desirable that
health services continue to expand to reach the whole of the population
it is certainly not desirable for the cost of drugs to the medical
services to continue rising at the rates they have been in recent
years.

In 1971 between 1,000 and 1,200 million tablets were consumed in
Tanzania. The size of the pharmaceutical market was estimated at £3.2
million, of which about £2.5 million was in the form of finished
pharmaceutical products. About half the £3.2 million of imported
medicaments was absorbed at government institutions, and half by
non-government agencies. Issues from central medical stores rose from
£375,000 in 1961/62 to £1,770,000 in 1971/72. Thus, over a ten year
period the value of the volume of issues from central medical stores
had become five times greater. (No data are available to show how much
of that increase resulted from price rises.) However, it took the first

seven years of that ten year period for the value of the issues to double from approximately £375,000 to just over £750,000. But, over the three years 1968/69 to 1971/72 the value of issues increased from just over £750,000 to over £1,750,000, representing an increase of 130% over the three year period. In fact, purchases, as opposed to issues by central medical stores had increased even more rapidly. Over the two years 1969/70 – 1971/72 there was more than a doubling of purchases by central medical stores, from almost £1.1 million to over £2.2 million. The sources of these imports might be of some interest: of the 1971 total 33% came from the United Kingdom and another 20% from mainly U.K. subsidiaries based in Kenya, another 22% came from Common Market countries, 9% from the United States, 5% from Eastern Europe, 4% from China and 7% from other sources.

This huge increase in drug consumption is not limited to Tanzania. The imports of medicaments for the three East African countries as a whole (Tanzania, Kenya and Uganda) rose by 117% over the years 1965-71; the rise for Tanzania was most rapid, Uganda followed and Kenya was last, which was only to be expected in the case of the one country of the three that was manufacturing a substantial volume of drugs within its own borders under licence. The estimated size of the Tanzanian pharmaceutical market in 1971, as stated above, came to £3.2 million. The comparable figures for other East African countries were Uganda £2.0 million, Kenya £3.5 million and Zambia £5.0 million. Even though the Tanzanian figures do not look quite so bad when compared to neighbouring countries, the rapid growth of drug consumption in Tanzania still constitutes a major problem for government.

The question of controlling the cost of drugs to the health services in countries all over the world is one of the most perplexing of all those facing health service planners and administrators. The basic situation is made worse in Third World countries as a result of their dependence upon international drug companies from whom they purchase their supplies. The influence of these large companies in Third World countries is particularly significant in that they control the sources of information available to health workers about new drugs and developments in the pharmaceutical industry to an even greater degree than in industrialised ones. It is also widely known that the possibilities of corruption in the purchase and supply of drugs are very great. The drug companies are also very successful in recruiting African doctors and other health workers into employment as representatives, at wages which are substantially greater than government is usually able to pay, thereby setting up another source of discontent for those remaining in government service.

In addition to the issues discussed above, there is the very nature of

173

the training of the medical doctor that encourages him to prescribe the most advanced drug irrespective of knowledge, or lack of knowledge of the costs of such drugs and the very specific priority requirement of any one patient for that very expensive drug. The basic pattern is the same as in the provision of expensive hospital beds and sophisticated manpower to meet all medical problems, even those requiring only much simpler levels of care. The effect of these medical attitudes upon the distribution of drugs is very substantial and the net result is the issue of a much greater volume of drugs, and more expensive drugs, to larger city hospitals where there are more doctors and specialists than smaller rural institutions; for example, Muhimbili Hospital in Dar es Salaam is able to absorb a far greater volume of drugs than any other hospital in the country. The lack of standardised treatment practices and effective cost accounting also contributes to the fact that there is usually little intended correlation between the volume of a particular hospital's in-patients and out-patients and the volume of drugs that it receives, from central medical stores.

Many modern drugs are extremely expensive, and yet it is not clear that these more expensive drugs are always more effective than alternative and less costly choices.* This problem is increased by the fact that identical compounds selling under different names have very different prices; many specific examples of this could be cited. For example, in anti-ulcer therapy 1,000 tablets of one particular drug can be purchased in Tanzania for £0.20, alternatively a very similar compound costs 40 times as much; or the cases in which aspirin costing £0.15 per 1,000 tablets can be used instead of very similar products that sell for as much as £20 to £25 per 1,000 tablets; or the case of certain tranquillizers available costing as little as £0.15 per 1,000 tablets as opposed to others costing £10 per 1,000. In all these cases there is little to choose between the various compounds in terms of proven therapeutic value. The savings inherent in the use of official as opposed to brand names is well known; however, many doctors, particularly in the Third World, continue to use brand name products thereby raising costs by as much as 20 times.

Very basic to this whole problem is the way in which medical students are trained and later practice their medicine, in that there is almost complete neglect of questions of cost in the approach to the selection of drugs. Students are usually taught therapeutics, and journals generally discuss recent advances in therapeutics without any reference to costs. When deciding to use a particular drug doctors often

---

*Part of the following discussion is freely drawn from Dr. A. N. P. Speight, 'Some Observations on the Cost of Commonly Used Drugs' a paper delivered at the East African Medical Research Council Annual Scientific Conference, Nairobi, Feb. 1973.

limit themselves almost entirely to considerations of efficacy and toxicity, thus one particular drug which may have only a marginal advantage over another is chosen despite the fact that it might cost 20 times as much. Such choices are in marked contrast to those made in the purchase of, say, an automobile where one vehicle costing 20 times more than another would never be chosen because it had only marginal advantages. The reason for this difference is surely that medical practices are concerned with life and death in a way that automobiles are not. It is right that doctors should be reluctant to consider economising on drugs in a case where a patient's life is at stake. However, the great majority of drug prescriptions are not life saving, so this question does not usually arise. Nonetheless, the medical profession vigorously defends its freedom to prescribe drugs irrespective of costs and the new or more expensive ones are being provided continuously for them by the pharmaceutical industry.

The problem for the planner is to discover ways of controlling the cost of drugs being used in the national health services without at the same time making economies in those areas which might adversely affect individual lives. The best and most fundamental way of meeting this problem would be the more appropriate training of medical students so that they could improve their own prescribing techniques. It would also be extremely helpful if the journals read by medical students and doctors required drug advertisers to include the prices of the drugs in the advertisements. It is the national health services, however, that are currently in the best position to take the lead in this matter. For example, information on drug costs could be widely disseminated to practising doctors by appropriate committees in ministries of health, although there are more steps than just the provision of information that must be taken by the relevant ministries — as can be seen from the fact that in Great Britain 70 per cent of prescriptions by general practitioners continue to be of brand name preparations, despite the encouragement of their Ministry of Health to do otherwise. Some such steps follow:—

1. A standard central medical stores drug list (a National Formulary) should be established with a view to reducing the number of different drugs circulating in the country at any one time; when additional drugs are added to the list it must clearly be shown that they are therapeutically necessary additions and well worth the additional cost.
2. The costs of the different drugs included on the standard list should be widely disseminated; and their generic names.
3. Attempts should be made to standardise drug prescribing for common ailments, especially at rural health centre and dispensary

level.

4. A consultant's signature should be required for prescription of the most expensive antibiotics, as well as certain other expensive drugs. This would mean a restricted drugs list.
5. Prepackaging of standardised drug dosages should be established.
6. More rigid control should be practised over drug company representatives.
7. Various drug control proposals need to be implemented by special drug committees e.g. restrictions on the import of certain drugs, and use of local purchase orders for expensive drugs.

All of the above suggestions have to do with controlling the supply of pharmaceuticals. The problem of controlling the demand for health services including drugs has been discussed earlier in the context of the charging of selected fees. The question of the control of drugs is very much related to that of the 'thinning out' of the health services in general: given the sharp constraint on the volume of available health resources means that drugs too must be thinned out to meet the widest possible requirements. Such a policy is in no way in contradiction with that of providing the minimal volume of drugs required for any particular, serious illness. This is so not only because the great bulk of drugs are unrelated to serious illness, but also that the fact that a very substantial part of drug prescribing is unrelated to illness at all, at least in the narrower physical sense.

The problem of control of drugs will not be solved quickly in Tanzania, nor anywhere else. One of the more obvious difficulties is the lack of sure knowledge as to how to proceed immediately. Probably even more important is the reluctance of administrators and others to interfere with the traditional right of the doctor to prescribe the 'drug of choice' without hindrance. This reluctance is linked to the understandable fear of damage being done to individual patients. It is one thing to agree that control of the use of very expensive drugs will lead to more efficient and equitable health services, but it is another matter to have to justify such policies in the face of a well publicised death. The training of Tanzanian pharmaceutical manpower is one prerequisite for the formulation of improved policies in this area. The number of citizen pharmacists will rise from less than a half dozen in 1972 to more than 75 by 1980. Over that same time period the number of pharmaceutical assistants will increase from 30 to 175, and pharmaceutical auxiliaries from less than 100 to 190.

A word might be included here about the uses of traditional drugs. There is increasing interest in very many parts of the world, and certainly in very many African countries, about the potential uses of traditional medicines within the organised health services. The testing of these drugs is generally turned over to chemists and other similarly trained people who proceed with their work in much the same ways that companies would go about testing any new pharmaceutical product. Not surprisingly such testing is extremely expensive and very slow. While such an approach may be sound it is not very practical, in that it tends to ignore the fact that these traditional drugs are currently being used in vast quantities irrespective of any laboratory findings about their efficacy. Therefore, the real question becomes not the use of modern or traditional drugs or even so much the need to test traditional drugs against the same criteria as modern drugs, but the continued use of traditional drugs as opposed to the use of no drug at all. This is a complex matter but it does seem that the starting point for the examination of these drugs should be one which begins with acceptance of the fact that they will, in any event, continue to be used very widely, as well as recognition that many of the drugs now being commonly prescribed within the modern health services also have only a limited therapeutic effect.

10. NON-GOVERNMENTAL SERVICES

A substantial proportion of all health services in Tanzania is provided by agencies other than government. The most important of these are the voluntary agencies, primarily related to the Christian churches, the occupational health services, and those in private practice in both the modern and traditional sectors.

A. Voluntary Agencies

The evangelical movements of the Christian churches, begun in East Africa in the latter part of the eighteenth century, were sufficiently active so that by the time the first Germans officially arrived in 1885 it was estimated that some 300 Europeans, primarily missionaries, had already lived and worked there. The first medical missionaries arrived in 1881, and grew steadily in number through the years of German and British colonial administration in Tanzania and the other parts of East Africa. Although the proselytising intentions of the early medical institutions were quite clear, with the passage of time the concept of evangelisation slowly became less important and by the time of African independence a much broader approach to medical work had become evident (which is of course not to say that the concept of evangelising had ever been completely lost).* Medical institutions were also frequently started for prestige purposes and sometimes even as a source of income to finance other missionary activities.

During the colonial period there was generally an easy relationship between the medical missionaries and government, which does not mean that their objectives were always the same, but relatively close personal contact did exist. With the coming of African independence certain strains began to be felt, although the situation varied widely in particular countries at different times. In Tanzania it is probably fair to say that the relationship remained fairly good although the situation fluctuated, especially with regard to different ministers of health. On the church side there was the tendency to be rather suspicious of government over the question of the future of their institutions, a

---

*For example, according to the Sumve Hospital Medical Report of 1937, "the Bishop of Mwanza did not give permission to Sumve Hospital [until] 1937 to build a male ward, because the nursing of females, especially in the obstetrical department, was more beneficial, as many babies could then be baptised." T. W. J. Schulpen, 'The Integration of Church Related Medical Service in the Policy of Tanzania', a thesis presented in July 1973 to the Royal Tropical Institute, Amsterdam, p.28.

suspicion that was strengthened after church educational institutions were nationalised. At independence approximately 70% of all educational services in Tanzania were run by the churches.

From the planner's point of view the question of coordinating the work of the voluntary institutions with government activities is of substantial importance. Because mission medical institutions are generally located in the rural areas they have the effect of making the availability of medical services more equitable, although this improved equity is reduced to some degree by the fact that fees are almost always charged. Their work is also usually as heavily curatively orientated as that of the government services. A particularly difficult problem arises from the fact that different Christian church groups have tended to work primarily within 'their own' geographic areas. The effect has been to concentrate mission health services in those parts of countries that are particularly Christian or made up of Christians of particular denominations. The results of this situation have been particularly serious in Africa where there are large numbers of Christians amongst mixed religious populations, rather than in most of the Asian countries where the number of Christian adherents is relatively small. To the degree that government does not integrate and organise the location of new hospital beds being built by Christian bodies it will have to concentrate more of its own building in the Moslem parts of a country in order to provide a proper balance with Christian areas. For example, in Tanzania the predominantly Moslem Coast Region has no voluntary agency hospital at all as is the case with about 40% of the country's more than 60 districts. However, in some regions voluntary agency beds represent a substantial majority of all hospital beds. This problem may be less significant in some countries with a more uniform religious structure, but in Tanzania where the number of Moslems and Christians is roughly equal and where both religions are actively proselytising, it is an important one. It must be stressed that government must have fore-knowledge of the building plans of the voluntary agencies if proper coordination of government and voluntary agency facilities is to be accomplished. This is especially important in situations where planning is meant to create a more equitable distribution of facilities throughout a country. Another aspect of this problem is that when planning for the siting of additional hospital beds in a situation in which government services are free but those offered by the churches are not, government is faced with the problem of accepting all beds — free and fee charging — as being equal, or of planning only for the more equitable distribution of government beds. This question becomes particularly important in places where it is recognised that sooner or later all hospital beds are likely to be incorporated into the government structure. This is not to suggest that this is likely to happen in the near future in Tanzania, or that it is government policy at this time to 'take over' any church institutions.

In 1946 the voluntary agencies provided a third of Tanzania's 6,300 hospital beds, and 18 of the 115 qualified doctors in the country. The following table shows the volume of health services provided by the voluntary agencies in 1961 and 1971 as percentages of total national services.

Table 13. Voluntary Agency Medical Services in Tanzania: 1961-1971

	1961 No.	% of National Total	1971 No.	% of National Total
Hospitals	46	47	59	49
Hospital Beds	4,600	41	7,950	45
Dispensaries	239	25	280	20
Registered Doctors	81	20	110	23
Hospital In-patients	85,000	38	167,000	34
All Out-patients (first attendances)	670,000	7	1,160,000	5

From the table it can be seen that over the decade there was relatively little shift in the share of national services provided by the voluntary agencies. They continued to offer almost half the country's hospitals and hospital beds; however, because those beds were less intensively utilised than beds in government hospitals they provided only a third of all hospital in-patient care. Only 5% of all new out-patient attendances were provided by voluntary agency institutions. The contribution of the agencies to training continues to be substantial; they operate 16 of the 20 B nursing schools, three of the six training centres for medical assistants, three schools for rural medical aids and a number of other schools and courses for paramedical auxiliaries. In addition to 110 medical doctors around 250 to 300 other expatriate health workers were employed by the voluntary agencies, the great bulk of them being senior nursing personnel.

Some sporadic attempts have been made to estimate the volume of health services being provided by the voluntary agency institutions in monetary terms. It would appear that in 1972/73 government grants of £700,000 were almost equivalent to the volume of fees collected by the voluntary agencies, and that between them these two sources of income covered the overwhelming bulk of the running costs of the voluntary

180

agency institutions. The amount of external support for operating costs represented only a small percentage of the whole. Those resources that do come into the country from outside are primarily for capital development. (This question will be discussed further in the chapter concerned with external aid to the health sector.) Government support to church medical institutions has always been substantial in Tanzania. Of the 59 voluntary agency hospitals, 46 were grant earning i.e. grants given by government on a per bed or per staff basis that enable voluntary agencies to charge much lower fees than they would otherwise. In addition 20 dispensaries, 5 leprosaria and 26 training schools are also grant earning. The schools receive grants equivalent to their training costs. The total value of these grants in 1971/72 came to around £450,000. This figure represents a three fold increase over the decade since independence. Government also makes available another £250,000 per annum for the running of 'designated district hospitals'. The first of these was established in 1965 and by 1973 there were eight such institutions. These are voluntary agency hospitals which continue to be managed by the churches, although they are given a grant sufficient to cover all running expenses and so do not charge any fees. This device has been hit upon for use in those districts of Tanzania in which there is a voluntary agency hospital but no government institution. It has thereby become possible to have an institution that functions in a similar way to other district hospitals without the necessity of government providing the capital costs required for additional construction. Although there have been some problems involved in the development of these designated hospitals, on the whole they have operated quite successfully. In passing it might be noted that over the years some of the hospitals originally built by the voluntary agencies were either offered to government, or, in one or two cases, taken by government and turned into government institutions — although in these cases the voluntary agencies continued to supply operating personnel and participate on the governing bodies of the institutions involved.

The major instrument of cooperation for the medical work of the many different Christian groups in Tanzania is the Tanzanian Christian Medical Association. This association goes back to the 'mission medical committee' set up in 1938. In addition to the coordinating association of the Christian medical bodies themselves there is a joint government-voluntary agency committee concerned with the question of grants and other areas of cooperation between government and the agencies. This committee is the key point at which government and voluntary agency interests meet in the area of health development. It is in such bodies that government can ensure that the voluntary agency bodies are really meeting national aspirations. For example, with regard to training

181

institutions, to plan for the gradual replacement of expatriate staff by citizens, or to ensure that choice of students is made from amongst the nationals of the country as a whole and is not drawn disproportionally from within the Christian community, or any particular group within that community. In fact, government is always in a position through its various subsidies (i.e. training staff and bed grants) to encourage the best utilisation of resources by the voluntary agencies e.g. in favour of more preventive and mobile work. In particular governments should take into account the overall availability of health services in particular regions or districts of the country in determining policy towards the subsidisation of specific voluntary agency hospitals and other health facilities. It is also necessary that government activity should discourage a standard of staffing and construction at voluntary agency institutions that is substantially higher than at comparable government facilities.

It is quite clear that the Christian churches can continue to play an important role in the development of health services in a country such as Tanzania; potential ideological differences need not be insurmountable. The essence of the matter is the degree of trust and confidence that medical mission personnel are able to place in the proper aspirations of independent African and other states. As is to be expected there may be substantial differences on these matters within the Church community itself, between different Christian sects and nationalities. Although some Christian churches appear to be constitutionally averse to any form of cooperation with government there are others that are quite capable and indeed even anxious to cooperate to the largest degree possible. The range of possibility and experience in the whole area of Church and government cooperation is very wide indeed.

B. Occupational Health Services

In many parts of the Third World, occupational health services provide an important part of all available health care. Because such services are generally linked to wage employment means that they are most extensively developed in the more industrialised parts of the Third World, in particular in the more economically developed parts of particular countries, and significantly less so in Africa. These services represent a particular problem for planners interested in the more equitable distribution of health resources because the provision of services through these schemes tends to create an unequal distribution of health services between those in and out of wage employment. It should be noted that although those in wage employment can be located either in the urban or rural areas, most of them will be in the cities although some are employed on large plantations in the rural areas. Many of these schemes are organised on an insurance basis paid

182

for in various ways by employer and employee contributions, and are therefore able to develop their own services almost independently of those being organised for the mass of the population by a ministry of health.

There can be no doubt about the essential need for occupational health services, especially as they relate to the safety of employment in which industrial and other wage employees are engaged. There is also the consideration that substantial production losses could be suffered if those in wage employment were not kept healthy: while this may also be true of those in subsistence agriculture, it is not nearly so clear and immediate an issue for those in wage employment. In fact it is the argument that there would be immediate losses in production as a result of the illness of industrial workers that at least partially justifies the very large expenditures on the occupational health services. Unfortunately, however, the health care being made available to industrial workers in Third World countries is essentially of a curative nature, so that although there may be a perfectly good argument for protecting industrial workers as a special concern, it does not necessarily follow that the curative services should continue to be given such a very high and expensive priority. In fact just because industrial workers are a highly organised group makes it much more possible to develop appropriate, preventive types of activities for them than it is for the bulk of the population. In fact all too often the occupational health services tend to be not much more than a palliative allowing employers the opportunity of offering their employees an 'aspirin' rather than having to come to grips with more basic problems that may be facing the worker and his family.

In Tanzania in 1970/71 the occupational health services covered around 165,000 employees — at an estimated cost of £600,000 — with facilities that included a wide range of clinics and dispensaries, but only five hospitals with a total of 320 beds. In Dar es Salaam the Group Occupational Health Service was established in 1967 and by 1970 was serving over 50 member firms with almost 15,000 workers. Similar schemes have been initiated in three other towns. Until now the question of occupational health services has been dealt with relatively little in Tanzania, mainly because there are no clear guidelines about how to create such services for any but that relatively small section of the population in wage employment. The influence of expatriates in the organisation and running of the occupational health services has been very substantial and will remain so at least until government finds itself better equipped to turn its attention to this area. However, even when government does come to serious grips with this question the basic contradiction between providing such relatively specialised services for the employed few, and the needs of the majority of the population

183

still remain.

Appropriate occupational health services, especially in poor countries, would be primarily directed towards the prevention of disease while at the same time avoiding taking a disproportionate share of national health resources for general curative activities. Two additional principles for the development of occupational health services which might usefully be followed are that such services become, to the greatest degree possible, self reliant in staff training and should charge an economic rate for services provided to upper income earners taking part in the schemes. In practice, the relationship between the occupational and the national health services and the sharing out of resources between them will largely be determined by the national pattern of industrial and other development; that is, if the larger industries are primarily in the public sector it will become somewhat easier to strike a better balance between the two health services.

Certain types of public health activities which have long been accepted in industrialised countries as extending the equality of health care provision do not play the same role in Africa and other parts of the Third World, although some of these services are absolutely essential. For example, when school health services were introduced in Europe in the latter part of the 19th century they played an important part in reducing the level of mortality and morbidity amongst the most impoverished parts of the population, the urban working class poor. However, in Africa today the urban working class does not comprise the most impoverished section of the population. In any event, merely to create special services for those children actually in school, as compared to the many who are not, could lead to increased inequality between the two groups. The same type of question arises in connection with the health of other special groups such as prisoners, who may enjoy a higher level of health care in many Third World countries than the mass of the population does. This comes about because as wards of the state prisoners are entitled to certain minimum levels of care, and that level may be more substantial than the level available to the average rural farmer. Of course it is right that those being held by the state should be entitled to care, but such services need not be allowed to become disproportionate to the limited services available to so much of the rural population. Other special health services are provided for the armed forces and the police. In many parts of the world these groups have the best health care available for any significant part of the population; the reasons are fairly obvious and it is not likely that the situation will change very rapidly in many places. Nonetheless, it would be possible to improve the health of the armed forces substantially at lower cost, if more attention were paid to the prevention of disease among them rather than its later curing. It is also

184

possible to encourage the armed forces to become responsible for the training of much of their own needed personnel and to extend their services to sections of the population not immediately connected with the forces. These types of anomalies are not easily done away with and answers to them can only be found within the context of specific situations in particular countries; but some principles are clear, the most obvious being that to whatever degree increasing short term inequality is justified in any particular situation, it should be kept to an absolute minimum. Also, that special services should, to the greatest degree possible, be self-financing while at the same time not being allowed to bid away scarce manpower resources in the health sector just because they are self financing.

C. Private Practice

There are in the Third World three categories of private practitioner; one is the formally educated and qualified doctor, a second is the traditional medical practitioner, and the third the many nurses, dressers and other former employees of the government health services engaged in various forms of private practice. Virtually nowhere in Africa is there any planning in relationship to the latter two categories, despite the fact that they comprise very significant numbers and are taking a substantial share of all private health sector expenditure. The bulk of the other type of private practitioner – the qualified doctor – is in general practice, basically outside the organised health services although some may be linked to the occupational health schemes. Nevertheless, there are a number of steps governments might take that could positively influence the work of these practitioners.

In general the services of private practitioners in most Third World countries are available only to the limited population who can afford them. However, there is evidence in some countries that the spread of private practice is beginning to extend to more of the population especially those people in some of the smaller towns. Although it is probably beyond the possibility of government action in most countries to draw private practitioners into rural practice itself, it might be possible to take steps that would further encourage them to open practices in the smaller urban centres. One way of accomplishing this is by declaring some towns closed to the opening of new practices, based upon already relatively high doctor to population ratios. And when new practices are to be opened in these larger towns they should be available only to those who have already put in a prescribed number of years of government service, followed by private practice in one of the smaller population centres. In fact if a government sees private practice as being valuable it is possible to subsidise the setting up of practices in the smaller population centres. This could be done through subsidies for office equipment etc., and perhaps even for the recurrent costs of the employment of an assistant to the private practitioner. In return government might require that the practitioner offer certain services at reduced rates or without charge to selected groups in the population.

Very many governments have taken the position that private practice is not an appropriate form of medical development for their countries, and although it might have to be tolerated it is not considered as desirable. In such countries it is not the policy of government to train doctors to go into private practice, but only for the government services. However, the pressure brought to bear on doctors in the public service by the existence of higher earnings in the private sector often leads to governments having to permit mixed private and public practice, at least to the more senior doctors in government service. In many parts of the world, as the pressure grows, such mixed practice is even permitted to the younger hospital doctors. Such a situation opens up many potential and actual distortions within the national health services, it is often the case that in such circumstances the public services are substantially subverted to the private ends of the doctors engaged in mixed public and private practice. It is difficult to offer ready remedies to the problems created by this sort of mixed practice and, although the situation might be alleviated in particular cases, the underlying difficulties will remain if public and private interests are allowed to become confused.

In Tanzania the environment for private business, including private medical practice is not as favourable as in many other places and the private, 'western educated' medical practitioner is beginning to disappear. Although the number of private practitioners rose from 38 in 1945/46 to 182 in 1960/61, that total declined to 73 in 1973. Only a few of those practitioners were Tanzanians, the others being expatriates — virtually all of them Asians born in East Africa. Many of these private practitioners find it relatively easy to emigrate to countries such as Canada, and with the increasing pressure of socialist development in Tanzania many have decided to leave. It should be emphasised that these doctors are not leaving for medical reasons but for business and social reasons that extend beyond the question of the amount of money they can make as private practitioners in Tanzania. The volume of potential earnings is still very substantial, but there is less that can be done with the money being earned. Also, they are no longer allowed to own large houses for rental purposes. The Acquisition of Housing Act of 1971 was a substantial blow to many of these practitioners, who had become quite wealthy, and were letting houses at high rentals. In addition, the difficulty of achieving foreign recognition for the schooling of their children was another serious blow; Tanzania is now

186

examining its own children, without reference to international standards; the diplomas being offered are not acceptable for higher education outside the country. The emigration of these private practitioners has probably had little effect upon the health situation of the country as a whole because they were located principally in Dar es Salaam and served a relatively select part of the population. It is probable that in time this private sector group will disappear almost entirely, at least insofar as the Asian born practitioners are concerned. The likelihood of the group being built up again as a result of Tanzanians joining it remains to be seen. It is certainly not the policy of government to train Tanzanians so they can eventually go into private practice. There has been no need until now to take any special steps in this direction as there have been so few who have left government service for this purpose. Should that situation change then government might find it necessary to take suitable steps.

Traditional Medical Practitioners

The question of traditional practitioners of African health care falls outside the scope of this work. However, a few figures will be given to indicate the volume of activity in this area.

One study* has shown that in Dar es Salaam there were about 700 full time traditional medical practitioners, which meant approximately one for each 400 of the Dar es Salaam population. These practitioners were seeing on average five to six patients per day. The fees for the services offered could be considerable. The lowest prices being charged for consultations were £.10 to £.20 although in the case of the most expensive medical condition, mental illness, patients paid anything from £.50 to £8 for a course of treatment. The estimates available for the overall number of traditional doctors practicing in Tanzania run from one for each 45 persons among rural Moslem populations, to one for each 400 of population in Dar es Salaam. If these averages are translated into national totals it could mean as many as 35,000 to 40,000 traditional practitioners in Tanzania. This figure is probably on the high side and certainly includes many practitioners who are only involved on a part time basis. One estimate suggests that around £1 million a year is spent in Tanzania for the services of traditional practitioners.+

It is obvious from the figures cited that the volume of traditional medical work and numbers of such practitioners in Tanzania is substantial. The relevant issue is the possibility of organising this large group of health workers into a coherent and more useful body, although

*An unpublished dissertation by Lloyd Swantz, University of Dar es Salaam.
+M. Gottlieb, Health Care Financing in Tanzania, Economic Research Bureau of the University of Dar es Salaam, seminar paper, March 1973, mimeo.

the question is complicated by the fact that they run the gamut from pure charlatans doing more harm than good to those capable of offering intelligent advice to people suffering from various forms of illness for which they are unable to receive help from any other source. There is no country in Africa that has worked out any reasonable approach to these traditional healers and it cannot be said that Tanzania has made very much progress in that direction either. At one point in the early 1970's an organisation representing some of the traditional practitioners had been recognised by government, but the experiment turned out badly and recognition was withdrawn. The difficulties involved in cooperation are extensive and deeply rooted both amongst the traditional and modern practitioners. On the traditional side there is, firstly, the widely mixed character of the skills these healers have to offer and, secondly, the fact that they are private practitioners who are in the habit of trading their skills freely in the market place, as are private practitioners everywhere. On the side of the modern doctors there is, as would be expected, the question of their basic attitudes with regard to the traditional healers, as well as the element of potential economic competition. The basic problem is to define and maximise that part of the work of this traditional group of health workers which can be turned to the use of the rural population among whom they mainly live, and whose confidence they retain. This is a long term question and it is highly unlikely that any African country, including Tanzania, will move very far on this question for some time to come.* The exception being that in some countries it is even now possible to utilise the traditional midwife, especially with some additional training. It is also generally agreed that the traditional practitioner could be immediately useful in the care of mental illness. In any event, it cannot be expected that much progress can be made in this area in the foreseeable future when so many countries continue to reject even the training of medical auxiliaries in favour of the exclusive use of graduate doctors.

---

*However, China, with its considerable experience in this area, is now assisting Tanzania with these questions.

11. EXTERNAL AID

The overall situation with regard to external aid to Tanzania has changed very rapidly during recent years. The first five year plan had to be financed primarily from Tanzania's own resources as a result of breaches between Tanzania and its then two major aid doners (the United Kingdom and West Germany). In the case of the second five year plan it was expected that 40% would be derived from external sources. In practice it has turned out that the first year of the plan, 1969/70, was 20% externally financed, the second year 37% and the third, fourth and fifth around 50%. The changed aid position reflects the growth of interest on the part of doners, in the rural development programmes and overall socio-political policies of the country. These factors have been particularly important with regard to the rapid expansion of the aid programmes of the Nordic countries and Canada. The previous break with the West Germans has been healed and a substantial volume of aid has been forthcoming from that country. China is the biggest single bilateral donor, mostly via the construction of the Tanzania-Zambia railway.

The entire question of the relationship of aid to the concept of self-reliance will not be reviewed here, but the issue must at least be mentioned. There can be little doubt that specific aid funding can be useful and need not jeopardise either self-reliance or national independence, but whether or not this will hold true in the face of the very large volume of aid which is now coming into Tanzania cannot easily be answered. The spectrum of possibilities in the relationships that can be developed between a recipient country and a number of donors is very great indeed. At this time Tanzania is certainly not a client state to any of its external donors, perhaps partly because the country has been involved with a wide variety of donors and the largest international donors have not been Tanzania's major cooperating partners. It is also the case that there is more or less 'only one Tanzania', thereby making it relatively easy for even the more conservative donors to support a range of activities which might not win such enthusiastic support if they were being demanded by a very great number of African countries militantly espousing socialist policies.

There is also the question of the intrinsic need for aid. Although it is relatively easy to reach agreement that external assistance for large hospital building in preference to rural health centres, is to be resisted, it is also true that in the stricter sense health centres do not absolutely require foreign aid as a precondition to their construction. Such centres could function perfectly well even if constructed with traditional building materials, which require very little external support except perhaps for the importation of equipment and vehicles. However such arguments remain rather theoretical, as even in the current Tanzanian political environment it is unlikely that a great number of health centres would be built in the absence of foreign aid. Therefore, in the short run at least external aid for health centres does assure their construction, although it remains possible that in the longer run it might deter the development of truly self-reliant attitudes. This question can be illustrated by a specific case; Tanzania is building eleven schools for the training of rural medical aids with external support. Because schools were planned to be opened as quickly as possible and not wait until construction was finished, the first half dozen schools were started in temporary accommodation. All the necessary buildings were located and converted, at small cost, for the use of the first year's intake into these training programmes. There is no doubt that this temporary accommodation was not very suitable, or comfortable, yet in the absence of foreign aid and with sufficient determination they could have been improved and turned into reasonably satisfactory permanent facilities, even though it is probable that they would have remained quite uncomfortable for both staff and students. Of course it should be asked how someone who doesn't have to take part in the training courses should ask others to put up with such uncomfortable facilities.

The questions raised above can only be answered by particular recipients and donors. From the recipient's point of view it will be essentially a political determination, made from within the perspective of a particular country. As for the donors, it is right that they be responsive to the requests of their cooperating partners – although of course they will always reserve the right to respond in particular ways to individual requests. Donors should lend support to projects which appear to be closest to the existing capability and environment of poor countries (requests of the sort that will be discussed below) even if there are some doubts about the ultimate effect of aid upon the development of self-reliant attitudes. Essentially this is a matter that can only be determined by recipients, and donors can only support the 'best' projects offered to them, by the 'best' recipients, at any particular time.

A. Health Sector Aid

Until recently external aid to the health sector in Tanzania had been limited almost entirely to support from the voluntary agencies, although a significant part of that support is based upon finance being made

190

available by government aid programmes channelled through the
agencies. In Tanzania this finance has resulted not only in an increase
in relatively small, mostly rural, church related health facilities but also
the construction of two large referral hospitals at Mwanza (New Mwanza
Hospital) and Moshi (Kilimanjaro Christian Medical Centre) at a cost of
not much less than £5 million. These voluntary agency aid inflows had
not been showing up in the usual aid statistics of either the ministries
of health, development or finance, or in Tanzania's annual development
budgets. The other 'traditional' sources of assistance to the health
sector have been the World Health Organisation and UNICEF. WHO
assistance primarily takes the form of technical assistance personnel,
while UNICEF support has comprised mainly vehicles, teaching
equipment and vaccines.

Reasons for a lack of conventional bilateral aid to the health sector
can be found on the side of both (potential) donors and recipients. On
the part of the donors there had been relatively little recent interest in
aid to the health sector as such; in fact during the later 1960's the
assistance which had previously gone into the health sector had largely
been transferred to population programmes specially with regard to
USAID. The general reluctance of donors to support the health sector
had been strengthened as a result of the sorts of requests that many
Third World countries, including Tanzania, had been making i.e. large
hospital construction. The experiences of those donors who had been
drawn into supporting the construction of large referral hospitals had
not been good. It was found that the new hospitals were not only taking
a very substantial proportion of the health budgets of small countries
but after construction were often inadequately staffed and indifferently
administered. Although many donors had turned away from large
hospital building, in those countries which channeled part of their aid
budgets through Christian bodies it was still possible to find funds for
such purposes. For example, two such countries, West Germany and
the Netherlands, were the primary donors for the construction of the
two large hospitals built in recent years in Tanzania. It seems that, at
least partly, because these countries have religious political parties it
had proved convenient for them to channel their 'humanitarian
assistance' through voluntary institutions, according to Protestant,
Catholic and non-sectarian (but voluntary) designations. At present it
appears that these agencies, too, have had second thoughts concerning
the question of supporting any more major hospital construction and
there are now relatively few aid donors still willing to fund such
hospital projects although there still are a few.

Not only did potential aid recipients find it convenient to ask for
large hospital projects but they also found it exceedingly difficult to
organise requests for more appropriate types of support, both in the

191

socio-political sense of defining 'more appropriate' and the technical sense of creating health plans containing projects that could win external support. Ministries of health almost everywhere in the Third World are among the last on the list of ministries to have support for strengthening their capability for administration and planning. The lack of planners within the health ministries means that there is little capacity for communicating with aid donors, who increasingly are demanding overall health sector plans into which requested aid projects can be seen to fit. Prospective donors are concerned with the ways in which the various components of the health sector are tied together; for example, the availability of manpower to staff the facilities being requested, or the capacity of the health ministry's budget to absorb the recurrent costs of aid projects, or the linkages between health service projects and other development activities. The Tanzanian Ministry of Health, too, had been faced with the same lack of a planning capacity as was practically every other country in Africa, very many of those in Asia, and more than a few in Latin America.

There was need, then, for donors to change their perspective as to the role of the health sector in development, and for ministries of health (representing prospective recipients) to change their views as to the sort of health aid that should hold the highest priority. This entire process has been helped by the fact that in recent years donors have been re-thinking the entire question of development. Growth of national product, which for many years had been seen to be virtually an end in itself, is now considered to be more the *result* of a broader policy of social change than the instigator of that change. Development should now be measured in terms of, say, the nutritional status of a population, or the ability of people to have work enough to support themselves and their families, or the creation of greater levels of equity within a society.* Given such measures of development rather than the more narrow view of growth of national product alone, it becomes clear that the health of populations and thus the health sector and the health services must begin to hold a higher priority in the eyes of donors than had previously been the case.

On the recipient side, at least in Tanzania, the question of the creation of a just society had also demanded new perspectives about health service development. It was then necessary to bring these fresh perspectives together in the context of a suitable health development plan for the country. That plan was developed, as discussed above, and it proved possible to win very substantial external funding for it. As a matter of fact, the volume of external aid now in the pipeline to the Tanzanian health sector may be the largest of its kind in Africa. The

---

*Dudley Seers, The Meaning of Development, *International Development Review,* December 1969, Vol. II, No.4, pp.2-6.

major bilateral participants in the programme of health aid to Tanzania are Sweden, Norway, Denmark, Finland, the United States and China. In addition, support is being received from the West Germans and the Swiss. Several other countries are making smaller contributions, and still others might become involved in the near future. Of course the WHO and UNICEF are extremely active, and recently the IBRD has been involved in the expansion of the medical school. In addition voluntary agency assistance continues to enter the country.

Of the almost £3 million capital budget of the Ministry of Health for the year 1973/74 over three-quarters was scheduled to come from external sources. Projects that fell within the scope of the Ministry's central administration (national projects) accounted for about 60% of the total value of the capital budget, with the other 40% being allocated at regional and district level. Two-thirds of the centralized budget was made up of expenditures for training institutions. Of the national projects almost 90% were to be externally financed, while of the regional projects about 70%. It might be noted that the total capital budget for health was about four times larger in 1973/74 than in the preceding year, in fact the capital budget for fiscal year 1973/74 was greater in size than the combined total of the first four years of the second five year plan.

In order to win such a large volume of funding for health sector projects it was necessary to approach prospective donors with a clearly defined health development plan. It was also necessary to 'assign' to each donor a clearly defined part of the entire plan. In approaching specific donors to take on particular parts of the plan it was also useful to take into consideration the peculiarities and interests of the different donors. It was clear that the easiest health sector projects to sell were those that appeared to relate most directly to the population question. Also relatively easy to 'sell' were those for preventive and promotive health care activities. All sorts of training activities were also likely to meet with a ready response from donors. However, projects concerned more directly with the delivery of health services were somewhat more difficult; although to the degree that they were smaller, village-based institutions, i.e. dispensaries and health centres, to that degree were donors more likely to be responsive. It must be stated quite categorically that all the donors who entered into cooperation with the Tanzanian health sector during the period under discussion were extremely cooperative and in point of fact there was virtually no project put forward for which it was really very difficult to win support. In approaching donors it is also important for recipients to bear in mind not only their overall priorities and consequent interests but also their different 'styles' of work, in this case in the health sector. For example, the fact that the U.S. and U.K. aid agencies contain health sections in the charge of medical doctors means that the decision making process with regard to health related projects will be different from that in the Scandinavian agencies, where medical doctors are primarily utilised on a consulting basis rather than as part of the administration machinery of the agency.

B. Bilateral Donors

The following discussion will review the programme of health aid to Tanzania developed in the years 1971-1973; although all major projects will be touched upon some relatively minor ones may be passed over (especially with regard to the provision of technical assistance personnel, including some from Eastern Europe and India). After China, Sweden is the largest overall bilateral donor to the Tanzanian aid programme. During 1973 Sweden and Tanzania signed an aid agreement in the health sector valued at about £3 million. Over the five years of the agreement the single largest component, representing about 80% of the total, provides for the construction of almost 100 rural health centres. Almost 10% of the total programme is set aside for the construction of student hostels and classrooms for the training of paramedical and auxiliary staff. Most of the balance of the programme money is set aside for technical assistance personnel, mainly in the area of health and medical service planning, although some smaller sums are also available for training courses, seminars and textbooks for paramedical and auxilliary staff, and for the purchase of vehicles and radio-communication equipment. In other separate, non-health ministry, agreements the Swedish Government has lent substantial support to the development of a nutrition programme for the whole of Tanzania and is supporting a massive national health education campaign that has been incorporated into the adult literacy programme of the country.

In passing it might be noted that in certain respects two non-health ministry projects being supported by Sweden i.e. the health education, and national nutrition programmes, are likely to have even more fundamental, although complementary effects upon the health status of the population than the specific Ministry of Health projects. The health education campaign already has been judged to be a substantial success, although it is still too early to comment on the nutrition programme. Sweden has also been involved in some support to the Tanzanian occupational health service and, through the voluntary agencies, to a number of church linked health facilities.

Until recently there had been only some relatively minor Norwegian involvement in Tanzanian health sector development. Such support was limited to some technical assistance personnel, a vaccination programme for one region of the country and assistance to voluntary agency institutions. In 1973, however, general agreement was reached on a substantial Norwegian contribution to the Tanzanian health sector. Just as Sweden will bear the brunt of the costs of rural health centre construction over forthcoming years, Norway will do so for dispensary construction. Over the four years 1973/74 - 1976/77 Norway will be constructing about 400 dispensaries at a cost of roughly three-quarters of a million pounds (the details of these dispensaries, the rural health centres discussed above, and some of the facilities that will be mentioned later have been described in earlier chapters). In addition to the dispensary programme Norway has become involved in the planning and development of the public health institute discussed earlier.

Past Danish involvement in the Tanzanian health sector had been limited to some technical assistance personnel and support to mission hospitals. There is now the expectation of considerable support in forthcoming years. Although no comprehensive longer term programme — as with Sweden and Norway — has as yet been developed, agreement has been reached for the support of a number of specific projects valued at about one-half million pounds. These included the construction of two district hospitals, one school for medical assistants, two schools for health auxiliaries, support for a hospital equipment maintenance unit and the opening stages of a campaign to control onchocerciasis (river blindness). Other projects were also under discussion. It might be noted that the two district hospitals Denmark has agreed to finance represented the only externally funded government hospital development in the country. It must be stressed that these particular hospital projects are well justified in terms of external support just because hospital expansion is to be so very limited in the overall Tanzanian context. Although in general it is right for aid agencies to resist requests for the construction of hospital buildings if, as is the case in Tanzania, there is a comprehensive development plan which allows for very limited hospital construction then it is not inappropriate for aid agencies to consider supporting such construction. Aid agencies must accept the fact that there may be specific and limited hospital requirements that cannot be avoided. The two district hospitals that Denmark is supporting in Tanzania are good cases in point because: 1) the hospitals fit into a pattern of extremely limited hospital development; 2) the cost of the two institutions is relatively small, about £100,000 each for these eighty bed institutions; 3) one of the hospitals will be constructed in a new district created when the most underbedded and populous district in the whole of the country, which had only one bed to each 3,500 of population, against a national average of roughly one to 800, was divided in two; and 4) the other district hospital to be built by the Danes will replace what is probably the oldest and least (physically) satisfactory government hospital in the country, originally built by the Germans during the early years of this century, also this particular hospital and the district it is in will be used for the teaching of district practice to medical students. (The World Bank will finance the construction of some student hostel and classroom facilities located in the area of the hospital.)

Although Finland is a relative newcomer to the aid business it has become heavily committed to Tanzania and has agreed to contribute almost three-quarters of a million pounds to the construction of eleven schools for rural medical aids. This programme is complementary to the Norwegian and Swedish dispensary and rural health centre construction programmes, in that the rural medical aids will be in charge of the work at dispensary level and will contribute in an important way to the staffing of the rural health centres. It is worth noting that aid agencies have not only cooperated with Tanzania in the development of health sector projects but have actively supported each other's work in this regard. They have been able to make use of each other's reports and other documentation in the development of their own contribution to the Tanzanian health sector. Of course the Nordic group have also cooperated with other donors involved in the health sector, but the special relationship that exists among them has made their cooperation particularly fruitful. (The Kibaha rural health centre and rural medical aid school is an earlier example of Nordic cooperation in the health sector.)

The largest of the non-Nordic donors to the Tanzanian health programme has been the United States. The American project mostly comprises finance for the construction of eighteen regional training centres for maternal and child health aids. This programme has been described earlier in some detail in the manpower chapter, and will not be discussed again here. The total agreed programme comes to over one million pounds, with the possible development of extensions at a later date. About 90% of the total sum is to go into the construction and equipping of the regional training centres; of the balance, most will be for equipment and supplies for rural health centres and dispensaries. This was a particularly important project for USAID as it was one of the first that specifically took into account the fact that it is likely to be the overall rural health care structure and not necessarily a family planning system as such that would be basic to changing the health and consequent demographic pattern of the African countryside.

In recent years the major contribution of West Germany to the health care system of Tanzania had been the financing of the central pathology laboratory in Dar es Salaam. Earlier there had been a very large contribution toward the construction of the two referral hospitals at Mwanza and Moshi. German health aid continues primarily in the form of support to a number of voluntary agency projects, and technical assistance personnel. The Dutch, too, have contributed to

196

many projects through the vehicle of the voluntary agencies, including the construction, several years ago, of a school for rural medical aids. They also offer support to technical assistance personnel in the health sector, and have made some contribution to the occupational health services in Dar es Salaam. The Swiss were also involved in the development of the central pathology laboratory and continue to support it with technical assistance personnel. In addition, the Swiss have recently allocated almost £200,000 for the construction of a school for the training of medical assistants. Discussions have been started with several other bilateral donors, in addition to those discussed above, which have covered such basic project areas as tuberculosis control, environmental sanitation and mental health.

Aid to the Tanzanian health sector from the socialist countries in Europe has come in the form of technical assistance personnel, primarily a number of doctors. The Chinese contribution to the health sector has been rather more significant: it has fallen into two categories. One has been the supply of expertise, equipment and raw materials for the construction, and operation for a specified time period of vaccine (1971) and pharmaceutical plants (1973). The second area of Chinese assistance to the health sector has been the supply of medical personnel. The Chinese have provided about 80 in all, of whom around 60 are medical doctors and most of the rest interpreters. These personnel are divided up into teams of about five, including a physician, surgeon, obstetrician-gynaecologist, ear, nose and throat specialist, and an interpreter. Although the teams are based at hospitals they spend the greater part of their time in the villages. The Chinese medical teams are much sought after by the districts and much admired for the spirit and quality of their work. They are extremely self-reliant and do almost everything required to keep themselves mobile, including driving their own vehicles.

C. Multilateral Donors

The World Health Organisation is, of course a major participant in health sector development in Tanzania. Their major direct activity is the supply of about 20 technical assistance personnel. As far as UNICEF is concerned, from a recipient's point of view they appear to be relatively flexible and able at comparatively short notice to meet requests. UNICEF is said to be exploring ways of diversifying their activities and, to some degree at least, getting out of the 'vehicle business' which until recently has been taking up much of their financial capacity. The United Nations Development Programme also supplies several people to the health sector in Tanzania, primarily in the form of teachers for the medical faculty. Several of the other UN agencies also touch on the work of a ministry of health from time to time. There is contact with various of the organisations based in Addis Abba, i.e. the Economic Commission for Africa and the Organisation for African Unity, most of which appears to take the form of answering requests for data and other information that often seem to duplicate each other. The World Bank has also been involved in health service development in Tanzania, primarily through support to the educational sector. The major result to date of the Bank's activities in this area has been a loan to cover a modest expansion of the facilities of the medical school and the salaries for some years of additional teachers.

D. Voluntary Agency Donors

Church-related

As has been indicated, church support to the health sector is very extensive in Tanzania. During any given year several voluntary agency hospitals are likely to be undergoing expansion and one may be under construction; in addition there will be contributions for new health centres and dispensaries. As mentioned, the two large referral centres at Mwanza and Moshi were also built through the voluntary agencies. There is also some support for part of the recurrent costs of most of the 60 voluntary agency hospitals in the country.

The major sources of church aid appear to be the Federal Republic of Germany, the Netherlands, the Nordic countries and the United States. In the case of the United States these funds are drawn primarily from internal church resources, although in the other countries a substantial part of the resources stem from national aid budgets. In addition, West Germany and some of the Nordic countries have national church taxes, part of which may be made available for aid projects. Some of this church aid is not being spent as effectively as it might be, partly because of a general lack of coordination, partly because Christian countries or Christian parts of countries tend to receive a disproportionate share of the available aid, and partly because some individual bishops, priests, pastors, etc., who sponsor specific health sector programmes, prefer the sort that are highly 'visible', e.g. a large hospital. There are a number of steps that governments could take in this regard. For example treasury, or whichever body is responsible for coordinating external aid, should have an officer responsible for developing and coordinating all voluntary agency aid. The first task of such an officer would be to become familiar with the entire pattern of church aid, e.g. sources, volume, types, etc., with a view to creating for the relevant ministries, especially those for health and education, a set of guidelines concerning such aid. It would also be useful for the government coordinating body to keep the voluntary agencies informed of the national requirements in

198

particular sectors. It should also be noted that the Christian aid effort covers a great variety of churches and a great many working styles. It is difficult to detail the 'ways' of each of these churches, but just as it is necessary to understand the particular interests and work styles of given bilateral and multilateral donors it is also necessary to be clear as to the interests and possibilities of the different Christian church bodies. Many of the external bodies providing support for voluntary agency programmes now require the approval of government before giving their own approval. In some countries this might be an extremely useful mechanism for preventing the development of the wrong sort of projects; however, in other countries it will not be enough to guarantee that inappropriate projects do not win support, as some governments appear to be willing to accept anything offered that appears to be 'free'. Nonetheless, new possibilities have been opened up with the institution of these procedures.

E. Other Voluntary Agencies

Aside from the Christian churches there are several other voluntary groups that participate in health sector development in the Third World; some, like OXFAM, have a particularly good record and can be extremely useful to a ministry of health. The usefulness of these groups arises particularly out of the fact that they are relatively unbureaucratic and generally quite flexible. In Tanzania OXFAM was particularly helpful several years ago in the development of a rural medical aid school. There are a number of other voluntary organisations that concentrate upon the supply of personnel, and Tanzania has benefited from very many excellent health sector volunteers from countries such as Canada, (particularly the Canadian Universities Service Organisation) Denmark, the Netherlands, etc.

SOME CONCLUSIONS

The Third Five-Year Plan

Tanzania has come a long way in planning for the development of its health services in a relatively short time although, of course, very much more remains to be done. The fact that 1972/73 represented a particularly successful year, when compared to previous ones, is reflected in the annual reports of the regional medical officers. Virtually all of these reports stressed the fact that one or another health development project had been implemented in their region during the course of the year, as well as there having been a more regular supply of drugs, more transport and the funds to keep it running, and somewhat improved staffing at district and regional level institutions. In succeeding years these annual reports should reflect still greater progress as the new plans gain momentum during the course of the third five year plan.

So far as hospital beds are concerned, it is clear that the planned constraint in their growth, in keeping with overall national priorities, is the key to future progress. The limited number of beds that will be added over the five years of the third plan will mainly be spread over those districts now showing the worst bed-population ratios. It is important to note that a strict policy of allocating beds against population will result in more beds being available for those who most need them than would otherwise have been the case. In practice what is being constrained are not hospital beds as such, but only the number available at a few large hospitals. What is necessary in relation to hospital development, in addition to a planned modest expansion, is the improvement of the services and administration of the existing institutions. The major stress will be put on improving the quality and referral capacity of the diagnostic and ancillary services available at the hospitals. In addition, the outpatient services must be extended and made more efficient. The training of hospital and health service administrators is an area of key importance. Other hospital related services that are likely to see significant development during the course of the next five year plan include the development of mental health units and the construction of urban MCH delivery units, as discussed earlier.

The rural sector has been well thought out and the targets for rural health centres and dispensaries are quite clear. Rural health centre construction will proceed at the rate of 25 per year and dispensaries at

200

100 per year. Services at village level, (below that of dispensaries), are likely to receive substantial encouragement. This is an area that had not been worked out in any detail but is now being given high priority. All kinds of mobile activities are also likely to be expanded during the course of the next plan period. Relatively little in the way of new construction for training centres is likely to be required during the next plan, given recent expansion, although some schools might need extension or replacement of outmoded facilities. The main problem in this area is improvement of the quality of training being carried out at existing schools. One important requirement is to guarantee an adequate supply of the best available teaching materials and books. Stress must also certainly be put on improving the teaching skills of instructors.

The development of preventive services is undoubtedly the most critical area of all those to be tackled during the course of the next five year plan. Specific quantitative targets for the preventive health services must be developed; for example, increasing the annual percentages of under-five's reached with required innoculations, or the number of people having access to and regularly using pit latrines, or the number of people involved in specific health education activities, or the preventive content of the occupational health services etc. The first need will be to quantify, on a district basis, the existing level of these sorts of services; only then will it be possible to set incremental goals to be accomplished on an annual basis.

Co-operation with the voluntary agencies will certainly continue and they will be encouraged to develop their services in conjunction with overall national health planning. The problem of expanding recurrent expenditures must be tackled, particularly the rising costs of drugs. Examination of the problems involved in the purchasing, proper utilisation and prescribing of drugs is of the highest priority.

The second five-year plan had a planned allocation of £4.7 million for the health sector. The growth of the development budget over recent years means that up to three to four times that figure should be made available during the third five year plan, provided of course, that individual projects are feasible and the entire plan internally consistent resulting in acceptable levels of recurrent budget requirements. About a third of the projected expenditure would go into hospital, urban and related services — including MCH delivery units and mental health units — and perhaps two-thirds into the rural intrastructure and preventive activities. Given the volume of external aid already in the pipeline it would probably be possible to achieve external finance for roughly two-thirds of the entire health sector programme.

Research

There are a number of high priority health sector data and research requirements in Tanzania. These include a proper survey of the physical conditions of the hospitals, and possibly health centres as well. More should be known about the country's mobile health activities. The volume of preventive activities must be quantified and a system set up for monitoring their development. Some detailed manpower studies are required, particularly concerning patterns of utilisation of such cadres as nurses. The quantification of resource allocation according to population groups would be extremely useful, i.e. by sex, age, occupation, etc., as well as by disease categories. The problems connected with drug allocation, distribution and utilisation have already been indicated. An extremely useful study would provide health baseline statistics for selected parts of the country: these could be developed in conjunction with detailed surveys of the workings of existing health institutions and manpower cadres. All of these studies and surveys should be organised on as simple a basis as possible with a view to providing practical planning data.

Ministries of Health or Ministries of Disease

In many respects ministries of health in most of the world might more correctly be termed ministries of disease. This can be argued because health ministries as we mainly know them are doing relatively little in relation to health itself; instead they mainly provide relief for those already suffering from disease. It is probably the case that ministries of health could do considerably more about health, as opposed to disease, than they are now doing, but it is also probably the case that the bulk of health inputs, as opposed to anti-disease inputs, are in fact beyond the scope of their conventional activities. There are two reasons for this: one is that the major factors influencing human health arise out of the services provided by such ministries as agriculture or education, rather than health; another is that much of that which has to do with health is not provided by governments, in the conventional sense at all; that is, people basically 'do for themselves' with regard to their own health requirements.

The implications of such an approach to health are far reaching. It means a departure from the accepted engineering and technological approach to health development, and inclusion of decision making in the health sector as part of the explicit subject matter of political economy. This is not to imply a totally negative approach to the possibilities of conventionally organised ministries of health, there is certainly much they can do now even within the constraints under which they operate (some of these possibilities have in fact been touched upon above); nonetheless, the limitations indicated here are certainly real.

It is at the village level itself that the best possibilities exist for rapid progress in health development. There are virtually no health ministries that know how to develop locally based health services; in fact, in the world over there are very few examples of such services, although reports from China indicate that substantial progress at least has been made in that country. In many countries there is talk of providing village level services through the planned activities of government. Of course such efforts are to be supported, but they do tend to beg the question of what government schemes alone can actually do in helping villagers to fulfill their own health care requirements. It may very well be that the cause of so much failure in the health sector stems from the fact that government planners either do not have as much wisdom and skill as is thought to be the case, or, at the very least, that this wisdom and these skills are not very relevant to local village level problems. There can be little doubt that villagers have at least the potential, if not the existing capacity, of organising their own lives in such a way as to produce sufficient skills so as to do most of that which is required to create a healthy environment in which to live, the proviso being that a form of social organisation exists at the national level that at the very least is not destructive of the possibilities of self-reliant village development. It is unfortunately the case that most ministries, and not only of health, are not only incapable of giving the kind of support needed at village level but are themselves part of larger national structures that are actually destructive of the possibilities of self-reliant village development. (Is it still not possible to agree that many, if not most, national governments and power structures are themselves the major cause of continuing underdevelopment in the Third World?)

The general problem under discussion can be illustrated in the context of manpower development. The usual thing is for ministries of health to train personnel who then join the civil service and draw wages on a monthly basis: but there are obvious limitations to the current possibilities of civil servants when dealing with the immense health care problems that exist in the villages of the Third World. What is needed rather, is a sense of participation on the part of village populations, including those selected for specific health care activities. Of course, such participation can become a real possibility only in the context of nations that have organised themselves in keeping with the needs of the whole of the population. What is required are people in each village who know something about the environmental health care needs of their fellow villagers: such people would come from the village and remain part of its day to day functioning. There is no way to put the large number of people that is needed for such work on ministerial payrolls; therefore, they must continue to make their livelihood from within the village itself. Preferably they would continue to have the possibility to grow their own food while being recompensed from community resources for the time they spend at their health work activities. Of course some will recognise here the Chinese concept of the 'barefoot doctor'. This is not to recommend that others follow what has been done in another country, but the basic principle of drawing health workers from the community itself does remain valid. However, the real problem is not merely to envisage some sort of 'ideal' structure but to make recommendations as to the accomplishment of that particular structure in the context of societies that are geared toward money wages, career promotion and escape from the village to the city. The question of how to create alternative sets of motivations for both national leaders and villagers remains probably the most important issue for future social and economic development, in both the general sense as well as when applied specifically to the development of health and health services.

In this connection there is no better way to close than with another reference to the speech by President Nyerere quoted in the introduction to this volume*.

"It cannot be denied that many difficulties face a Third World country which chooses the socialist alternative of development. Not least among these are its own past, the dynamism of capitalist initiative techniques, and the gambler instinct which every human being seems to possess, so that we all hope we shall be among the privileged not the exploited! But I believe that we can choose the socialist path, and that by so doing we can develop ourselves in freedom, and towards those conditions which allow dignity and self-respect for every one of our citizens.

"I believe that this prospect must be pursued, with vigour and determination. We shall not create socialist societies overnight; because we have to start from where we are, we shall have to take risks in our development. But I am convinced that Third World countries have the power to transform themselves, over time, into socialist societies in which their peoples can live in harmony and co-operation as they work together for their common benefit."

---

*J. K. Nyerere, Socialism: The Rational Choice, as reprinted in the *Daily News*, 6 January 1973.

INDEX